COBOL Programmer's Notebook

Jim Keogh

ISBN 0-13-977414-9

90000

 Prentice Hall PTR
Upper Saddle River, NJ 07458
http://www.phptr.com

9 780139 774140

Editorial/Production Supervision: Nick Radhuber
Acquisitions Editor: Jeffrey Pepper
Editorial Assistant: Christy Schaack
Marketing Manager: Kaylie Smith
Buyer: Alexis Heydt
Cover Design: Wee Design
Cover Design Direction: Jerry Votta

© 1998 Prentice Hall PTR
Prentice-Hall, Inc.
A Simon & Schuster Company
Upper Saddle River, NJ 07458

The publisher offers discounts on this book when ordered in bulk quantities. For more information, contact: Phone: 800-382-3419; FAX: 201-236-714; E-mail (Internet): corpsales@prenhall.com

or write:
Corporate Sales Department,
Prentice Hall PTR
One Lake Street
Upper Saddle River, NJ 07458

Printed in the United States of America

10 9 8 7 6 5 4 3 2 1

ISBN 0-13-977414-9

Prentice-Hall International (UK) Limited, London
Prentice-Hall of Australia Pty. Limited, Sydney
Prentice-Hall Canada Inc., Toronto
Prentice-Hall Hispanoamericana, S.A., Mexico
Prentice-Hall of India Private Limited, New Delhi
Prentice-Hall of Japan, Inc., Tokyo
Simon & Schuster Asia Pte. Ltd., Singapore
Editora Prentice-Hall do Brasil, Ltda., Rio de Janeiro

*This book is dedicated to Little Grandma,
who was taken from us suddenly,
but who will live in our hearts and memories forever.*
- Anne, Sandra, Joanne, and Jim

---

*Many thanks to
Eric Carmeli who was the technical reviewer of this book.*

Contents

Chapter Two

Working with Constants and Variables 31

Chapter Three

Working with Data Structures 67

Chapter Four

Working with Program Control 95

Chapter Five

Working with Operators and Expressions   123

Chapter Six

Working with Data Input and Screens   147

Chapter Seven

Working with Other Programs   165

Chapter Eight

Working with Files   177

Chapter Nine

Working with File Errors   229

Chapter Ten

Working with Sorting and Merging   241

Chapter Eleven

Working with the Printer   269

Chapter Twelve

Working to Solve the Year 2000 Problem

307

Programmer's Checklist

331

Index   **341**

Preface

Many readers associate COBOL (Common Business Oriented Language) will older applications that have been running successfully for decades on mainframe computer and with applications containing the Year 2000 Problem.

COBOL is at the center of the Year 2000 Problem because many applications written in COBOL fail to use the century digits. Instead they use the year digit such as 99 rather than 1999. This works well until the year 2000 when the year becomes 00.

Does 00 represent the year 2000 or 1900? If the COBOL program subtracts dates, will 00 - 99 result in a -99 or will the program stop running altogether?

How long will it take a programmer to locate and fix the problem if this occurs? Remember, business and government operations might stop until the problem is fixed. Will it take an hour, a day? Or will this occur in several programs requiring a team of programmers a week or more to address the problem?

The answer is no one really knows because the computer industry has never experienced such a problem before. Every line of code in every COBOL program must be reviewed, and fixed if necessary.

This book is designed to bring novice COBOL programmers up to speed quickly using COBOL and fixing the Year 2000 Problem. The clock is ticking. There's less than 1000 days remaining.

The Picture Book Approach

COBOL, as any computer language, is complex and has many rules that must be obeyed. Learning those rules can be timeconsuming, especially for readers who already know how to program in a language other than COBOL. Those readers want to jump into the language and begin writing simple code almost immediately.

Many programmers who learn COBOL as their second language have their own philosophy about learning the language. "Show me sample code and I'll figure out the rest," is a statement that summarizes their approach. And that's what I do in this book.

The picture book concept places the focus of the book on a picture of the code. Around this picture are callouts that describe each keyword and statement. The rules are presented in tables that are positioned near the picture. Furthermore, there is a picture for each variation of the topic that is discussed in the chapter.

A reader who wants to jump into COBOL can study the picture, then copy the code into a compiler and make the executable program without having to sift through pages of text. The rules can be referenced later, when the reader needs to expand the use of the routine.

This approach is not intended to circumvent a thorough presentation of the COBOL language. In fact, this book presents COBOL in its completion. Instead, the picture book approach presents material in the way programmers want to learn a new computer language.

Each example is a complete program that is unlike many computer books that show snippets of code, then expect you to know how to assemble all the other necessary pieces into a program that will compile.

Navigating This Book

I organized this book into traditional chapters. Each chapter covers a topic of COBOL in a logical progression. So, if you are not familiar with the basics of COBOL, then begin with the first chapter and continue through each chapter in progression. At the end of the last chapter you will have a good foundation in COBOL and how to begin solving the year 2000 problem.

However, these chapters can be used also for quick reference. Jump to the chapter that discusses the topic that you want to review. The topic within the chapter is presented in its completion with a focus on examples of code.

Each chapter is further divided into two page spreads. That is, careful attention is given to the relationship between the left and right pages. The left page contains text that describes the topic that is illustrated on the right page. The right page focuses on COBOL code that contains callouts describing each facet of the example.

The most efficient way to use a two-page spread is to first study the example on the right page. If you understand the function of each statement in the example, then you can continue and write your own program. However, if a statement or keyword is confusing, then read the callout that describes the item. Still confused? Read the text on the left page.

Careful attention is given to clarity of the code example, the right page. You will notice that the syntax of the COBOL code is shown in bold. Parts of the statements that are not bold are pieces that the programmer creates.

For example, the statement **ACCEPT** LNAME**.** reads data from the keyboard and stores it in the variable LNAME. Notice **ACCEPT** is bold as is the period after the LNAME. They are part of the syntactic of COBOL. The word LNAME, however, is a name of a variable that can be any name that complies with the rules of COBOL.

Working with the Editor, Compiler, and Linker

- Dissecting a Simple COBOL Program
- Editors
- Naming Files
- Compiler Errors
- COBOL Areas
- COBOL Organization
- Identification Division
- Environment Division Configuration Section
- Environment Division Input-Output Section
- Environment Division Input-Output Section I-O Control Paragraph
- Data Division
- Data Division Linkage Section
- Communication Section
- Report Section
- Procedure Division
- Words to Avoid Using

Dissecting a
Simple COBOL Program

Every COBOL program has four parts called *divisions*. A division breaks up your program into functional groups. These are the Identification Division, Environment Division, Data Division, and Procedure Division.

The *Identification Division* contains information that identifies the program. The Identification Division in the example on the next page identifies the program as FIRST.

000200 PROGRAM-ID. FIRST.

The *Environment Division* lists any special equipment needed to run the program. We have none in this example which will be the case in most COBOL programs you create. Special equipment is typically used in unique kinds of operations where the same program will run on different computers.

The *Data Division* contains the definition of variables used by the program. You'll learn how to use the Data Division to define variables in the next chapter. No data is used in the example on the next page, therefore the Data Division is empty.

The *Procedure Division* is where statements are entered to tell the computer what to do. In this example, the computer is told to display a simple message on the screen.

Two lines are used to identify where the code of the Procedure Division begins (BEGIN-MY-PROGRAM.) and where it ends (STOP-MY-PROGRAM.). You can use any text to describe this segment of code. Each is a *paragraph name*. Programming statements are entered below a paragraph name.

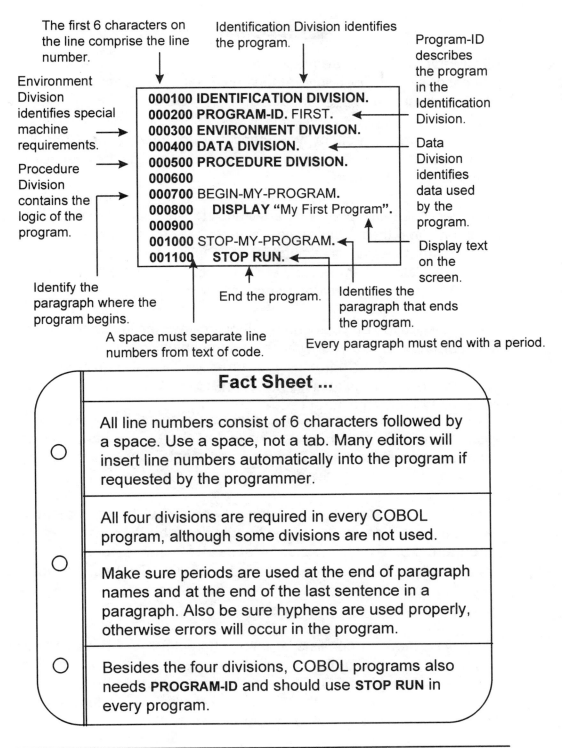

The first 6 characters on the line comprise the line number.

Identification Division identifies the program.

Program-ID describes the program in the Identification Division.

Environment Division identifies special machine requirements.

Procedure Division contains the logic of the program.

```
000100 IDENTIFICATION DIVISION.
000200 PROGRAM-ID. FIRST.
000300 ENVIRONMENT DIVISION.
000400 DATA DIVISION.
000500 PROCEDURE DIVISION.
000600
000700 BEGIN-MY-PROGRAM.
000800    DISPLAY "My First Program".
000900
001000 STOP-MY-PROGRAM.
001100    STOP RUN.
```

Data Division identifies data used by the program.

Display text on the screen.

Identify the paragraph where the program begins.

End the program.

Identifies the paragraph that ends the program.

A space must separate line numbers from text of code.

Every paragraph must end with a period.

Fact Sheet ...

○ All line numbers consist of 6 characters followed by a space. Use a space, not a tab. Many editors will insert line numbers automatically into the program if requested by the programmer.

All four divisions are required in every COBOL program, although some divisions are not used.

○ Make sure periods are used at the end of paragraph names and at the end of the last sentence in a paragraph. Also be sure hyphens are used properly, otherwise errors will occur in the program.

○ Besides the four divisions, COBOL programs also needs **PROGRAM-ID** and should use **STOP RUN** in every program.

Editors

All COBOL code is written using an editor. An *editor* is like a word processor except most editors don't have fancy features such as a spelling checker and text formatting.

There are many editors you can use to write your COBOL programs. You can even use a word processor as long as you save the file in the text format.

However, COBOL programmers tend to use editors that are common to their operating system. For example, UNIX programmers use vi or emacs. DOS COBOL programmers use EDIT. VAX VMS offers several editors including EDIT and EMACS. IBM/MVS mainframe environments use ISPF.

Select the editor of your choice, then review the documentation and learn how to find your way around the editor.

Naming Files

The file containing your COBOL program is called the *source code file*, sometimes called *source code* for short. The name of the source code file consists of two components. These are the file name and the file extension.

The *file name* can be any characters permitted by the operating system. However, the file name should describe the function of the program. For example, abcd is a valid file name, but tells you nothing about the program contained in the file. On the other hand, the file name payroll implies the file contains the source code for the payroll program.

The *file extension* consists of three characters and is sometimes specified by the COBOL compiler. For example, COB is used for the VAX VMS. Most COBOL programmers use cbl as the extension if none is required by the COBOL compiler. This identifies the source code file as a COBOL program.

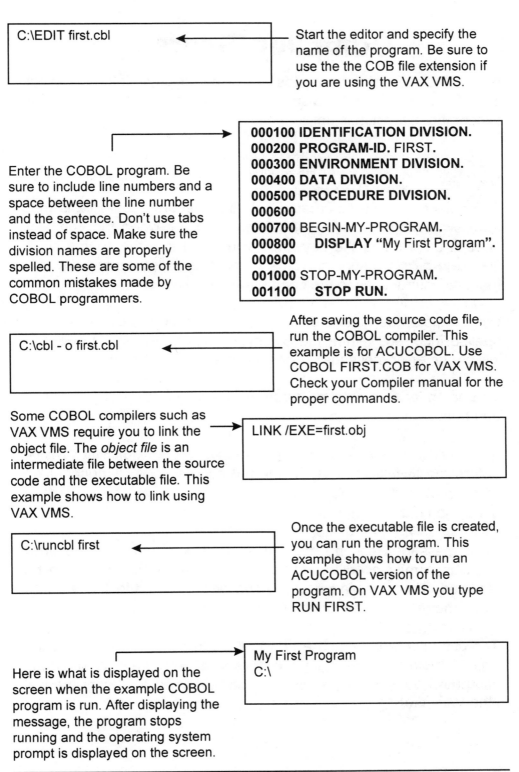

C:\EDIT first.cbl

Start the editor and specify the name of the program. Be sure to use the the COB file extension if you are using the VAX VMS.

```
000100 IDENTIFICATION DIVISION.
000200 PROGRAM-ID. FIRST.
000300 ENVIRONMENT DIVISION.
000400 DATA DIVISION.
000500 PROCEDURE DIVISION.
000600
000700 BEGIN-MY-PROGRAM.
000800    DISPLAY "My First Program".
000900
001000 STOP-MY-PROGRAM.
001100    STOP RUN.
```

Enter the COBOL program. Be sure to include line numbers and a space between the line number and the sentence. Don't use tabs instead of space. Make sure the division names are properly spelled. These are some of the common mistakes made by COBOL programmers.

C:\cbl - o first.cbl

After saving the source code file, run the COBOL compiler. This example is for ACUCOBOL. Use COBOL FIRST.COB for VAX VMS. Check your Compiler manual for the proper commands.

Some COBOL compilers such as VAX VMS require you to link the object file. The *object file* is an intermediate file between the source code and the executable file. This example shows how to link using VAX VMS.

LINK /EXE=first.obj

C:\runcbl first

Once the executable file is created, you can run the program. This example shows how to run an ACUCOBOL version of the program. On VAX VMS you type RUN FIRST.

My First Program
C:\

Here is what is displayed on the screen when the example COBOL program is run. After displaying the message, the program stops running and the operating system prompt is displayed on the screen.

Working with the Editor, Compiler, and Linker

Compiler Errors

A COBOL Compiler translates your source code into an object code file that contains the same file name as the source code file except the extension is obj.

FIRST.COB
FIRST.OBJ

The object code file is created only if the source code file is free from syntactic errors. A *syntactic error* occurs when the compiler doesn't understand the keywords you typed into the source code file. *Keywords* are special words sometimes called *reserved words* that give instructions to the computer.

For example, the names of the divisions are keywords. If they are spelled incorrectly, then the compiler won't know what to do and will create error messages instead of creating the object file.

The compiler also catches errors in the sequencing of sentences and punctuation used in the source code.

A *sequencing error* occurs if you placed the **Environment Division** before the **Identification Division** in the source code. A *punctuation error* occurs if you failed to place a period at the end of a paragraph name or at the end of a paragraph.

Error messages can be misleading. It is common that one error such as a misplaced period can cause many other errors to be reported. This is called a *cascading error*. Once the first error is fixed, the rest go away on the next compile.

The compiler won't catch errors in logic in your COBOL program. For example an error in logic occurs if your program instructs the computer to display a person's first name, when you want the last name displayed.

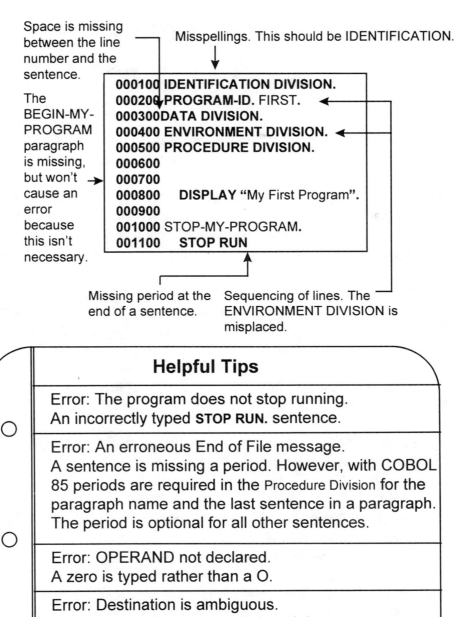

Space is missing between the line number and the sentence.

Misspellings. This should be IDENTIFICATION.

The BEGIN-MY-PROGRAM paragraph is missing, but won't cause an error because this isn't necessary.

```
000100 IDENTIFICATION DIVISION.
000200 PROGRAM-ID. FIRST.
000300DATA DIVISION.
000400 ENVIRONMENT DIVISION.
000500 PROCEDURE DIVISION.
000600
000700
000800      DISPLAY "My First Program".
000900
001000 STOP-MY-PROGRAM.
001100      STOP RUN
```

Missing period at the end of a sentence.

Sequencing of lines. The ENVIRONMENT DIVISION is misplaced.

Helpful Tips

○	Error: The program does not stop running. An incorrectly typed **STOP RUN.** sentence.
	Error: An erroneous End of File message. A sentence is missing a period. However, with COBOL 85 periods are required in the Procedure Division for the paragraph name and the last sentence in a paragraph. The period is optional for all other sentences.
○	Error: OPERAND not declared. A zero is typed rather than a O.
	Error: Destination is ambiguous. Two variables have been assigned the same name.
○	Error: Invalid paragraph name, but name looks correct. The same name is used for a variable in the DATA DIVISION.

COBOL Areas

In addition to divisions, a COBOL program is organized into areas. An *area* refers to character positions on a line of the source code that is shown in the example on the next page.

There are five areas of a COBOL program. These are the Sequence Number area, the Indicator area, Area A, Area B, and the Identification area.

The *Sequence Number* area consists of the first six character positions on the line and contains the line number. Some COBOL compilers do not use the Sequence Number area for processing, but requires you to include this area in your source code.

The *Indicator* area is the seventh character position and typically consists of a space. You can replace the space with an asterisk that will cause the COBOL compiler to ignore the entire line; a forward slash (/) is used to indicate that a comment follows; a hyphen (-) continues the previous line; and a D is the debug directive. You'll learn how to use these characters later in this book.

Area A is defined as character positions eight through eleven. Divisions, sections, and paragraphs must begin anywhere in this area.

Area B is defined as character positions 12 through 72. All sentences must be contained within Area B. No part of a sentence is permitted in character position 73 or beyond.

The *Identification* area is defined as character positions 73 through 80. This area is used to store modification code. *Modification codes* are eight-character codes that identify code changes made to the line and help track changes made to large COBOL programs worked on by more than one programmer. You don't need to insert modification codes in your source code if you are the only programmer working on the program.

Did You Know ...

COBOL was created at a time when editors were not available. Each line of code was represented as a series of strategically place-holes in an indexlike card called a *punch card*.

Programs were assembled by placing punch cards in a pile called a *stack*. The punch cards would then be executed in sequence by the computer when the program was run.

Line numbers helped programmers to reassemble the punch card stack if they became out of order. The computer registered a warning if the stack was executed out of line number sequence.

Today, line numbers are used by compilers to identify the location of errors in the program, and editors can insert the numbers in the code if requested by the programmer.

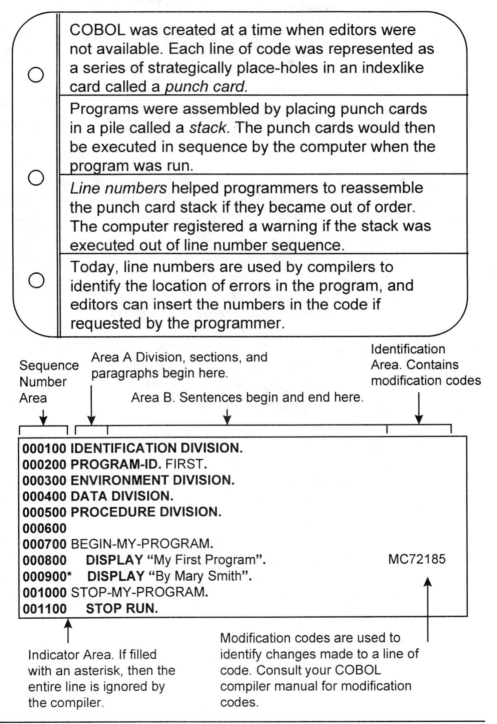

Sequence Number Area

Area A Division, sections, and paragraphs begin here.

Identification Area. Contains modification codes

Area B. Sentences begin and end here.

```
000100 IDENTIFICATION DIVISION.
000200 PROGRAM-ID. FIRST.
000300 ENVIRONMENT DIVISION.
000400 DATA DIVISION.
000500 PROCEDURE DIVISION.
000600
000700 BEGIN-MY-PROGRAM.
000800    DISPLAY "My First Program".                    MC72185
000900*   DISPLAY "By Mary Smith".
001000 STOP-MY-PROGRAM.
001100    STOP RUN.
```

Indicator Area. If filled with an asterisk, then the entire line is ignored by the compiler.

Modification codes are used to identify changes made to a line of code. Consult your COBOL compiler manual for modification codes.

COBOL Organization

You've learned that a COBOL program is organized into major groups called division. Divisions are further organized into smaller groups called sections, paragraphs, and sentences.

A *division* can contain several sections, although most division don't require any sections in a simple COBOL program such as the examples shown previously in this book.

A *section* segregates a subset of information stored in a division and contains specific types of paragraphs. The most frequently used section is the Working-Storage Section that is required if variables are used in the program as illustrated in the example on the next page.

> **DATA DIVISION.**
> **WORKING-STORAGE SECTION.**

Some sections can be excluded from a division depending on the functionality of the program. For example, the Working-Storage Section is only required if your program uses variables, otherwise the section can be excluded from your program.

A *paragraph* is a subgroup within a section and can contain one or more sentences. Some paragraphs can be used without identifying a section such as **PROGRAM-ID**. You'll learn when this is possible in examples throughout this book.

Some paragraphs are also required such as **PROGRAM-ID** and others are left to the programmer's discretion. You can create your own paragraphs to help identify parts of your code. For example, BEGIN-MY-PROGRAM and STOP-MY-PROGRAM are not required by COBOL, but are used to make the code readable.

A *sentence* contains COBOL commands such as **DISPLAY** "My First Program."

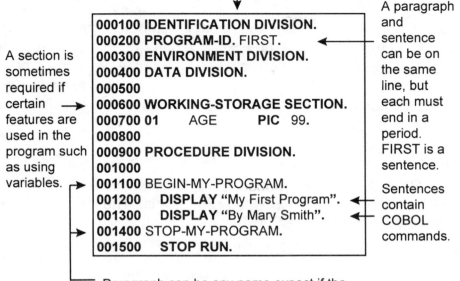

Division is a major segment of a COBOL program.

A section is sometimes required if certain features are used in the program such as using variables.

```
000100 IDENTIFICATION DIVISION.
000200 PROGRAM-ID. FIRST.
000300 ENVIRONMENT DIVISION.
000400 DATA DIVISION.
000500
000600 WORKING-STORAGE SECTION.
000700 01    AGE        PIC  99.
000800
000900 PROCEDURE DIVISION.
001000
001100 BEGIN-MY-PROGRAM.
001200    DISPLAY "My First Program".
001300    DISPLAY "By Mary Smith".
001400 STOP-MY-PROGRAM.
001500    STOP RUN.
```

A paragraph and sentence can be on the same line, but each must end in a period. FIRST is a sentence.

Sentences contain COBOL commands.

Paragraph can be any name expect if the paragraph is required. These paragraphs are not required, but make the program easier to read.

Tricks Of The Trade ...

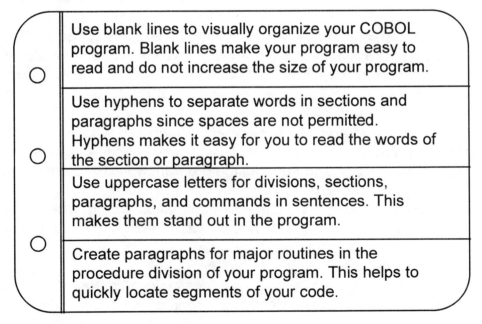

○ Use blank lines to visually organize your COBOL program. Blank lines make your program easy to read and do not increase the size of your program.

○ Use hyphens to separate words in sections and paragraphs since spaces are not permitted. Hyphens makes it easy for you to read the words of the section or paragraph.

Use uppercase letters for divisions, sections, paragraphs, and commands in sentences. This makes them stand out in the program.

○ Create paragraphs for major routines in the procedure division of your program. This helps to quickly locate segments of your code.

Identification Division

We'll begin a closer look at each division with the Identification Division. You must include the Program-Id paragraph in the Identification Division of every COBOL program you write, otherwise, the program won't compile. The Program-Id paragraph must be followed by a sentence containing the name of the program as shown on the next page.

The Program-Id paragraph and sentence can accept parameters. A *parameter* is information that tells the program how to perform under specific circumstances. Two parameters used with the Program-Id are **Common** and **Initial**

The *Common* parameter is used if the program is called from within another program. You'll learn how to do this later in the book. Once the **Common** parameter is set, the programmer is no longer able to call itself.

The *Iinitial* parameter is used to reset data items to their original values each time the program is called. Data items of programs called by your program are also reset to their original values.

There are also optional paragraphs that should be included in your **Identification Division** because they provide important information about the program. These optional paragraphs are Author, Installation, Date-Written, Date-Compiled, and Security.

The *Author paragraph* identifies the programmer who wrote the program and the *Date-Written* and *Date-Compile* specify the date the program was written and the date the program was compiled.

The *Installation paragraph* contains information about where the program was installed and any other information the programmer might find useful in installing the program.

The *Security paragraph* tells of any restrictions imposed by the program such as limiting access to a selected user group.

COMMON and INITIAL are parameters to the Program-Id paragraph.

Identifies the author, installation instructions, date written, and date compiled.

Identifies security restrictions required by of program.

```
000100 IDENTIFICATION DIVISION.
000200 PROGRAM-ID. FIRST IS COMMON INITIAL PROGRAM.
000300 AUTHOR. Mary Smith.
000400 INSTALLATION. Contact Mary Smith before installing.
000500 DATE-WRITTEN. March 17, 1999.
000600 DATE-COMPILED. March 17, 1999.
000700 SECURITY. Only officer level has permission to run
000800              this program.
000900 ENVIRONMENT DIVISION.
001000 DATA DIVISION.
001100
001200 WORKING-STORAGE SECTION.
001300 01    AGE         PIC 99.
001400
001500 PROCEDURE DIVISION.
001600
001700 BEGIN-MY-PROGRAM.
001800     DISPLAY "My First Program".
001900     DISPLAY "By Mary Smith".
002000 STOP-MY-PROGRAM.
002100     STOP RUN.
```

Text can be extended to more than one line by placing the period only at the end of the last line of the sentence.

Fact Sheet ...

○

ANSI-97 COBOL won't allow the Author, Date-Compiled, Date-Written, Installation, Security paragraphs.

○

○

Sentences in these paragraphs cannot be extended to more than one line by placing a hyphen in the Indicator Area. Instead, let the text wrap around, then place the period at the end of the multiline sentence.

Environment Division
Configuration Section

The Environment Division is divided into two sections. These are the Configuration Section and the Input-Output Section. Each of these sections are optional.

The Configuration Section has three optional paragraphs that are mostly used in large COBOL computer applications where several programmers work on the same program and the program is used on more than one computer. These are the Source-Computer, the Object-Computer, and Special-Names.

The Source-Computer paragraph identifies the computer used to compile the program that may be different from the computer running the program.

The program can be compiled with debugging code by using the With Debugging clause with the Source-Computer paragraph. Later in the book you'll learn how to debug your programs. Debugging code is ignored by the compiler if this clause is not used.

The Object-Computer paragraph identifies the computer that will run the program.

There are several optional clauses that are used in older versions of COBOL as part of the Object-Computer paragraph. All of these will be obsolete in the next version of COBOL. Consult documentation that came with your COBOL compiler for more information on these clauses.

The Special-Names paragraph contains sentences that define mnemonic names used in the program as shown on the next page. Special clauses are used with the Special-Names paragraph to identify common mnemonics. These are Alphabet, Symbolic Characters, Class, Decimal-Point, and Currency Sign.

The name of the computer that will compile the program.

Include debugging lines in the compile.

The name of the computer that will run the program.

Create an alias for a printer. Name the alphabet to use and the sorting method.

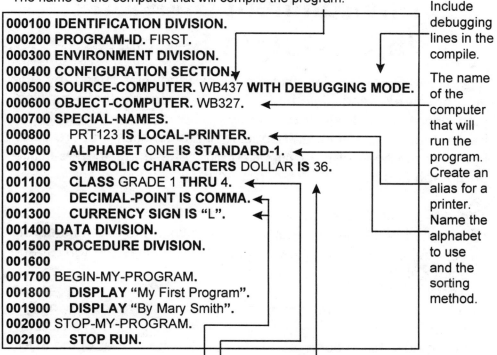

```
000100 IDENTIFICATION DIVISION.
000200 PROGRAM-ID. FIRST.
000300 ENVIRONMENT DIVISION.
000400 CONFIGURATION SECTION.
000500 SOURCE-COMPUTER. WB437 WITH DEBUGGING MODE.
000600 OBJECT-COMPUTER. WB327.
000700 SPECIAL-NAMES.
000800     PRT123 IS LOCAL-PRINTER.
000900     ALPHABET ONE IS STANDARD-1.
001000     SYMBOLIC CHARACTERS DOLLAR IS 36.
001100     CLASS GRADE 1 THRU 4.
001200     DECIMAL-POINT IS COMMA.
001300     CURRENCY SIGN IS "L".
001400 DATA DIVISION.
001500 PROCEDURE DIVISION.
001600
001700 BEGIN-MY-PROGRAM.
001800     DISPLAY "My First Program".
001900     DISPLAY "By Mary Smith".
002000 STOP-MY-PROGRAM.
002100     STOP RUN.
```

Replace default decimal and currency symbol.

Replace the word DOLLAR in the program with the ASCII character 36 that is $.

Assign a range of values to a name (GRADE). Use the name to test a condition such as determining if a data item is within the range of GRADE.

Fact Sheet ...

○ Alphabet clause can use three types of alphabets: **STANDARD-1 is ANSI ASCII,;STANDARD-2 is IOS; NATIVE** is the system default, or literally defined an in the clause.

○ You can assign a name to any ASCII code by using the Symbolic Characters clause.

○ The Class clause defines a condition that is considered true if the value being tested appears in the values of the Class.

Environment Division
Input-Output Section

The *Input-Out Section* identifies devices and files used by the program to exchange information. You'll recognize these as files, tape drives, and disks drives among other devices. Each device has a name, a location, and specific characteristics that are listed in two paragraphs of the Input-Out Section. These are the File-Control paragraph and the I-O-Control paragraph.

The *File-Control paragraph* relates system file names with devices files named in the Select statement as shown in the example on the next page. The File-Control paragraph also identifies the format and structure of the files.

The *Select statement* relates a real file name to an alias which is referred to in the program whenever the file is used. You'll learn more on how this is done later in the book. The format of the **Select** statement is dependent on the type of file used by the program. There are five types: sequential files, relative files, indexed files, sort-merge files, and report files.

A *sequential file* contains records that are written and read in sequential order. Records can't be accessed out of order.

A *relative file* contains records that are accessed by referencing the record's position in the file.

An *indexed file* contains records stored sequentially, but accessed randomly, using an index table similar to an index of a book.

A *sort-merge file* is a temporary file created as a result of a sort or the merging of files. This file can't be accessed without using the sort and merger commands. More on this later in this book.

A *report file* is created by using the Report Writer Control System and is typically not accessed, but rather sent to a printer.

```
000100 ENVIRONMENT DIVISION.
000200 INPUT-OUTPUT SECTION.
000300 FILE-CONTROL.
000400 SELECT PAYROLL
000500 ASSIGN TO "PAYROLL.DAT"
000600 RESERVE 5 AREAS
000700 ORGANIZATION IS SEQUENTIAL
000800 PADDING IS "*"
000900 RECORD DELIMITER STANDARD-1
001000 ACCESS MODE IS SEQUENTIAL.
```

Sequential File and Report File

Use PAYROLL in the program to refer to the PAYROLL.DAT file.

Each area is a file buffer.

Defines the character to use to fill in unused character positions.

Refer to your COBOL documentation for record delimiters.

Relative File

Access Mode can be Random to access records in any order or Dynamic to access either sequentially or randomly.

Relative Key is the key used to access the file randomly.

```
000100 ENVIRONMENT DIVISION.
000200 INPUT-OUTPUT SECTION.
000300 FILE-CONTROL.
000400 SELECT PAYROLL
000500 ASSIGN TO "PAYROLL.DAT"
000600 RESERVE 5 AREAS
000700 ORGANIZATION IS RELATIVE
00800 ACCESS MODE IS RELATIVE RANDOM
000900 RELATIVE KEY IS KEY-1.
```

```
000100 ENVIRONMENT DIVISION.
000200 INPUT-OUTPUT SECTION.
000300 FILE-CONTROL.
000400 SELECT PAYROLL
000500 ASSIGN TO "PAYROLL.DAT"
000600 RESERVE 5 AREAS
000700 ORGANIZATION IS INDEXED
000800 ACCESS MODE IS RANDOM
000900 RECORD KEY IS KEY-1
001000 ALTERNATE RECORD KEY IS KEY-2
001100 WITH DUPLICATES.
```

Indexed File

Access Mode can be Random to access records in any order, Dynamic to access either sequentially or randomly, or Sequential.

Specify the primary key and the alternate key to find records in the file.

Allow duplicate key values in the file for alternate keys only.

Sort or Merge File

No clauses can be used with a file created using the sort or merge commands.

```
000100 ENVIRONMENT DIVISION.
000200 INPUT-OUTPUT SECTION.
000300 FILE-CONTROL.
000400 SELECT PAYROLL
000500 ASSIGN TO "PAYROLL.DAT".
```

Environment Division
Input-Output Section
I-O Control Paragraph

The *I-O-Control* paragraph defines files on devices such as tape drivers and disks. The are several statements that can be used to create these definitions. These are Rerun, Same, Sort-Merge, Record, and Multiple File Tape Contains.

The *Rerun* statement identifies where the program is to store rerun information whenever an event occurs such as the end of a file, specified number of records, a time period, or a specific condition is met.

The *Same* statement tells the computer to use the same memory area for more than one file as a way to share resources. Typically, this statement is used in conjunction with Sort and Merge phrases.

The Same statement is also used with Record phrases that require a memory area to be shared when files are read.

The *Multiple File Tape Contains* statement identifies the location of files used by the programs that are stored on tape. The Position phrase is used with this statement to specify the file's position if the necessary files are not in sequential order on the tape as shown on the next page.

All statements can be placed in any order within the I-O control paragraph and only statements necessary for running the program should be included. For example, Multiple File Tape Contains statement is unnecessary if files are not stored on a tape or if only one file is used by the program.

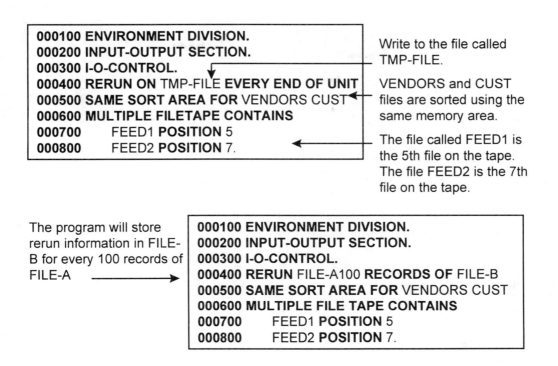

```
000100 ENVIRONMENT DIVISION.
000200 INPUT-OUTPUT SECTION.
000300 I-O-CONTROL.
000400 RERUN ON TMP-FILE EVERY END OF UNIT
000500 SAME SORT AREA FOR VENDORS CUST
000600 MULTIPLE FILETAPE CONTAINS
000700     FEED1 POSITION 5
000800     FEED2 POSITION 7.
```

Write to the file called TMP-FILE.

VENDORS and CUST files are sorted using the same memory area.

The file called FEED1 is the 5th file on the tape. The file FEED2 is the 7th file on the tape.

The program will store rerun information in FILE-B for every 100 records of FILE-A

```
000100 ENVIRONMENT DIVISION.
000200 INPUT-OUTPUT SECTION.
000300 I-O-CONTROL.
000400 RERUN FILE-A100 RECORDS OF FILE-B
000500 SAME SORT AREA FOR VENDORS CUST
000600 MULTIPLE FILE TAPE CONTAINS
000700     FEED1 POSITION 5
000800     FEED2 POSITION 7.
```

```
000100 ENVIRONMENT DIVISION.
000200 INPUT-OUTPUT SECTION.
000300 I-O-CONTROL.
000400 RERUN ON TMP-FILE  CONDITION COND-1
000500 SAME SORT AREA FOR VENDORS CUST
000600 MULTIPLE FILE TAPE CONTAINS
000700     FEED1 POSITION 5
000800     FEED2 POSITION 7.
```

Store rerun information each time the condition specified in COND-1 is encountered.

The program will store rerun information in FILE-B for every 100 records of FILE-A

```
000100 ENVIRONMENT DIVISION.
000200 INPUT-OUTPUT SECTION.
000300 I-O-CONTROL.
000400 RERUN FILE-A100 RECORDS OF FILE-B
000500 SAME SORT AREA FOR VENDORS CUST
000600 MULTIPLE FILE TAPE CONTAINS
000700     FEED1 POSITION 5
000800     FEED2 POSITION 7.
```

Data Division

The *Data Division* is the location where you define data elements and data files that will be used in your program. This division is grouped into six sections each used to describe a particular kind of data.

The *File Section* is the section where you define data used in files. This is called the *structure of the files*. Data in files are organized into records. A *record* is a set of data such as a person's name and address. There are three methods used to organize records in a file. These are sequentially, relatively, and indexed.

A *sequential file* contains records written and read sequentially. The first record written to the file is always the first record read from the file.

In a *relative file*, records are accessed by referencing their position in the file that permits random access of records. For example, you can ask for the fifth record in the file without having to read the first four records.

An *indexed file* uses an indexed table to locate a record. The index table contains search criteria called a *key* and the relative position of the record in the file. Once the key is located in the indexed table, the record is located using the record's relative position.

You'll learn more about how to use the File Section later in the book when you write and read data to and from a file.

The *Working-Storage Section* is the place where you define data elements that are not related to files. It is in this section where you define variables and constants used throughout your program.

The example on the next page briefly illustrates how this section is used in your program. You'll be shown other ways to use the Working-Storage Section in the next chapter.

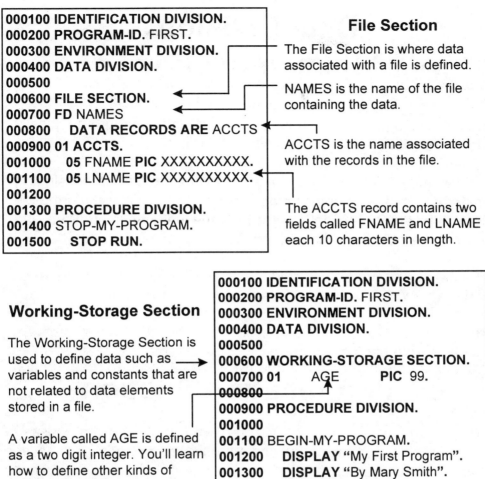

File Section

The File Section is where data associated with a file is defined.

NAMES is the name of the file containing the data.

ACCTS is the name associated with the records in the file.

The ACCTS record contains two fields called FNAME and LNAME each 10 characters in length.

```
000100 IDENTIFICATION DIVISION.
000200 PROGRAM-ID. FIRST.
000300 ENVIRONMENT DIVISION.
000400 DATA DIVISION.
000500
000600 FILE SECTION.
000700 FD NAMES
000800    DATA RECORDS ARE ACCTS
000900 01 ACCTS.
001000    05 FNAME PIC XXXXXXXXXX.
001100    05 LNAME PIC XXXXXXXXXX.
001200
001300 PROCEDURE DIVISION.
001400 STOP-MY-PROGRAM.
001500    STOP RUN.
```

Working-Storage Section

The Working-Storage Section is used to define data such as variables and constants that are not related to data elements stored in a file.

A variable called AGE is defined as a two digit integer. You'll learn how to define other kinds of variables and constants in the next chapter.

```
000100 IDENTIFICATION DIVISION.
000200 PROGRAM-ID. FIRST.
000300 ENVIRONMENT DIVISION.
000400 DATA DIVISION.
000500
000600 WORKING-STORAGE SECTION.
000700 01    AGE       PIC  99.
000800
000900 PROCEDURE DIVISION.
001000
001100 BEGIN-MY-PROGRAM.
001200    DISPLAY "My First Program".
001300    DISPLAY "By Mary Smith".
001400 STOP-MY-PROGRAM.
001500    STOP RUN.
```

Did You Know ...

○ The 01 in examples on this page are called levels. The first level is 01 as you surmised. The 02 level data items are associated with the level 01. The level 03 is

○ related to the level 02 of the same set. The sequence continues.

○ There are 49 levels you can use in your program, although most programmers never come close to using this number. There are also special levels above 49 that you'll learn about in the next chapter.

Data Division
Linkage Section

Your COBOL program can be called by another program typically to process data passed by the other program.

For example, your program may perform special processing of salary information. Another program may collect salary information from data entry. The data entry program calls your program and makes available the salary information for processing.

The data entry program is said to call your program using the **CALL** command. You'll see how this is done later in the book.

The *Linkage Section* is used to identify the data your program receives from another program.

Communication Section

Data can be transmitted and received to and from message queues by using the **SEND** and **RECEIVE** commands. A *message queue* is a memory buffer that exchanges data with systems communications devices.

Data elements designed to be used with the **Send** and **Receive** commands must be defined in the Communication Section. You'll learn the proper formats of these definitions later in this book.

Report Section

You'll find many of your programs are required to print data in a report. Reports are assembled by your program and written to a report file. A *report file* contains the report description. The Report Section is where you define the report and define data used in the report.

Linkage Section

```
000100 IDENTIFICATION DIVISION.
000200 PROGRAM-ID. FIRST.
000300 ENVIRONMENT DIVISION.
000400 DATA DIVISION.
000500
000600 LINKAGE SECTION USING FNAME LNAME.
000700 77 NAMES    PIC X(20).
000800
000900 01 FNAME PIC X(10).
001000 01 LNAME PIC X(10).
001100
001200
001300 PROCEDURE DIVISION.
001400 STOP-MY-PROGRAM.
001500    STOP RUN.
```

The Linkage Section is where data passed to your program by another program is defined.

The definition must start at the special level 77.

The data definition in your program must be defined as used in the calling program.

The calling program uses these names for the data.

Communication Section

The Communication Section is where data is defined for communicating with systems devices.

COM1 is the name of the device and the program will receive data from the device.

Incoming data will be stored on the queue called Q1.

```
000100 IDENTIFICATION DIVISION.
000200 PROGRAM-ID. FIRST.
000300 ENVIRONMENT DIVISION.
000400 DATA DIVISION.
000500
000600 COMMUNICATION SECTION.
000700 CD COM1 FOR INPUT
000800 SYMBOLIC QUEUE IS Q1.
000900
001000 PROCEDURE DIVISION.
001100 STOP-MY-PROGRAM.
001200    STOP RUN.
```

Report Section

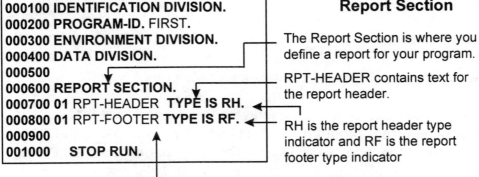

```
000100 IDENTIFICATION DIVISION.
000200 PROGRAM-ID. FIRST.
000300 ENVIRONMENT DIVISION.
000400 DATA DIVISION.
000500
000600 REPORT SECTION.
000700 01 RPT-HEADER  TYPE IS RH.
000800 01 RPT-FOOTER TYPE IS RF.
000900
001000    STOP RUN.
```

The Report Section is where you define a report for your program.

RPT-HEADER contains text for the report header.

RH is the report header type indicator and RF is the report footer type indicator

RPT-FOOTER contains text for the report footer.

Procedure Division

The focus of most of your COBOL programming will be within the Procedure Division. This is where you write instructions into your program to tell the computer to do something such as to manipulate data and display information on the screen.

You can immediately enter instructions following the Procedure Division header in your program without the need to enter section headers or paragraphs.

Notice the first code example on the next page does not contain any section or paragraphs in the Procedure Division. This program will compile without errors, although this is not good coding style.

Always use paragraphs to segregate the Procedure Division into functional sentence groups as illustrated in the second example on the opposite page. Two paragraphs are used in this division to identify the purpose of the sentences within the paragraph.

There is a section commonly used in the Procedure Division to group together special purpose procedures. This section is called *Declaratives*.

Special purpose procedures include those for exceptions, reporting, and debugging. You'll learn how to create and use these procedures later in this book.

The third example on the next page shows a debugging special procedures that is declared in the Declaratives Section. Notice this section must end with an *End Declaratives* statement.

The Procedure Division can be used with the *Using phrase* that passes data values from programs that call your program using the **CALL** command. The third example on the next page receives FNAME and LNAME values from another program that calls this program.

```
000100 IDENTIFICATION DIVISION.
000200 PROGRAM-ID. FIRST.
000300 ENVIRONMENT DIVISION.
000400 DATA DIVISION.
000500 PROCEDURE DIVISION.
000600
000700 DISPLAY "My First Program".
000800 DISPLAY "By Mary Smith".
000900
001000 STOP RUN.
```

The Procedure Division is where you write most of your COBOL instructions.

No required sections and paragraphs are necessary in this division.

Enter your COBOL commands here.

```
000100 IDENTIFICATION DIVISION.
000200 PROGRAM-ID. FIRST.
000300 ENVIRONMENT DIVISION.
000400 DATA DIVISION.
000500 PROCEDURE DIVISION.
000600
000700 DISPLAY-TEXT.
000800    DISPLAY "My First Program".
000900    DISPLAY "By Mary Smith".
001000 STOP-MY-PROGRAM.
001100    STOP RUN.
```

Create your own paragraphs to better organize your program.

The Using phrase identifies data passed by a calling program.

The Declaratives Section is used to define special procedures.

The debug information is gathered each time the communications device is referenced.

```
000100 IDENTIFICATION DIVISION.
000200 PROGRAM-ID. FIRST.
000300 ENVIRONMENT DIVISION.
000400 DATA DIVISION.
000500 PROCEDURE DIVISION USING FNAME LNAME.
000600 DECLARATIVES.
000700    USE FOR DEBUGGING ON
000800       COM1.
000900 END DECLARATIVES.
001000 DISPLAY-TEXT.
001100    DISPLAY FNAME.
001200    DISPLAY LNAME.
001300 STOP-MY-PROGRAM.
001400    STOP RUN.
```

The Declaratives Section must terminate using then End Declaratives sentence.

Words To Avoid Using

You've learned throughout this chapter that you can create your own names for sections, paragraphs, and data names. You'll learn about this in the next chapter.

There are restrictions, however. The words you choose must not be words that are used in the COBOL language. These words are called *reserved words* and will likely cause a compiler error in your program if they are used incorrectly such as a name of your own section, paragraph or data.

The following pages contain a list of words recognized by most COBOL compilers as reserved words. Refer to this list before creating any names.

A

ACCEPT
ACCESS
ADD
ADVANCING
AFTER
ALL
ALPHABET
ALPHABETIC
ALPHABETIC-LOWER
ALPHABETIC-UPPER
ALPHANUMERIC
ALPHANUMERIC-EDITED
ALSO
ALTER
ALTERNATE
AND
ANY
ARE
AREA
AREAS
ASCENDING
ASSIGN
AT
AUTHOR

B

BEFORE
BINARY
BLANK
BLOCK
BOTTOM
BY

C

CALL
CANCEL
CD
CF
CH
CHARACTER
CHARACTERS
CLASS
CLOCK-UNITS
CLOSE
COBOL
CODE
CODE-SET
COLLATING
COLUMN
COMMA

COMMUNICATIONS
COMP
COMPUTATIONAL
COMPUTE
CONFIGURATION
CONTAINS
CONTENT
CONTINUE
CONTROL
CONTROLS
CONVERTING
COPY
CORR
CORRESPONDING
COUNT
CURRENCY

D

DATA
DATE
DATE-COMPILED
DATE-WRITTEN
DAY
DAY-OF-WEEK
DE

DEBUG-CONTENTS
DEBUG-ITEM
DEBUG-LINE
DEBUG-NAME
DEBUG-SUB-1
DEBUG-SUB-2
DEBUG-SUB-3
DEBUGGING
DECIMAL-POINT
DECLARATIVES
DELETE
DELIMITED
DELIMITER
DEPENDING
DESCENDING
DESTINATION
DETAIL
DISABLE
DISPLAY
DIVIDE
DIVISION
DOWN
DUPLICATES
DYNAMIC

E

EGI
ELSE
EMI
ENABLE
END
END-ADD
END-CALL
END-COMPUTE
END-DELETE
END-DIVIDE
END-EVALUATE
END-IF
END-MULTIPLY
END-OF-PAGE
END-PERFORM
END-READ
END-RECEIVE
END-RETURN

END-REWRITE
END-SEARCH
END-START
END-STRING
END-SUBTRACT
END-UNSTRING
END-WRITE
ENTER
ENVIRONMENT
EOP
EQUAL
ERROR
ESI
EVALUATE
EVERY
EXCEPTION
EXIT
EXTEND
EXTERNAL

F

FALSE
FD
FILE
FILE-CONTROL
FILLER
FINAL
FIRST
FOOTING
FOR
FROM

G

GENERATE
GIVING
GLOBAL
GO
GREATER
GROUP

H

HEADING
HIGH-VALUE
HIGH-VALUES

I

I-O
I-O-CONTROL
IDENTIFICATION
IF
IN
INDEX
INDEXED
INDICATE
INITIAL
INITIALIZE
INITIATE
INPUT
INPUT-OUTPUT
INSPECT
INSTALLATION
INTO
INVALID
IS

J

JUST
JUSTIFIED

K

KEY

L

LABEL
LAST
LEADING
LEFT
LENGTH
LESS
LIMIT
LIMITS
LINAGE
LINAGE-COUNTER
LINE
LINE-COUNTER
LINES
LINKAGE
LOCK
LOW-VALUE

LOW-VALUES

M
MEMORY
MERGE
MESSAGE
MODE
MODULES
MOVE
MULTIPLE
MULTIPLY

N
NATIVE
NEGATIVE
NEXT
NO
NOT
NUMBER
NUMERIC
NUMERIC-EDITED

O
OBJECT-COMPUTER
OCCURS
OF
OFF
OMITTED
ON
OPEN
OPTIONAL
OR
ORDER
ORGANIZATION
OTHER
OUTPUT
OVERFLOW

P
PACKED-DECIMAL
PADDING
PAGE
PAGE-COUNTER
PERFORM

PF
PH
PIC
PICTURE
PLUS
POINTER
POSITION
POSITIVE
PRINTING
PROCEDURE
PROCEDURES
PROCEED
PROGRAM
PROGRAM-ID
PURGE

Q
QUEUE
QUOTE
QUOTES

R
RANDOM
RD
READ
RECEIVE
RECORD
RECORDS
REDEFINES
REEL
REFERENCE
REFERENCES
RELATIVE
RELEASE
REMAINDER
REMOVAL
RENAMES
REPLACE
REPLACING
REPORT
REPORTING
REPORTS
RERUN
RESERVE
RESET

RETURN
REVERSED
REWIND
REWRITE
RF
RH
RIGHT
ROUNDED
RUN

S
SAME
SEARCH
SECTION
SECURITY
SEGMENT
SEGMENT-LIMIT
SELECT
SEND
SENTENCE
SEPARATE
SEQUENCE
SEQUENTIAL
SET
SIGN
SIZE
SORT
SORT-MERGE
SOURCE
SOURCE-COMPUTER
SPACE
SPACES
SPECIAL-NAMES
STANDARD
STANDARD-1
STANDARD-2
START
STATUS
STOP
STRING
SUB-QUEUE-1
SUB-QUEUE-2
SUB-QUEUE-3
SUBTRACT
SUM

SUPPRESS
SYMBOLIC
SYNC
SYNCHRONIZED

T
TABLE
TALLYING
TAPE
TERMINAL
TERMINATE
TEST
TEXT
THAN
THEN
THROUGH
THRU
TIME
TIMES
TD
TOP
TRAILING
TRUE
TYPE

U
UNIT
UNSTRING
UNTIL
UP
UPON
USAGE
USE
USING

V
VALUE
VALUES
VARYING

W
WHEN
WITH
WORDS

WORKING-STORAGE
WRITE

Z
ZERO
ZEROES
ZEROS

Chapter
Two

Working with Constants and Variables

- Constants and Variables
- Naming Variables
- Defining Variables
- Assigning Values to Variables
- Displaying the Value of Variables
- Using a Variable as a Constant
- Dealing with Alphanumeric Variables
- Initializing Variables
- Initializing Variables with Zeros and Spaces
- Truncation
- Decimal Variables
- Displaying Decimal Values
- Suppressing Zeros
- Limit Variables to Alphabetic Characters
- Insert a Blank into the Data
- Currency Data
- Insert Commas into the Data
- Indicating Debit or Credit
- Changing the Currency Symbol
- Changing the Decimal Point Symbol
- Replace Leading Zeros with Asterisks
- Date Data
- Use Blanks Instead of Zeros
- Signed Numbers
- Ways to Store Data.
- Assign Values to Many Variables

Constants and Variables

Information is stored in your program in one of two ways: as a constant or as a variable. A *constant* is a value that doesn't change while your program is running. You saw programs in the last chapter use the value "My First Program". This is a constant.

In contrast, a *variable* is a place-holder for data. You give this place-holder a name within your program. The name is called the *name of the variable*.

The value inside the place-holder can change as your program runs. For example, a person might enter a street address at the keyboard that your program stores in a variable until the information is processed. The street address entered by the next person is also stored in the same variable.

Instructions written in your program to receive and process the street address refers to the name of the variable rather than the value of the variable.

Let's call the variable STREET and the first value of the variable is "Main Street". The program uses the sentence **DISPLAY** STREET to show the current value of the variable. The program can prompt the user to enter another street that replaces "Main Street" as the value of the variable STREET. However, the program uses the same sentence to display the new value.

The first example on the next page illustrates the use of a constant in a program. Constants are used whenever a value is not going to change in a program.

The second example shows the use of a variable in a program. Notice the value of the variable changes although the program references the same variable name to display both values of the variable on the screen.

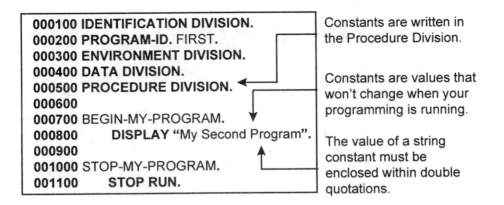

```
000100 IDENTIFICATION DIVISION.
000200 PROGRAM-ID. FIRST.
000300 ENVIRONMENT DIVISION.
000400 DATA DIVISION.
000500 PROCEDURE DIVISION.
000600
000700 BEGIN-MY-PROGRAM.
000800     DISPLAY "My Second Program".
000900
001000 STOP-MY-PROGRAM.
001100     STOP RUN.
```

Constants are written in the Procedure Division.

Constants are values that won't change when your programming is running.

The value of a string constant must be enclosed within double quotations.

Numeric constants should only be used to display a numeric value that is not intended to be used in mathematical operations.

Numeric constants are entered without double quotation marks.

```
000100 IDENTIFICATION DIVISION.
000200 PROGRAM-ID. FIRST.
000300 ENVIRONMENT DIVISION.
000400 DATA DIVISION.
000500 PROCEDURE DIVISION.
000600
000700 BEGIN-MY-PROGRAM.
000800     DISPLAY 1999.
000900
001000 STOP-MY-PROGRAM.
001100     STOP RUN.
```

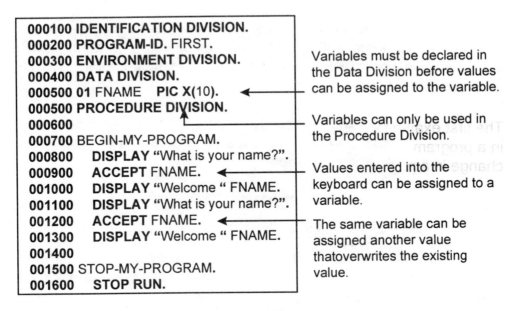

```
000100 IDENTIFICATION DIVISION.
000200 PROGRAM-ID. FIRST.
000300 ENVIRONMENT DIVISION.
000400 DATA DIVISION.
000500 01 FNAME    PIC X(10).
000500 PROCEDURE DIVISION.
000600
000700 BEGIN-MY-PROGRAM.
000800     DISPLAY "What is your name?".
000900     ACCEPT FNAME.
001000     DISPLAY "Welcome " FNAME.
001100     DISPLAY "What is your name?".
001200     ACCEPT FNAME.
001300     DISPLAY "Welcome " FNAME.
001400
001500 STOP-MY-PROGRAM.
001600     STOP RUN.
```

Variables must be declared in the Data Division before values can be assigned to the variable.

Variables can only be used in the Procedure Division.

Values entered into the keyboard can be assigned to a variable.

The same variable can be assigned another value that overwrites the existing value.

Naming Variables

Before a variable can be used in your program, you must tell the computer to reserve a place in memory for the variable. This is called *defining the variable* and is written in the Data Division.

The compiler needs to know three facts about the variable. These are the name of the variable, the kind of data you intend to store in the variable, and the amount of space you want to reserve.

The *name of the variable* should reflect the value stored in the variable. For example, a variable containing a person's first name shouldn't be named STREET, although there is nothing stopping you from doing so. FIRST-NAME or FNAME might be a better alternative.

Variable names are limited to no more than 30 characters and can consist of uppercase letters, digits zero through nine, and hyphens. However, a hyphen cannot be used at the first character of the variable name.

There are also a few other characters that cannot be used in the name of a variable such as the underscore and the dollar sign($).

Variable names should be unique. You can't have two variables with the same name defined on the same level. The name also can't be a reserved word (see Chapter 1 for a complete list of reserved words).

You should consider the readability of the variable name whenever you create a variable. Always separate the words in the name with a hyphen such as in this example:

FIRST-NAME
FIRSTNAME

Notice the first variable in this example is easier to read than the second because your mind does not have to decipher where the first word ends and the second word begins.

Unacceptable name because lowercase letters are used in the variable name. All variable names must be in uppercase letters. A solution is to use FNAME.

```
000100 IDENTIFICATION DIVISION.
000200 PROGRAM-ID. FIRST.
000300 ENVIRONMENT DIVISION.
000400 DATA DIVISION.
000500 01 Fname   PIC XXXXXXXXX.
000600 PROCEDURE DIVISION.
000700
000800 STOP-MY-PROGRAM.
000900    STOP RUN.
```

```
000100 IDENTIFICATION DIVISION.
000200 PROGRAM-ID. FIRST.
000300 ENVIRONMENT DIVISION.
000400 DATA DIVISION.
000500 01 7-2-99   PIC 999.
000600 PROCEDURE DIVISION.
000700
000800 STOP-MY-PROGRAM.
000900    STOP RUN.
```

Acceptable name. Numbers can be used as the name of a variable, although the name does not indicate the value stored in the variable. A better name is TODAYS-SALES or whatever best describes the value of the variable.

Unacceptable name. The dollar sign cannot be used in the name of the variable. A solution is to use DOLLAR-AMOUNT.

```
000100 IDENTIFICATION DIVISION.
000200 PROGRAM-ID. FIRST.
000300 ENVIRONMENT DIVISION.
000400 DATA DIVISION.
000500 01 $-AMOUNT   PIC 99.
000600 PROCEDURE DIVISION.
000700
000800 STOP-MY-PROGRAM.
000900    STOP RUN.
```

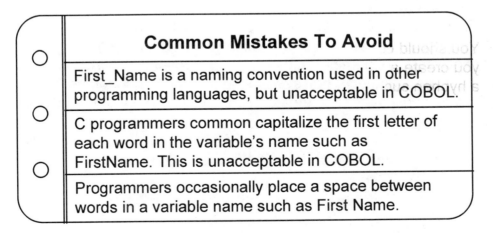

Common Mistakes To Avoid

○ First_Name is a naming convention used in other programming languages, but unacceptable in COBOL.

○ C programmers common capitalize the first letter of each word in the variable's name such as FirstName. This is unacceptable in COBOL.

○ Programmers occasionally place a space between words in a variable name such as First Name.

Defining Variables

In addition to properly naming a variable, you must also describe the kind of the data you intend to store in the variable and the size of the data.

The kind of data stored in the variable is called the *data type* and can be either a string or a numeric value. Alphanumeric characters are characters and numbers stored in an *alphanumeric variable*. Numeric values are stored in a *numeric variable*.

Variables are defined in the **Working-Storage Section** of the **Data Division** as shown in the examples on the next page. A variable definition is created in a sentence that begins with a level number. A variable definition must begin with a level specification and be followed by a valid variable name.

The data type of a variable is defined in the sentence using either the **PICTURE IS** or **PIC** clause shown on the next page. Either is correct, although many programmers use the shorter version (**PIC**) to save unnecessary typing.

The data type of the variable is identified by using either an X or a 9 in the **PIC** clause. An X indicates the variable is an alphanumeric variable and a 9 tells the compiler the variable is a numeric variable.

Each X reserves space for one character in memory. If 10 X is used, then the alphanumeric variable can have a value up to ten characters. Characters can be any alphanumeric character including numbers, however these numbers cannot be used in calculations. Instead, they are used in values like a street address.

Each 9 reserves space for a digit from 0 through 9. If 99 is used, then the numeric variable can hold a value from 0 to 99.

```
000100 IDENTIFICATION DIVISION.
000200 PROGRAM-ID. FIRST.
000300 ENVIRONMENT DIVISION.
000400 DATA DIVISION.
000500
000600 WORKING-STORAGE SECTION.
000700
000800 01 FNAME   PICTURE IS XXXXXXX.
000900 PROCEDURE DIVISION.
001000
001100 STOP-MY-PROGRAM.
001200    STOP RUN.
```

Variables must be defined in the Working-Storage Section of the Data Division.

Variables must specify the level such as level 01.

Each X reserves space for one character in memory.

Each 9 reserves space for one digit of a number. Values from 0 to 9 can be assigned for each 9.

The PIC clause is an abbreviation for PICTURE IS and can be used for both numeric variables and alphanumeric variables.

```
000100 IDENTIFICATION DIVISION.
000200 PROGRAM-ID. FIRST.
000300 ENVIRONMENT DIVISION.
000400 DATA DIVISION.
000500
000600 WORKING-STORAGE SECTION.
000700
000800 01 AGE   PIC 99.
000900 PROCEDURE DIVISION.
001000
001100 STOP-MY-PROGRAM.
001000    STOP RUN.
```

```
000100 IDENTIFICATION DIVISION.
000200 PROGRAM-ID. FIRST.
000300 ENVIRONMENT DIVISION.
000400 DATA DIVISION.
000500
000600 WORKING-STORAGE SECTION.
000700
000800 01 QUANTITY   PIC 9(15).
000900 01 FNAME       PIC X(10).
001000 PROCEDURE DIVISION.
001100
001200 STOP-MY-PROGRAM.
001300    STOP RUN.
```

Parentheses are used as an alternative to writing a series of Xs and 9s.

This is the same as writing 15 9s.

This is the same as writing 10 Xs.

Assigning Values to Variables

Values can be stored in a variable once the variable is defined. This is called *assigning* a value to the variable. Only values that meet the definition of the variable can be assigned to it.

For example, you cannot assign a character to a numeric variable. Likewise, you cannot assign a number value to an alphanumeric variable unless the number is enclosed within quotations.

The command used to assign a value to a variable is called the **MOVE** command that is illustrated in examples on the next page. The *MOVE command* copies the value from one memory location and stores the value into the variable. Remember, the name of the variable is the name of a location in memory where the value of the variable is stored.

The value being moved into the variable can be a constant value. A *constant value* is a value that does not change while your program is running such as the number 25 or "My First Program".

The value being moved can also be the value of another variable. In such cases, the name of each variable is used within the sentence containing the **MOVE** command.

The sentence containing the **MOVE** command must be written in the Procedure Division of your program at the point in your program when you what to store the value in the variable.

The **MOVE** command can be written within any section or paragraph in the Procedure Division. However, many COBOL programmers create their own paragraphs below which they write the assignment sentence.

Values being moved are not moved at all. Instead they are copied from one location to another. Once copied, the values appear in both locations.

```
000100 IDENTIFICATION DIVISION.
000200 PROGRAM-ID. FIRST.
000300 ENVIRONMENT DIVISION.
000400 DATA DIVISION.
000500
000600 WORKING-STORAGE SECTION.
000700
000800 01 FNAME    PIC X(15).
000900 PROCEDURE DIVISION.
001000
001100    MOVE "Bob" TO FNAME.
001200 STOP-MY-PROGRAM.
001300    STOP RUN.
```

Variables must be defined before they can be used in your program.

The MOVE command must be used in the Procedure Division.

A alphanumeric constant is assigned to the FNAME alphanumeric variable.

Make sure the TO clause is used with the MOVE command to indicate the target location of the move.

```
000100 IDENTIFICATION DIVISION.
000200 PROGRAM-ID. FIRST.
000300 ENVIRONMENT DIVISION.
000400 DATA DIVISION.
000500
000600 WORKING-STORAGE SECTION.
000700
000800 01 AGE   PIC 99.
000900 PROCEDURE DIVISION.
001000
001100    MOVE 25 TO AGE.
001200 STOP-MY-PROGRAM.
001300    STOP RUN.
```

A numeric constant is assigned to the AGE numeric variable.

```
000100 IDENTIFICATION DIVISION.
000200 PROGRAM-ID. FIRST.
000300 ENVIRONMENT DIVISION.
000400 DATA DIVISION.
000500
000600 WORKING-STORAGE SECTION.
000700
000800 01 QUANTITY    PIC 9(15).
000900 01 INVENTORY   PIC 9(15).
001000 PROCEDURE DIVISION.
001100
001200    MOVE 295 TO QUANTITY.
001300    MOVE QUANTITY TO INVENTORY.
001400 STOP-MY-PROGRAM.
001500    STOP RUN.
```

A numeric constant is assigned to the QUANTITY numeric variable.

The value of the QUANTITY numeric variable is copied to the INVENTORY numeric variable.

Displaying the Value of Variables

Values stored in variables can be displayed on the screen by using the **DISPLAY** command followed by the name of the variable. This technique is shown in examples on the next page.

The *DISPLAY command* is used to show the value of either an alphanumeric variable or a numeric variable without changing the syntax of the command.

The **DISPLAY** command must be written into the Procedure Division of your program and can only refer to variables that are defined in the **Working-Storage Section** of the **Data Division**.

More than one variable can be referenced by the same instance of the **DISPLAY** command by using the name of the variables in the same sentence. Each name must be separated by.

However, the space has no effect on how the value of the variables will appear on the screen. Look at the following lines of code. Assume the value of FNAME is Bob and the value of LNAME is Smith. Notice there isn't a space between them when the values are displayed.

> **DISPLAY** FNAME LNAME
> Output: BobSmith

Values of variables can be combined with a literal character such as a space to properly display values on the screen. A *literal character* is an alphanumeric value or a symbol that does not represent another value. Examples on the following page illustrates how to combine a literal and variables using the **DISPLAY** command.

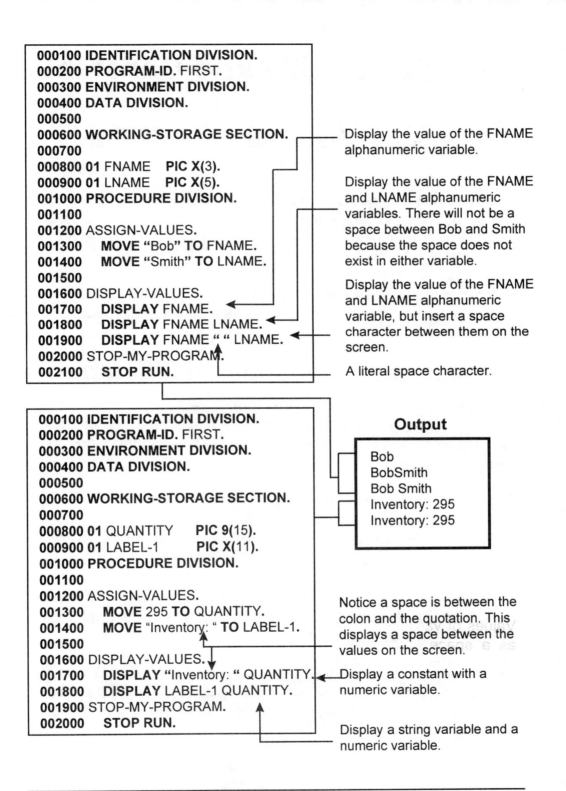

```
000100 IDENTIFICATION DIVISION.
000200 PROGRAM-ID. FIRST.
000300 ENVIRONMENT DIVISION.
000400 DATA DIVISION.
000500
000600 WORKING-STORAGE SECTION.
000700
000800 01 FNAME    PIC X(3).
000900 01 LNAME    PIC X(5).
001000 PROCEDURE DIVISION.
001100
001200 ASSIGN-VALUES.
001300     MOVE "Bob" TO FNAME.
001400     MOVE "Smith" TO LNAME.
001500
001600 DISPLAY-VALUES.
001700     DISPLAY FNAME.
001800     DISPLAY FNAME LNAME.
001900     DISPLAY FNAME " " LNAME.
002000 STOP-MY-PROGRAM.
002100     STOP RUN.
```

Display the value of the FNAME alphanumeric variable.

Display the value of the FNAME and LNAME alphanumeric variables. There will not be a space between Bob and Smith because the space does not exist in either variable.

Display the value of the FNAME and LNAME alphanumeric variable, but insert a space character between them on the screen.

A literal space character.

```
000100 IDENTIFICATION DIVISION.
000200 PROGRAM-ID. FIRST.
000300 ENVIRONMENT DIVISION.
000400 DATA DIVISION.
000500
000600 WORKING-STORAGE SECTION.
000700
000800 01 QUANTITY    PIC 9(15).
000900 01 LABEL-1     PIC X(11).
001000 PROCEDURE DIVISION.
001100
001200 ASSIGN-VALUES.
001300     MOVE 295 TO QUANTITY.
001400     MOVE "Inventory: " TO LABEL-1.
001500
001600 DISPLAY-VALUES.
001700     DISPLAY "Inventory: " QUANTITY.
001800     DISPLAY LABEL-1 QUANTITY.
001900 STOP-MY-PROGRAM.
002000     STOP RUN.
```

Output

```
Bob
BobSmith
Bob Smith
Inventory: 295
Inventory: 295
```

Notice a space is between the colon and the quotation. This displays a space between the values on the screen.

Display a constant with a numeric variable.

Display a string variable and a numeric variable.

Using a Variable as a Constant

You'll recall a constant is a value that does not change while your program is running. For example, "..." is a alphanumeric constant. You've seen a series of periods used in text to indicate more text will follow.

If you use one or a series of characters frequently in your program, you do not have to retype the character(s) as a constant. Instead you can type the character(s) once, then assign the character(s) to a variable.

Reference the variable each time you want to use the character(s) in your program. The first example on the opposite page illustrates this technique.

Dealing with Alphanumeric Variables

A common problem COBOL programmers face is a lack of space when assigning a string to a variable. Simply stated, the string is too long to fit on the same line with the **MOVE** command and the name of the variable.

The solution is to extend the length of the sentence. Most COBOL sentences fit on a line of code. However, a sentence can bridge more than one line. You can see how this is done in the second example on the next page.

A sentence is not a line, but a series of characters that end with a period. Notice in lines 001400 and 001800 in the second example they do not end with a period.

The sentence continues to the next line that ends with a period. The compiler treats both lines as one sentence. This is the same as if you were able to type both lines on a single line in your program.

```
000100 IDENTIFICATION DIVISION.
000200 PROGRAM-ID. FIRST.
000300 ENVIRONMENT DIVISION.
000400 DATA DIVISION.
000500
000600 WORKING-STORAGE SECTION.
000700
000800 01 ONE-COLON          PIC  X.
000900 01 SEVERAL-PERIODS     PIC X(3).
001000 PROCEDURE DIVISION.
001100
001200 ASSIGN-VALUES.
001300     MOVE ":" TO ONE-COLON.
001400     MOVE "..." TO SEVERAL-PERIODS.
001500
001600 DISPLAY-VALUES.
001700     DISPLAY AGE ONE-COLON.
001800     DISPLAY "Tips" SEVERAL-PERIODS.
001900 STOP-MY-PROGRAM.
002000     STOP RUN.
```

Use a variable as a constant by assigning the value of the constant to the variable.

A colon is assigned to an alphanumeric variable.
Three periods are assigned to an alphanumeric variable.

Whenever you want to use the constant, use the variable instead.

```
000100 IDENTIFICATION DIVISION.
000200 PROGRAM-ID. FIRST.
000300 ENVIRONMENT DIVISION.
000400 DATA DIVISION.
000500
000600 WORKING-STORAGE SECTION.
000700
000800 01 QUANTITY      PIC 9(15).
000900 01 LABEL-1       PIC X(25).
001000 PROCEDURE DIVISION.
001100
001200 ASSIGN-VALUES.
001300     MOVE 295 TO QUANTITY.
001400     MOVE "Inventory for July 1999:
001500     TO LABEL-1.
001600
001700 DISPLAY-VALUES.
001800     DISPLAY "Inventory July 1999"
001900       QUANTITY.
002000     DISPLAY LABEL-1 QUANTITY.
002100 STOP-MY-PROGRAM.
002200     STOP RUN.
```

Assign a long alphanumeric literal to an alphanumeric variable by extending the sentence to the next line.

No period.

Period is inserted on next line.

Display a long alphanumeric variable literal and a variable by extending the sentence to the next line.

No period.

Period is inserted on next line.

Working with Constants and Variables

Initializing Variables

When you define a variable in the Data Division, the compiler reserves space in the computer's memory for the value you'll later assign to the variable.

You'll recall the PIC clause tells the compiler how much room to reserve. Although memory is available for the value, no value is placed into memory. The variable has no value assigned to it.

The assumption you make each time you define a variable is you'll assign a value to it some place in the Procedure Division of your program. However, sometimes the assumption isn't correct especially in large COBOL programs that contain hundreds of lines of code.

You may actually try to use the variable before assigning the variable a value. This can cause problems when you run your program and produce unpredictable results.

Experienced COBOL programmers avoid this problem by assigning a value to a variable at the time the variable is defined. This technique is called *initializing* the variable.

Variables are initialized using the VALUE IS clause as illustrated in the examples on the next page. You'll notice the VALUE IS clause has a similar result as using the MOVE command to assign a value to a variable.

Some COBOL programmers prefer to create an initialization paragraph at the beginning of the Working-Storage Section of the Procedure Division. They use the MOVE command to assign initial values to all the variables created in the program..

You should develop the habit of initializing variables at the time you define them so you avoid encountering a bug in your program.

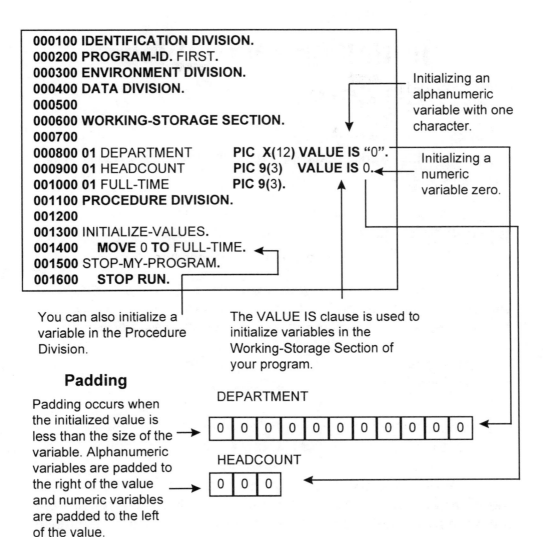

```
000100 IDENTIFICATION DIVISION.
000200 PROGRAM-ID. FIRST.
000300 ENVIRONMENT DIVISION.
000400 DATA DIVISION.
000500
000600 WORKING-STORAGE SECTION.
000700
000800 01 DEPARTMENT      PIC  X(12) VALUE IS "0".
000900 01 HEADCOUNT       PIC 9(3)   VALUE IS 0.
001000 01 FULL-TIME       PIC 9(3).
001100 PROCEDURE DIVISION.
001200
001300 INITIALIZE-VALUES.
001400    MOVE 0 TO FULL-TIME.
001500 STOP-MY-PROGRAM.
001600    STOP RUN.
```

Initializing an alphanumeric variable with one character.

Initializing a numeric variable zero.

You can also initialize a variable in the Procedure Division.

The VALUE IS clause is used to initialize variables in the Working-Storage Section of your program.

Padding

Padding occurs when the initialized value is less than the size of the variable. Alphanumeric variables are padded to the right of the value and numeric variables are padded to the left of the value.

DEPARTMENT

| 0 | 0 | 0 | 0 | 0 | 0 | 0 | 0 | 0 | 0 | 0 |

HEADCOUNT

| 0 | 0 | 0 |

Facts You Should Know...

Your program will compile without error if you use an uninitialized numeric variable in a calculation. However, the program will stop running after trying to perform the calculation.

You can use either the PIC or the PICTURE IS clause with the VALUE IS clause in your program.

Initializing Variables with Zeros and Spaces

On the previous page you learned the techniques for initializing variables in the **Working-Storage Section** of the **Data Division** when you define the variable.

It is common for programmers to initialize variables with either a zero or a space depending on if the variable is a numeric variable or a string variable.

Instead of initializing with your own value, you can initialize a variable using one of the two COBOL keywords. These are **ZEROES** and **SPACES** as illustrated in the example on the next page.

When **ZEROES** and **SPACES** are used, the compiler pads all the positions of the variable with either zeros or spaces.

Truncation

Values assigned to a variable must be small enough to be stored in the memory location reserved for the variable. You'll recall from earlier in this chapter, the **PIC** clause tells the compiler how much room to reserve in memory for the data.

If the data is too large for the variable, then the data will truncate the data. *Truncation* means some of the data will be discarded.

If you reserved 5 characters for the variable FNAME and tried to assign "Joseph", only "Josep" will be stored in the variable. The "h" will be discarded. The right characters are truncated.

Likewise, if you reserved space for 2 digits for the variable AGE and tried to assign 100, only 00 will be stored. The 1 is discarded. The left characters are truncated.

Use the reserved word SPACES to fill the variable with spaces.

Use the reserved word ZEROES to fill the variable with zeros.

The reserved words ZEROES and SPACES can be used with the MOVE command.

Values too large for the variable will be truncated. You will lose data.

```
000100 IDENTIFICATION DIVISION.
000200 PROGRAM-ID. FIRST.
000300 ENVIRONMENT DIVISION.
000400 DATA DIVISION.
000500
000600 WORKING-STORAGE SECTION.
000700
000800 01 DEPARTMENT      PIC X(12) VALUE SPACES.
000900 01 HEADCOUNT       PIC 9(3)   VALUE ZEROES.
001000 01 FULL-TIME       PIC 9(3)
001100 01 FNAME           PIC X(5).
001200 PROCEDURE DIVISION.
001300
001400 INITIALIZE-VALUES.
001500     MOVE ZEROES TO FULL-TIME.
001600     MOVE SPACES TO FNAME.
001700
001800 ASSIGN-VALUES.
001900     MOVE "Joseph" TO FNAME.
002000     MOVE 1000 TO HEADCOUNT.
002100 STOP-MY-PROGRAM.
002200     STOP RUN.
```

ZEROES, ZEROS, AND ZERO are reserved words and all have the same effect.

Padding

The ZEROES reserved word will pad a variable with zeros and the SPACES reserved word will pad a variable with spaces.

HEADCOUNT

0	0	0

There is a space between the double quotation marks. The quotation marks are used for an illustrative purpose. They are not stored when the SPACES reserved word is used.

DEPARTMENT

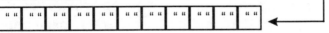

Truncation

Date too large to be stored in the variable will be discarded.

HEADCOUNT

0	0	0

FNAME

J	o	s	e	p

Decimal Variables

Variables can be assigned a decimal value as long as you reserve space for the decimal when the variable is defined. The decimal value will be discarded if you don't define a decimal before assigning a decimal to the variable.

Decimals are defined using the **PIC** clause in the **Working-Storage Section** of the **Data Division**. The letter **V** is used in place of the decimal in the definition of the variable.

You must be sure to include sufficient number of decimal places for whatever value is to be assigned to the variable. Remember, values will be truncated if there isn't sufficient storage space.

A truncated decimal value can give you an erroneous result in a calculation. Truncation is not rounding, so if the results of a calculation is 2.259 and you reserved two decimal places, the value of the variable will be 2.25 and not 2.26. This difference could be significant.

This is also true when integers are used in a calculation. The results will also be truncated and not round up or down if there is insufficient room in the variable to contain the results of the calculation.

Numeric variables defined to store a decimal value can be initialized using techniques illustrated previously in this chapter. The initial value of the decimal should contain a decimal point and not the letter **V**. The letter **V** is only used in the **PIC** clause.

PIC 99V99 VALUE 32.67

The letter **V** can only be used in a numeric variable definition. You cannot use the letter **V** to represent a decimal in the definition of a string variable.

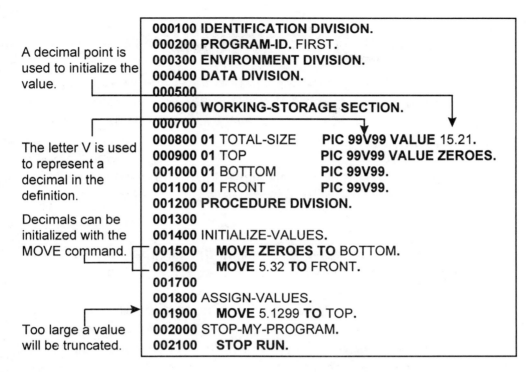

A decimal point is used to initialize the value.

The letter V is used to represent a decimal in the definition.

Decimals can be initialized with the MOVE command.

Too large a value will be truncated.

```
000100 IDENTIFICATION DIVISION.
000200 PROGRAM-ID. FIRST.
000300 ENVIRONMENT DIVISION.
000400 DATA DIVISION.
000500
000600 WORKING-STORAGE SECTION.
000700
000800 01 TOTAL-SIZE    PIC 99V99 VALUE 15.21.
000900 01 TOP           PIC 99V99 VALUE ZEROES.
001000 01 BOTTOM        PIC 99V99.
001100 01 FRONT         PIC 99V99.
001200 PROCEDURE DIVISION.
001300
001400 INITIALIZE-VALUES.
001500     MOVE ZEROES TO BOTTOM.
001600     MOVE 5.32 TO FRONT.
001700
001800 ASSIGN-VALUES.
001900     MOVE 5.1299 TO TOP.
002000 STOP-MY-PROGRAM.
002100     STOP RUN.
```

Padding

The ZEROES reserved word will pad a variable with zeros including the decimal places.

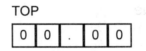

TOP

| 0 | 0 | . | 0 | 0 |

Truncation

Data too large to be stored in the variable will be discarded.

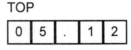

TOP

| 0 | 5 | . | 1 | 2 |

Facts You Should Know...

○

○ The compiler stores decimal values differently than integers are stored in memory. This difference increases the speed at which the computer can calculate expressions using decimal values.

Displaying Decimal Variables

Decimal values are stored by the compiler in a different format than integers are stored in memory. Decimals are treated differently to increase the performance of calculating an expression that uses decimal values.

The method the compiler uses to store decimal values in memory shouldn't concern you except when you want to display a decimal value on the screen.

You must tell the compiler the format of the decimal value before using the **DISPLAY** command to display the decimal value.

The format is defined in the definition of a numeric variable whose sole purpose is for displaying a decimal value. This variable is defined in the **Working-Storage Section** of the **Data Division** using the **PIC** clause. However, the decimal point is used in the **PIC** clause instead of the letter **V** to mark the decimal position in the value.

PIC 99.99

A decimal value must be assigned to the display variable, then the display variable is used with the **DISPLAY** command to properly show the decimal value on the screen. An example of this technique is illustrated on the next page.

Remember to use the display variable and not the decimal variable with the **DISPLAY** command, otherwise you will see unexpected results on the screen that could cause you to spend hours debugging your program.

You can avoid making this mistake by naming the display variable the same name as the decimal variable except begin the variable name with the word **DISPLAY**. You'll always be able to distinguish between the display variable and the decimal variable by the name.

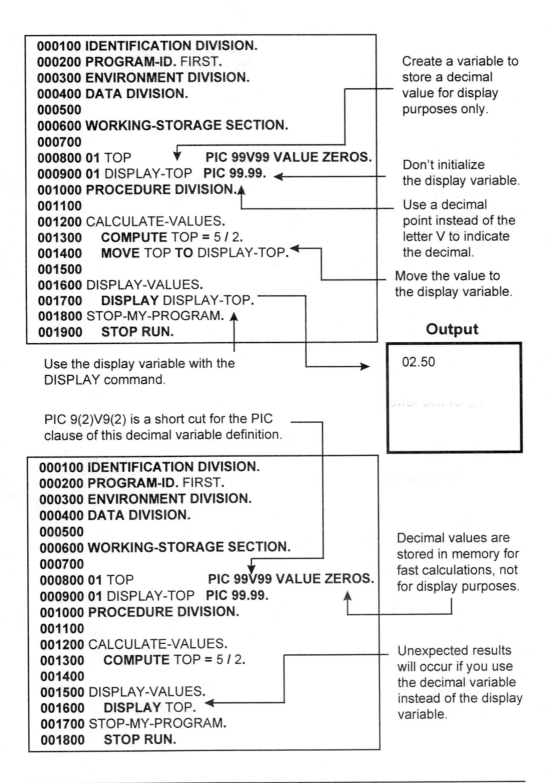

```
000100 IDENTIFICATION DIVISION.
000200 PROGRAM-ID. FIRST.
000300 ENVIRONMENT DIVISION.
000400 DATA DIVISION.
000500
000600 WORKING-STORAGE SECTION.
000700
000800 01 TOP          PIC 99V99 VALUE ZEROS.
000900 01 DISPLAY-TOP  PIC 99.99.
001000 PROCEDURE DIVISION.
001100
001200 CALCULATE-VALUES.
001300     COMPUTE TOP = 5 / 2.
001400     MOVE TOP TO DISPLAY-TOP.
001500
001600 DISPLAY-VALUES.
001700     DISPLAY DISPLAY-TOP.
001800 STOP-MY-PROGRAM.
001900     STOP RUN.
```

Create a variable to store a decimal value for display purposes only.

Don't initialize the display variable.

Use a decimal point instead of the letter V to indicate the decimal.

Move the value to the display variable.

Use the display variable with the DISPLAY command.

Output

```
02.50
```

PIC 9(2)V9(2) is a short cut for the PIC clause of this decimal variable definition.

```
000100 IDENTIFICATION DIVISION.
000200 PROGRAM-ID. FIRST.
000300 ENVIRONMENT DIVISION.
000400 DATA DIVISION.
000500
000600 WORKING-STORAGE SECTION.
000700
000800 01 TOP          PIC 99V99 VALUE ZEROS.
000900 01 DISPLAY-TOP  PIC 99.99.
001000 PROCEDURE DIVISION.
001100
001200 CALCULATE-VALUES.
001300     COMPUTE TOP = 5 / 2.
001400
001500 DISPLAY-VALUES.
001600     DISPLAY TOP.
001700 STOP-MY-PROGRAM.
001800     STOP RUN.
```

Decimal values are stored in memory for fast calculations, not for display purposes.

Unexpected results will occur if you use the decimal variable instead of the display variable.

Suppressing Zeros

Numeric variable are filled with zeros whenever you define and initialize the variable. Values assigned to the variable replaces some or all of the zeros with other values.

You'll notice after some assignments, the value of the variable will contain more zeros than is required to represent the value. For example, a six-digit variable assigned a two-digit value still has zeros in the other four digits.

000024

Likewise, when a variable with room to store a three-digit decimal value is assigned a one-digit decimal value, two decimal values are filled with zeros.

00.200

The zeros are referred to as leading zeros and trailing zeros. *Leading zeros* appear to the left of the integer value and *trailing zeros* appear to the right of the last decimal digit. You'll see this illustrated in the examples on the next page.

Leading and trailing zeros don't increase or decrease the value of the variable. You can remove the zeros and the value of the variable won't change.

However, leading and trailing zeros make the value of the variable difficult to read when displayed on the screen. You should have your program drop leading and trailing zeros before the values are displayed.

Tell the compiler to drop leading and trailing zero from the value of the variable by replacing the **9** in the **PIC** clause with **Z**.

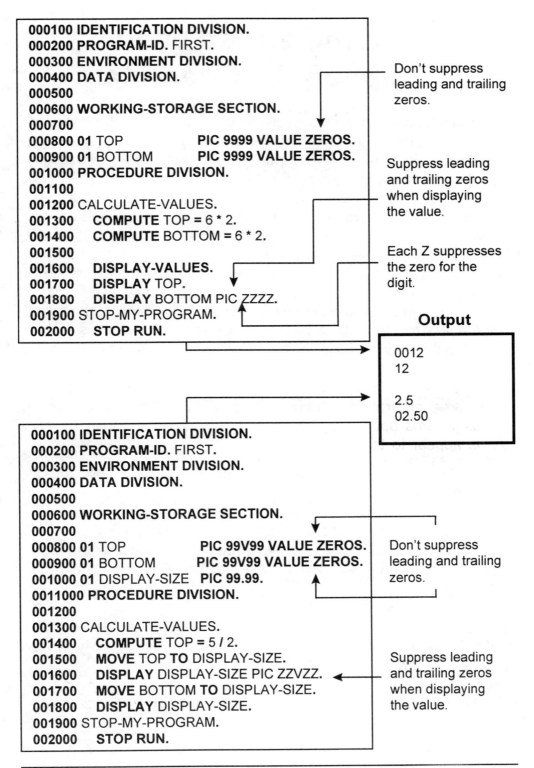

```
000100 IDENTIFICATION DIVISION.
000200 PROGRAM-ID. FIRST.
000300 ENVIRONMENT DIVISION.
000400 DATA DIVISION.
000500
000600 WORKING-STORAGE SECTION.
000700
000800 01 TOP          PIC 9999 VALUE ZEROS.
000900 01 BOTTOM       PIC 9999 VALUE ZEROS.
001000 PROCEDURE DIVISION.
001100
001200 CALCULATE-VALUES.
001300    COMPUTE TOP = 6 * 2.
001400    COMPUTE BOTTOM = 6 * 2.
001500
001600    DISPLAY-VALUES.
001700    DISPLAY TOP.
001800    DISPLAY BOTTOM PIC ZZZZ.
001900 STOP-MY-PROGRAM.
002000    STOP RUN.
```

Don't suppress leading and trailing zeros.

Suppress leading and trailing zeros when displaying the value.

Each Z suppresses the zero for the digit.

Output

```
0012
12

2.5
02.50
```

```
000100 IDENTIFICATION DIVISION.
000200 PROGRAM-ID. FIRST.
000300 ENVIRONMENT DIVISION.
000400 DATA DIVISION.
000500
000600 WORKING-STORAGE SECTION.
000700
000800 01 TOP          PIC 99V99 VALUE ZEROS.
000900 01 BOTTOM       PIC 99V99 VALUE ZEROS.
001000 01 DISPLAY-SIZE  PIC 99.99.
0011000 PROCEDURE DIVISION.
001200
001300 CALCULATE-VALUES.
001400    COMPUTE TOP = 5 / 2.
001500    MOVE TOP TO DISPLAY-SIZE.
001600    DISPLAY DISPLAY-SIZE PIC ZZVZZ.
001700    MOVE BOTTOM TO DISPLAY-SIZE.
001800    DISPLAY DISPLAY-SIZE.
001900 STOP-MY-PROGRAM.
002000    STOP RUN.
```

Don't suppress leading and trailing zeros.

Suppress leading and trailing zeros when displaying the value.

Working with Constants and Variables

Limit Variables to Alphabetic Characters

Alphanumeric variables discussed in this chapter can be assigned any alphanumeric character. However, an application may require a variable to contain only alphabetical characters and exclude numbers from being stored in the variable.

Remember, numbers stored in an alphanumeric variable are character representations of numbers rather than digits and cannot be used in calculations. For example, they could be used to represent a house number, but not used in an addition expression.

You can limit an alphanumeric variable to only alphabetical characters by using an **A** instead of an **X** in the **PIC** clause when defining the variable as is illustrated in examples on the next page.

Insert a Blank into the Data

COBOL applications require data to be displayed in a specific format that could include blank characters used to separate a series of characters.

One such format is with a telephone number where the value stored in the variable is divided into three sets of numbers: the area code, the exchange, and the unique telephone number within the exchange.

Insert the letter **B** in the **PIC** clause to indicate a blank when defining the variable. A blank will appear in that position whenever the value of the variable is displayed on the screen.

The same technique can be used to insert fixed spaces in an alphanumeric variable.

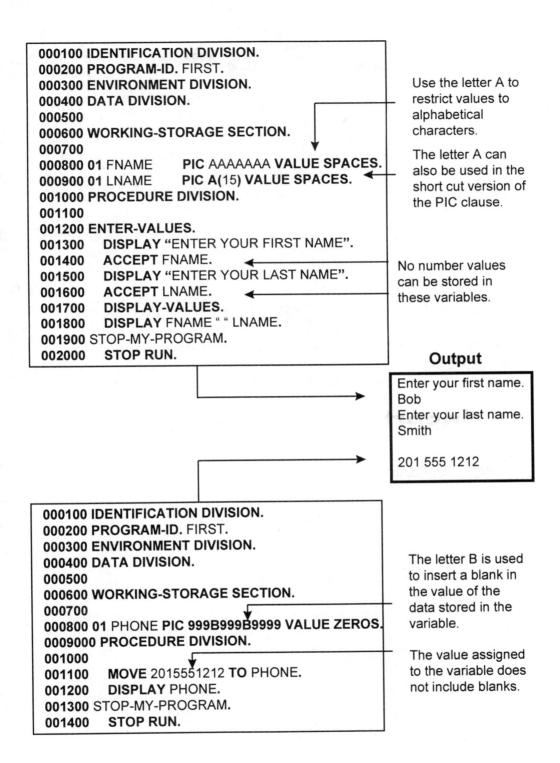

```
000100 IDENTIFICATION DIVISION.
000200 PROGRAM-ID. FIRST.
000300 ENVIRONMENT DIVISION.
000400 DATA DIVISION.
000500
000600 WORKING-STORAGE SECTION.
000700
000800 01 FNAME      PIC AAAAAAA VALUE SPACES.
000900 01 LNAME      PIC A(15) VALUE SPACES.
001000 PROCEDURE DIVISION.
001100
001200 ENTER-VALUES.
001300    DISPLAY "ENTER YOUR FIRST NAME".
001400    ACCEPT FNAME.
001500    DISPLAY "ENTER YOUR LAST NAME".
001600    ACCEPT LNAME.
001700    DISPLAY-VALUES.
001800    DISPLAY FNAME " " LNAME.
001900 STOP-MY-PROGRAM.
002000    STOP RUN.
```

Use the letter A to restrict values to alphabetical characters.

The letter A can also be used in the short cut version of the PIC clause.

No number values can be stored in these variables.

Output

```
Enter your first name.
Bob
Enter your last name.
Smith

201 555 1212
```

```
000100 IDENTIFICATION DIVISION.
000200 PROGRAM-ID. FIRST.
000300 ENVIRONMENT DIVISION.
000400 DATA DIVISION.
000500
000600 WORKING-STORAGE SECTION.
000700
000800 01 PHONE PIC 999B999B9999 VALUE ZEROS.
0009000 PROCEDURE DIVISION.
001000
001100    MOVE 2015551212 TO PHONE.
001200    DISPLAY PHONE.
001300 STOP-MY-PROGRAM.
001400    STOP RUN.
```

The letter B is used to insert a blank in the value of the data stored in the variable.

The value assigned to the variable does not include blanks.

Currency Data

Numeric variables that contain currency amounts typically require the use of the currency symbol and the decimal point to represent cents. The dollar sign is used to represent any currency symbol. Later in this chapter you'll learn how to change the currency sign.

The currency sign is displayed automatically when you place the dollar sign in the PIC clause of a numeric variable. This is shown in the example on the next page. The decimal point is identified by using the letter V in the PIC clause as is shown in the previous chapter.

Insert Commas into the Data

One of the most common ways to format data is to separate a series of digits by a comma. Commas are used in the United States to make large numbers easy to read.

You can include commas in the format of a variable by inserting commas in the desired position in the PIC clause. This is shown in the example on the next page.

Commas are used with numeric variables and can be used with either 9 or Z as the character position identifier.

Indicating Debit or Credit

A currency calculation can result in a negative value indicated by a minus sign. In some accounting applications, the negative sign is replaced by a debit or credit indicator as show on the next page.

You can insert the symbol DB at the end of the PIC clause to indicate that the variable contains a debit value and insert the symbol CR to indicate that the variable contains a credit amount. These symbols are displayed only if the value is a negative.

Insert a dollar sign in the definition of a numeric variable to have the currency symbol displayed whenever the data is displayed. ⟶

```
000100 IDENTIFICATION DIVISION.
000200 PROGRAM-ID. FIRST.
000300 ENVIRONMENT DIVISION.
000400 DATA DIVISION.
000500
000600 WORKING-STORAGE SECTION.
000700
000800 01 AMOUNT  PIC $Z(4) ZV(2) VALUE ZEROES.
000900 01 DISP-AMT PIC $9999.99.
001000 PROCEDURE DIVISION.
001100
001200 CALCULATE-VALUES.
001300     MOVE 150.99 TO AMOUNT.
001400     MOVE AMOUNT TO DISP-AMT.
001500     DISPLAY-VALUES.
001600     DISPLAY DISP-AMT.
001700 STOP-MY-PROGRAM.
001800     STOP RUN.
```

$ 150.99 is the value displayed on the screen. ⟶

Insert CR if the variable will contain a credit value. ⟶

Insert commas to separate values of numeric variables. ⟶

```
000100 IDENTIFICATION DIVISION.
000200 PROGRAM-ID. FIRST.
000300 ENVIRONMENT DIVISION.
000400 DATA DIVISION.
000500
000600 WORKING-STORAGE SECTION.
000700
000800 01 CREDITS  PIC $Z(2) VALUE ZEROES.
000900 01 DEBITS PIC $Z(2) VALUE ZEROES.
001000 01 DISP-CR PIC $9(2) CR.
001100 01 DISP-DB PIC $9(2) DB.
001200 PROCEDURE DIVISION.
001300
001400 CALCULATE-VALUES.
001500     MOVE 5 TO CREDITS.
001600     MOVE 10 TO DEBITS.
001700     COMPUTE DISP-CR = CREDITS - 7.
001800     COMPUTE DISP-DB = DEBITS - 20.
001900 DISPLAY-VALUES.
002000     DISPLAY DISP-CR.
002100     DISPLAY DISP-DB.
002200 STOP-MY-PROGRAM.
002300     STOP RUN.
```

Insert DB if the variable will contain a debit value. ⟶

$2CR is displayed. ⟶

$10DB is displayed. ⟶

Changing the Currency Symbol

COBOL applications that display currency in other than dollar denominations must be able to display the appropriate currency symbol.

The default currency symbol is the dollar sign. You can change the currency symbol to another sign in the **Configuration Section** of the **Environment Division** as illustrated in the example on the next page.

The dollar sign used in the **PIC** clause tells the compiler to use the current currency symbol that may be something other than the dollar sign.

Changing the Decimal Point Symbol

The fractional part of the value is separated from the integer by the decimal point. However, some countries use a different symbol in place of the decimal point such as a comma.

You can change the default decimal point symbol to another character by redefining the decimal point in the **Configuration Section** of the **Environment Division** as shown on the next page.

Replace Leading Zeros with Asterisks

Applications such as those that print checks require all character positions in the amount to be filled making it hard for someone to change the value of the check.

Typically, character positions to the left of the amount are filled with asterisks. You can fill empty positions in a numeric variable with asterisks by using the asterisk in place of the **9** or **Z** in the **PIC** clause when defining the variable. This technique is shown in an example on the next page.

F*150,99

```
000100 IDENTIFICATION DIVISION.
000200 PROGRAM-ID. FIRST.
000300 ENVIRONMENT DIVISION.
000400
000500 CONFIGURATION-SECTION.
000600
000700 SPECIAL-NAMES
000800  CURRENCY SIGN IS 'F'.
000900  DECIMAL-POINT IS COMMA.
001000
001100 DATA DIVISION.
001200
001300 WORKING-STORAGE SECTION.
001400
001500 01 AMOUNT  PIC $*(4) ZV(2) VALUE ZEROES.
001600 01 DISP-AMT PIC $9999.99.
001700 PROCEDURE DIVISION.
001800
001900 CALCULATE-VALUES.
002000    MOVE 150.99 TO AMOUNT.
002100    MOVE AMOUNT TO DISP-AMT.
002200 DISPLAY-VALUES.
002300    DISPLAY DISP-AMT.
002400 STOP-MY-PROGRAM.
002500    STOP RUN.
```

Use the F as the new currency sign which isthe French Franc.

Use a comma in place of the decimal point.

Replace leading zeros with asterisks.

The $ and V are still used as symbols within the program to indicate that you want to use the currency symbol and the decimal point.

Did You Know ...

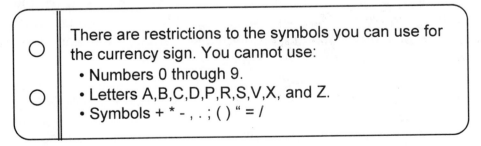

There are restrictions to the symbols you can use for the currency sign. You cannot use:
- Numbers 0 through 9.
- Letters A,B,C,D,P,R,S,V,X, and Z.
- Symbols + * - , . ; ( ) " = /

Date Data

A date is composed of three elements. These are the month, day, and year and are commonly treated as separate numeric variables within a COBOL program. These elements can be defined as members of a data structure that will be discussed later in this book.

A date displayed on the screen looks something like this:

12/31/99

However, the date is likely to be stored in the program as individual variables such as: MONTH, DAY, and YEAR. The slashes are not included in these variables.

You must insert the slashes when the elements of the date are displayed on the screen.

In the example on the next page, variables are defined for each element of the date at level 05. Collectively, the elements can be referenced in the program by using the name **DATE-VARIABLE** that is defined at level 01. The date element variables are a subset of the DATE-VARIABLE variable.

Date values are assigned to each variable using the **MOVE** command after which the variables are displayed along with slashes separating the elements of the date.

Notice the year is represented in four digits. This is probably something you won't find in existing applications because until recently many programmers dropped the century digit and used only the year. This is called the *Year 2000 Problem*.

Programs that perform date calculations commonly subtract one year from another. In the year 2000, programs will attempt to subtract 97 from 00 and are likely to crash. More on this problem later in the book.

Output

12/31/1999

Create a variable for each element of the date.

Be sure all dates contain the century digits, otherwise the program will not be compatible with the year 2000.

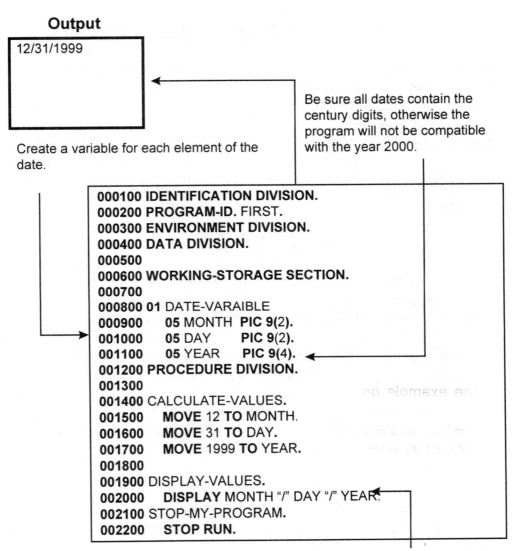

```
000100 IDENTIFICATION DIVISION.
000200 PROGRAM-ID. FIRST.
000300 ENVIRONMENT DIVISION.
000400 DATA DIVISION.
000500
000600 WORKING-STORAGE SECTION.
000700
000800 01 DATE-VARAIBLE
000900     05 MONTH  PIC 9(2).
001000     05 DAY    PIC 9(2).
001100     05 YEAR    PIC 9(4).
001200 PROCEDURE DIVISION.
001300
001400 CALCULATE-VALUES.
001500     MOVE 12 TO MONTH.
001600     MOVE 31 TO DAY.
001700     MOVE 1999 TO YEAR.
001800
001900 DISPLAY-VALUES.
002000     DISPLAY MONTH "/" DAY "/" YEAR.
002100 STOP-MY-PROGRAM.
002200     STOP RUN.
```

Display date values with slasshes.

Did You Know ...

Date variables are at the heart of the Year 2000 Problem. Date variables in many COBOL programs have room for only a two-digit year. The century digits are dropped from the date. Errors could occur if such variables are used in date calculations because a good date is subtracted from 00.

Use Blanks Instead of Zeros

You can suppress leading and trailing zeros by using the letter **Z** in the **PIC** clause in place of the **9** when defining a numeric variable. This technique is illustrated earlier in the chapter.

You can also replace zeros with spaces called *blanks* even if the are no leading or trailing zeros by using the **BLANK WHEN ZERO** phrase in the **PIC** clause. You see this used in an example on the next page.

Signed Numbers

Numbers used in your COBOL application can be a positive number or a *negative number. Positive numbers are greater than or equal to zero and negative numbers* are less than zero.

The plus sign is used to indicate a number is positive and a minus sign is used to signify a negative number. Values that display these signs are called *signed numbers*.

Any numeric variable can be stored a signed number if you insert the letter **S** before the **9** or **Z** in the **PIC** clause when you define the numeric variable. This is shown on the next page.

The plus or minus sign is displayed when values of signed numeric variables are displayed. The sign is always trailing the value such as:

55-

You can change the location of the sign by using the **SIGN IS LEADING** or **SIGN IS TRAILING** phrases in the **PIC** clause.

Another way to make sure signs are used is to insert the plus sign before the **9** or **Z** in the **PIC** clause. This is illustrated on the next page.

```
000100 IDENTIFICATION DIVISION.
000200 PROGRAM-ID. FIRST.
000300 ENVIRONMENT DIVISION.
000400 DATA DIVISION.
000500
000600 WORKING-STORAGE SECTION.
000700
000800 01 SIZE  PIC 9(5) BLANK WHEN ZERO.
000900 PROCEDURE DIVISION.
001000
001100 CALCULATE-VALUES.
001200     COMPUTE SIZE = 10 + 3.
001300
001400 DISPLAY-VALUES.
001500     DISPLAY SIZE.
001600 STOP-MY-PROGRAM.
001700     STOP RUN.
```

Replace zeros with a blank space.

No leading zeros will appear when this variable is displayed on the screen.

Output

```
13

+9
-8
```

```
000100 IDENTIFICATION DIVISION.
000200 PROGRAM-ID. FIRST.
000300 ENVIRONMENT DIVISION.
000400 DATA DIVISION.
000500
000600 WORKING-STORAGE SECTION.
000700
000800 01 DIFF-1  PIC S9(4) VALUE ZEROES.
000900 01 DIFF-2 PIC +9(4) VALUE ZEROES.
001000 PROCEDURE DIVISION.
001100
001200 CALCULATE-VALUES.
001300     COMPUTE DIFF-1 = 10 - 1.
001400     MOVE DIFF-1 TO DIFF-2.
001500     DISPLAY DIFF-2.
001600     COMPUTE DIFF-2 = 10 - 18.
001700     MOVE DIFF-1 TO DIFF-2.
001800     DISPLAY DIFF-2.
001900 STOP-MY-PROGRAM.
002000     STOP RUN.
```

The letter S tells the compiler to include the sign of numbers assigned to this variable. Don't include space for the sign.

The plus sign also ensures the sign of the number is used with the variable.

The variable contains negative numbers.

Ways to Store Data

The compiler stores data in a different way than what you see on the screen. Data is represented in memory as a sequence of binary values. A *binary value* is either zero or one.

Most COBOL programmers don't need to know how data is stored in memory since the compiler uses the default values to store data.

However, you can specify the method used to store data by using the **USAGE** clause with the **PIC** clause. The most frequently used phrase in the **USAGE** clause is **COMP**. **COMP**, which is an abbreviation for computational leaves, it up to the compiler to determine the best method to store the data. Most compilers will store the data in binary form.

You can explicitly tell the compiler to store the data in binary values by using the phrase **BINARY** with the **USAGE** clause.

A commonly used method of storing decimal values is as a packed decimal that reduces memory space to nearly half. Many COBOL programmers routinely set the **USAGE** clause to **PACKED-DECIMAL** whenever they define a decimal variable.

Another use of the **USAGE** clause is to specify the alignment of string data by using the **JUSTIFIED RIGHT** and **JUSTIFIED LEFT** phrases. All alphanumeric data starts at the left-most position called *justified left*, You can start alphanumeric data at the right-most position by using the **JUSTIFIED RIGHT** phrase. **JUSTIFIED** can be shortened to **JUST** also.

Assign Values to Many Variables

The same value can be assigned to multiple variables using a single **MOVE** command. The trick is to place all the target variables in the same sentence as the **MOVE** command. This is illustrated in examples on the next page.

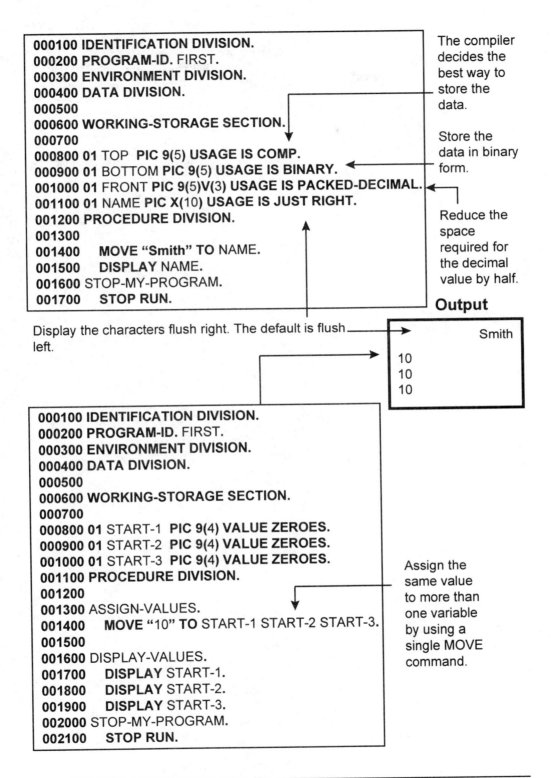

The compiler decides the best way to store the data.

```
000100 IDENTIFICATION DIVISION.
000200 PROGRAM-ID. FIRST.
000300 ENVIRONMENT DIVISION.
000400 DATA DIVISION.
000500
000600 WORKING-STORAGE SECTION.
000700
000800 01 TOP  PIC 9(5) USAGE IS COMP.
000900 01 BOTTOM PIC 9(5) USAGE IS BINARY.
001000 01 FRONT PIC 9(5)V(3) USAGE IS PACKED-DECIMAL.
001100 01 NAME PIC X(10) USAGE IS JUST RIGHT.
001200 PROCEDURE DIVISION.
001300
001400     MOVE "Smith" TO NAME.
001500     DISPLAY NAME.
001600 STOP-MY-PROGRAM.
001700     STOP RUN.
```

Store the data in binary form.

Reduce the space required for the decimal value by half.

Output

```
                    Smith
10
10
10
```

Display the characters flush right. The default is flush left.

```
000100 IDENTIFICATION DIVISION.
000200 PROGRAM-ID. FIRST.
000300 ENVIRONMENT DIVISION.
000400 DATA DIVISION.
000500
000600 WORKING-STORAGE SECTION.
000700
000800 01 START-1  PIC 9(4) VALUE ZEROES.
000900 01 START-2  PIC 9(4) VALUE ZEROES.
001000 01 START-3  PIC 9(4) VALUE ZEROES.
001100 PROCEDURE DIVISION.
001200
001300 ASSIGN-VALUES.
001400     MOVE "10" TO START-1 START-2 START-3.
001500
001600 DISPLAY-VALUES.
001700     DISPLAY START-1.
001800     DISPLAY START-2.
001900     DISPLAY START-3.
002000 STOP-MY-PROGRAM.
002100     STOP RUN.
```

Assign the same value to more than one variable by using a single MOVE command.

Working with Data Structures

- Creating a Data Structure
- Using a Data Structure
- Formatting a Data Structure
- A Common Mistake Using Data Structures
- Nested Data Structures
- RENAMES
- REDEFINES
- Identifying Member Variables
- Creating an Array
- Accessing an Array
- Looping Through an Array
- Assigning Values to an Array from the Keyboard
- Defining an Index Variable

Creating a Data Structure

A *Variable* is a reserved space in memory where data used by your program is stored. *Data* is a piece of information that typically describes something such as a person's first name.

Rarely does a data item provide a full description of anything. For example, a person's first name may help you identify a person in a small group, but won't help you identify the person in a population.

A more thorough description requires more data about the person such as the person's last name, state, city, and street. Collectively these data items enable you to reduce the chance of error when trying to identify a person.

Your program can group related information together in the form of a data structure. A *data structure* is a collection of variables that relate to each other.

For example, variables called FNAME, LNAME, STREET, CITY, and STATE are a set of variables that identify a single entity called a person. These variables can be defined as a data structure and the name of the data structure can be called PERSON.

The compiler groups together any variables you designate into the data structure without regard to the logic of your selection. For example, you could include a variable that isn't related to the other variables in the data structure.

Another name for a data structure is a *record*. Some programmers refer to a collection of related data in a file as a record and a data structure when the data is used in memory.

You create a data structure in the Working-Storage Section of the Data Division by defining the name of the data structure in Area A at level 01. Variables associated with the data structure are defined in Area B at a lower level than level 01.

```
000100 IDENTIFICATION DIVISION.
000200 PROGRAM-ID. FIRST.
000300 ENVIRONMENT DIVISION.
000400 DATA DIVISION.
000500
000600 WORKING-STORAGE SECTION
000700 01 STUDENT.
000800     05 FNAME    PIC X(10) VALUE SPACES.
000900     05 LNAME    PIC X(15) VALUE SPACES.
001000     05 STREET   PIC X(20) VALUE SPACES.
001100     05 CITY     PIC X(20) VALUE SPACES.
001200     05 STATE    PIC X(2)  VALUE SPACES.
001300     05 ZIP      PIC X(10) VALUE SPACES.
001400     05 ID-NUM   PIC X(9)  VALUE SPACES.
001500     05 TV-SHOW  PIC X(20) VALUE SPACES.
001600 PROCEDURE DIVISION.
001700
001800 STOP-MY-PROGRAM.
001900    STOP RUN.
```

Define the name of the data structure at level 01 in Area A.

Define variables of the data structure at a lower level than 01 in Area B. Typically, level 05 is used.

The value of all variables in the data structure should be logically related to each other.

You can include irrelevant variables in the data structure, but this must be avoided.

Don't use the PIC clause when you define the name of the data structure. The variables actually define the data structure.

The name of the data structure must conform to the same naming restrictions as a variable. See Chapter 2 for the rules.

The values of all the variables in this data structure are related to each other.

All the techniques used to define a variable can be used to define a data structure.

```
000100 IDENTIFICATION DIVISION.
000200 PROGRAM-ID. FIRST.
000300 ENVIRONMENT DIVISION.
000400 DATA DIVISION.
000500
000600 WORKING-STORAGE SECTION
000700 01 STUDENT.
000800     05 FNAME    PIC X(10)  VALUE SPACES.
000900     05 LNAME    PIC X(15)  VALUE SPACES.
001000     05 STREET   PIC X(20)  VALUE SPACES.
001100     05 CITY     PIC X(20)  VALUE SPACES.
001200     05 STATE    PIC X(2)   VALUE SPACES.
001300     05 ZIP      PIC X(10)  VALUE SPACES.
001400     05 ID-NUM   PIC X(9)   VALUE SPACES.
001500 PROCEDURE DIVISION.
001600
001700 STOP-MY-PROGRAM.
001800    STOP RUN.
```

Using a Data Structure

The purpose of a data structure is to organize data used by your program. You've seen on the previous pages how a group of related variables are defined below the name of the data structure in the Working-Storage Section of the Data Division.

Variables defined within the data structure can be used as if they were not a member of the data structure. For example, you can assign values to a variable in the same way as you would if the variable was independent of the other variables.

Member variables can be accessed without referencing the data structure. This is different than in other computer languages such as C or C++ where the name of the data structure must be used in conjunction with the name of the member variable whenever the variable is used in the program.

In this example, student is the name of the instance of the structure in the C language.

C: student.FirstName

COBOL: FIRSTNAME

A data structure provides a visual grouping of variables within the code of your program and identifies a functional relationship. You can refer to the name of the structure whenever you want to do something with all the variables defined within the data structure.

It is common for a COBOL program to assign values to members of a data structure, then refer to the name of the data structure to display or print all the member variables.

The compiler treats the name of the data structure as one variable that has several parts. This enables you to cut down on code writing by using the name of the data structure in a **DISPLAY** command rather than typing the names of member variables.

```
000100 IDENTIFICATION DIVISION.
000200 PROGRAM-ID. FIRST.
000300 ENVIRONMENT DIVISION.
000400 DATA DIVISION.
000500
000600 WORKING-STORAGE SECTION.
000700 01 STUDENT.
000800    05 FNAME    PIC X(4)  VALUE SPACES.
000900    05 LNAME    PIC X(5)  VALUE SPACES.
001000    05 STREET   PIC X(12) VALUE SPACES.
001100    05 CITY     PIC X(9)  VALUE SPACES.
001200    05 STATE    PIC X(2)  VALUE SPACES.
001300    05 ZIP      PIC X(5)  VALUE SPACES.
001400    05 ID-NUM   PIC X(9)  VALUE SPACES.
001500 PROCEDURE DIVISION.
001600
001700 ASSIGN-VALUES.
001800   MOVE "Bob" TO FNAME.
001900   MOVE "Smith" TO LNAME.
002000   MOVE "555 Anywhere" TO STREET.
002100   MOVE "Any Place" TO CITY.
002200   MOVE "NJ" TO STATE.
002300   MOVE "07502" TO ZIP.
002400   MOVE "123456789" TO ID-NUM.
002500
002600 DISPLAY-VALUES.
002700   DISPLAY STUDENT.
002800
002900 STOP-MY-PROGRAM.
003000    STOP RUN.
```

Define the data structure.

Define member variables of the data structure.

Assign values to member variables without referring to the name of the data structure.

Display all the member variables on the screen using the name of the data structure.

Output

BobSmith555 AnywhereAny PlaceNJ07502123456789

Formatting a Data Structure

A data structure is considered one variable made up of one or more smaller variables. When the name of a data structure is used with a **DISPLAY** command, the compiler shows each member variable one after the other in the order the variable is listed in the data structure definition.

You'll notice in the first example on the next page that values assigned to member variables are jumbled together so it is difficult to identify where one variable ends and the other begins.

You can improve the readability of the data by using a **FILLER** as part of the data structure. A *FILLER* is included in the definition of a data structure as a way to format member variables. This is optional inCOBOL-II where you can leave out the name **FILLER**.

The second program on the next page shows how to use the **FILLER** in the data structure. The **FILLER** is not a member variable of the data structure, although it is treated in a similar fashion within the definition of the data structure.

You can use the **PIC** clause and the **VALUE** clause to define the format used between member variables. The compiler will insert the contents of the **VALUE** clause between the member variables above and below the **FILLER** when the data structure is displayed.

There is no limit to the number of **FILLER**s you can use in a data structure. However, keep in mind that each **FILLER** defines the delimiter between one set of variables.

A **FILLER** can only hold literal values that are assigned when the data structure is defined. You cannot assign a new value to a **FILTER** by using the **MOVE** command.

The **FILLER** is a member of the data structure. All member variables and all **FILLER**s are displayed whenever reference is made to the name of the data structure.

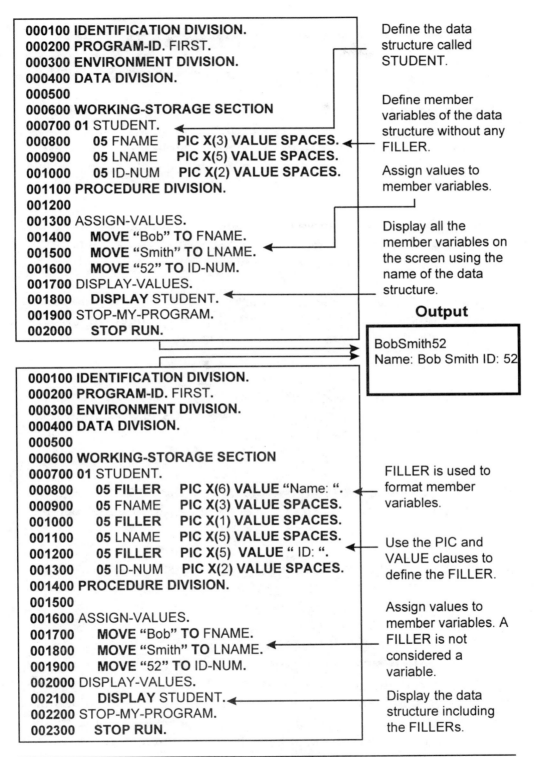

```
000100 IDENTIFICATION DIVISION.
000200 PROGRAM-ID. FIRST.
000300 ENVIRONMENT DIVISION.
000400 DATA DIVISION.
000500
000600 WORKING-STORAGE SECTION
000700 01 STUDENT.
000800     05 FNAME     PIC X(3) VALUE SPACES.
000900     05 LNAME     PIC X(5) VALUE SPACES.
001000     05 ID-NUM    PIC X(2) VALUE SPACES.
001100 PROCEDURE DIVISION.
001200
001300 ASSIGN-VALUES.
001400     MOVE "Bob" TO FNAME.
001500     MOVE "Smith" TO LNAME.
001600     MOVE "52" TO ID-NUM.
001700 DISPLAY-VALUES.
001800     DISPLAY STUDENT.
001900 STOP-MY-PROGRAM.
002000     STOP RUN.
```

Define the data structure called STUDENT.

Define member variables of the data structure without any FILLER.

Assign values to member variables.

Display all the member variables on the screen using the name of the data structure.

Output

```
BobSmith52
Name: Bob Smith ID: 52
```

```
000100 IDENTIFICATION DIVISION.
000200 PROGRAM-ID. FIRST.
000300 ENVIRONMENT DIVISION.
000400 DATA DIVISION.
000500
000600 WORKING-STORAGE SECTION
000700 01 STUDENT.
000800     05 FILLER    PIC X(6) VALUE "Name: ".
000900     05 FNAME     PIC X(3) VALUE SPACES.
001000     05 FILLER    PIC X(1) VALUE SPACES.
001100     05 LNAME     PIC X(5) VALUE SPACES.
001200     05 FILLER    PIC X(5) VALUE " ID: ".
001300     05 ID-NUM    PIC X(2) VALUE SPACES.
001400 PROCEDURE DIVISION.
001500
001600 ASSIGN-VALUES.
001700     MOVE "Bob" TO FNAME.
001800     MOVE "Smith" TO LNAME.
001900     MOVE "52" TO ID-NUM.
002000 DISPLAY-VALUES.
002100     DISPLAY STUDENT.
002200 STOP-MY-PROGRAM.
002300     STOP RUN.
```

FILLER is used to format member variables.

Use the PIC and VALUE clauses to define the FILLER.

Assign values to member variables. A FILLER is not considered a variable.

Display the data structure including the FILLERs.

A Common Mistake Using Data Structures

The name of a data structure is used to identify a group of related variables as you've seen throughout this chapter. The compiler treats the entire data structure as one variable that can have serious repercussions if you use the name of the data structure as a variable.

A common mistake when working with a data structure in a program having hundreds of lines of code is that you assume the name of a data structure is the name of a variable.

Technically, the assumption is correct because the compiler reserves continuous space in memory for all member variables. You can refer to this space by referring to the name of the data structure.

The example on the next page conceptually shows how the data structure appears in memory. Member variables and FILLERs are laid out in the order that they are defined in the data structure definition.

The length of the data structure is the sum of the lengths of all the member variables and FILLERs. In this example, the data structure is 22 characters in length.

The compiler treats the data structure as a single, string variable having a length of 22 characters. Whenever you refer to the name of the data structure, the compiler assumes you are referring to a variable.

You can use the MOVE command to assign a value to the entire data structure by using the name of the data structure as the target of the MOVE command. This would be an error because values of member variables will be overwritten. The data is lost and cannot be recovered until the data is stored elsewhere in your program.

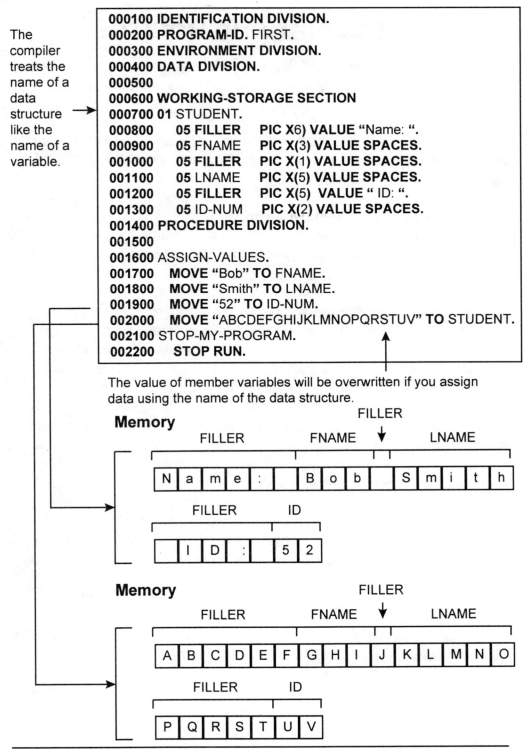

The compiler treats the name of a data structure like the name of a variable.

```
000100 IDENTIFICATION DIVISION.
000200 PROGRAM-ID. FIRST.
000300 ENVIRONMENT DIVISION.
000400 DATA DIVISION.
000500
000600 WORKING-STORAGE SECTION
000700 01 STUDENT.
000800     05 FILLER     PIC X6) VALUE "Name: ".
000900     05 FNAME      PIC X(3) VALUE SPACES.
001000     05 FILLER     PIC X(1) VALUE SPACES.
001100     05 LNAME      PIC X(5) VALUE SPACES.
001200     05 FILLER     PIC X(5)  VALUE " ID: ".
001300     05 ID-NUM     PIC X(2) VALUE SPACES.
001400 PROCEDURE DIVISION.
001500
001600 ASSIGN-VALUES.
001700    MOVE "Bob" TO FNAME.
001800    MOVE "Smith" TO LNAME.
001900    MOVE "52" TO ID-NUM.
002000    MOVE "ABCDEFGHIJKLMNOPQRSTUV" TO STUDENT.
002100 STOP-MY-PROGRAM.
002200    STOP RUN.
```

The value of member variables will be overwritten if you assign data using the name of the data structure.

Memory

FILLER   FNAME   FILLER   LNAME

| N | a | m | e | : | | B | o | b | | S | m | i | t | h |

FILLER   ID

| | I | D | : | | 5 | 2 |

Memory

FILLER   FNAME   FILLER   LNAME

| A | B | C | D | E | F | G | H | I | J | K | L | M | N | O |

FILLER   ID

| P | Q | R | S | T | U | V |

Nested Data Structures

A data structure contains variables and FILLERs as is shown on the previous pages. A data structure can also contain one or more other data structures.

For example, you can call the data structure STUDENT that indicates data stored in the data structure variables contains information about a student.

You can create a data structure within the STUDENT data structure and call it STATUS, then within the STATUS data structure defines member variables such as MAJOR, MINOR, and CREDITS. These variables describe the status of the student.

Some COBOL programmers choose to group member variables into data structures within a larger data structure. In this example besides STATUS, you can define another data structure called PERSONAL that contains information such as the student's name, address, and ID.

A data structure defined within another data structure is called *nesting* data structures. The name of the nested data structure is written at the same level as member variables of the larger data structure that is commonly at level 05.

Member variables of the nested data structure are written at a lower level than the name of the nested data structure. Typically this is at level 10 although any lower level is acceptable to the compiler.

The compiler treats the larger data structure and all its members including nested data structures as one variable that is illustrated on the previous pages.

A nested data structure and its member variables are also considered one variable by the compiler.

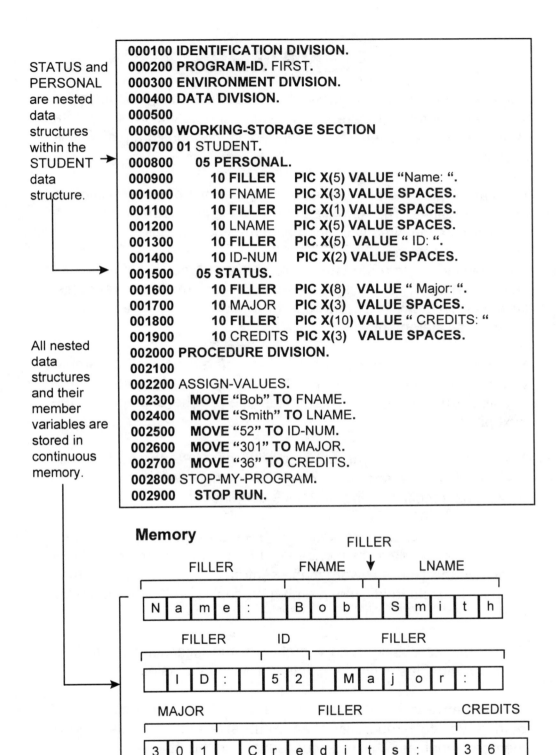

STATUS and PERSONAL are nested data structures within the STUDENT data structure.

```
000100 IDENTIFICATION DIVISION.
000200 PROGRAM-ID. FIRST.
000300 ENVIRONMENT DIVISION.
000400 DATA DIVISION.
000500
000600 WORKING-STORAGE SECTION
000700 01 STUDENT.
000800     05 PERSONAL.
000900        10 FILLER    PIC X(5) VALUE "Name: ".
001000        10 FNAME     PIC X(3) VALUE SPACES.
001100        10 FILLER    PIC X(1) VALUE SPACES.
001200        10 LNAME     PIC X(5) VALUE SPACES.
001300        10 FILLER    PIC X(5) VALUE " ID: ".
001400        10 ID-NUM    PIC X(2) VALUE SPACES.
001500     05 STATUS.
001600        10 FILLER    PIC X(8)  VALUE " Major: ".
001700        10 MAJOR     PIC X(3)  VALUE SPACES.
001800        10 FILLER    PIC X(10) VALUE " CREDITS: "
001900        10 CREDITS   PIC X(3)  VALUE SPACES.
002000 PROCEDURE DIVISION.
002100
002200 ASSIGN-VALUES.
002300     MOVE "Bob" TO FNAME.
002400     MOVE "Smith" TO LNAME.
002500     MOVE "52" TO ID-NUM.
002600     MOVE "301" TO MAJOR.
002700     MOVE "36" TO CREDITS.
002800 STOP-MY-PROGRAM.
002900     STOP RUN.
```

All nested data structures and their member variables are stored in continuous memory.

Memory

FILLER

FILLER   FNAME   LNAME

| N | a | m | e | : | | B | o | b | | S | m | i | t | h |

FILLER   ID   FILLER

| | I | D | : | | 5 | 2 | | M | a | j | o | r | : | |

MAJOR   FILLER   CREDITS

| 3 | 0 | 1 | | C | r | e | d | i | t | s | : | | 3 | 6 |

RENAMES

Variables defined as a member of a data structure are displayed in the sequence that they are defined within the definition of the data structure. You've seen this illustrated in previous pages in this chapter.

You can display member variables in a different order by using the **RENAMES** clause. The *RENAMES* clause assigns another name for a memory location already defined as a member variable.

For example, a data structure called STUDENT could have FNAME, LNAME, STREET, CITY, STATE, and ZIP as member variables. However, let's say you want to refer to just the FNAME and LNAME in a display statement.

You can create another name that references both member variables by using the **RENAMES** clause. Let's say the second name is called STUDENT-NAME. This is illustrated in the example on the next page.

The **RENAMES** clause can be used with the *THRU* phrase that tells the compiler to associate a range of member variables with the new name specified in the **RENAMES** sentence.

For example, the data structure on the next page defines **FNAME**, **FILLER**, and **LNAME** in sequence. You don't need to specify **FILLER** if you use the **THRU** keyword in the sentence. The compiler is smart enough to include all the member variables that fall within the range.

The **RENAMES** clause does not change the size nor data type of member variables. It simply points to existing variables.

An alternative to the **RENAME** clause is the *REDEFINES* clause that permits you to temporarily change the size and the data type of member variables. This is discussed later in this chapter.

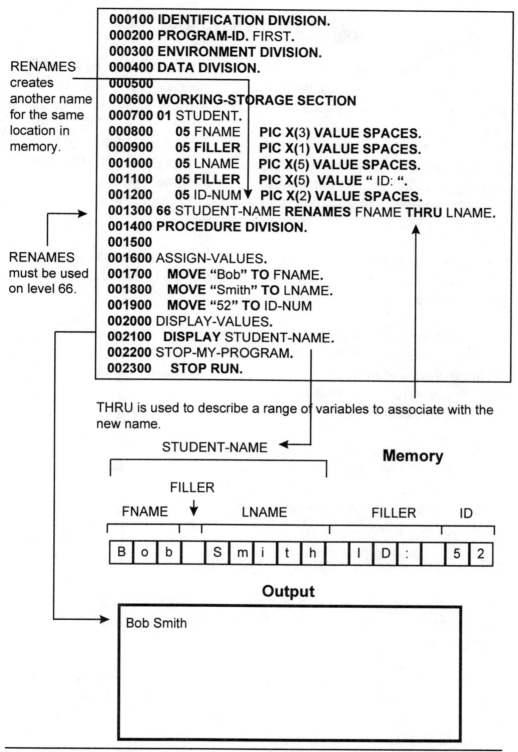

RENAMES creates another name for the same location in memory.

```
000100 IDENTIFICATION DIVISION.
000200 PROGRAM-ID. FIRST.
000300 ENVIRONMENT DIVISION.
000400 DATA DIVISION.
000500
000600 WORKING-STORAGE SECTION
000700 01 STUDENT.
000800    05 FNAME    PIC X(3) VALUE SPACES.
000900    05 FILLER   PIC X(1) VALUE SPACES.
001000    05 LNAME    PIC X(5) VALUE SPACES.
001100    05 FILLER   PIC X(5)  VALUE " ID: ".
001200    05 ID-NUM   PIC X(2) VALUE SPACES.
001300 66 STUDENT-NAME RENAMES FNAME THRU LNAME.
001400 PROCEDURE DIVISION.
001500
001600 ASSIGN-VALUES.
001700    MOVE "Bob" TO FNAME.
001800    MOVE "Smith" TO LNAME.
001900    MOVE "52" TO ID-NUM
002000 DISPLAY-VALUES.
002100    DISPLAY STUDENT-NAME.
002200 STOP-MY-PROGRAM.
002300    STOP RUN.
```

RENAMES must be used on level 66.

THRU is used to describe a range of variables to associate with the new name.

STUDENT-NAME

Memory

FILLER

FNAME   LNAME   FILLER   ID

| B | o | b | | S | m | i | t | h | I | D | : | | 5 | 2 |

Output

Bob Smith

REDEFINES

The **REDEFINES** clause performs a similar job as the **RENAMES** clause you saw on the previous page. However, there are some major differences that make **REDEFINES** a more powerful tool to use.

The *REDEFINES* clause enables you to create another word for an existing location in memory that is represented by a previously defined variable. This clause also lets you change the data type, the data size, and format of the data.

Changes to the data type, data size, and data format only affect the data when it is referenced by the new name. These changes do not affect the existing variable.

Data type changes only instruct the compiler to read the value of the variable differently than the definition of the data type when the variable was defined. Typically, data type changes are used to read a numeric value in a string variable as if it were stored in a numeric variable.

Data size changes can only be less than the size of the variable. When the compiler encounters a change in size, it begins reading the value of the variable with the left-most character (right-most for a numeric variable) and stops reading when it exhausts the new size. This is a method to copy parts of data from a variable.

These techniques are illustrated in examples on the next page.

REDEFINES must occur at the same level used to define the variable and must immediately follow the definition of the variable in the Data Division.

REDEFINES cannot be used for variables that are defined with the **VALUE** or **OCCURS** clauses. Also **REDEFINES** are prohibited from being used in level 01 in the **File Section** and the Communication Section of the Data Division.

REDEFINES creates another name for a previously defined variable.

The new name references the first three characters of the variable.

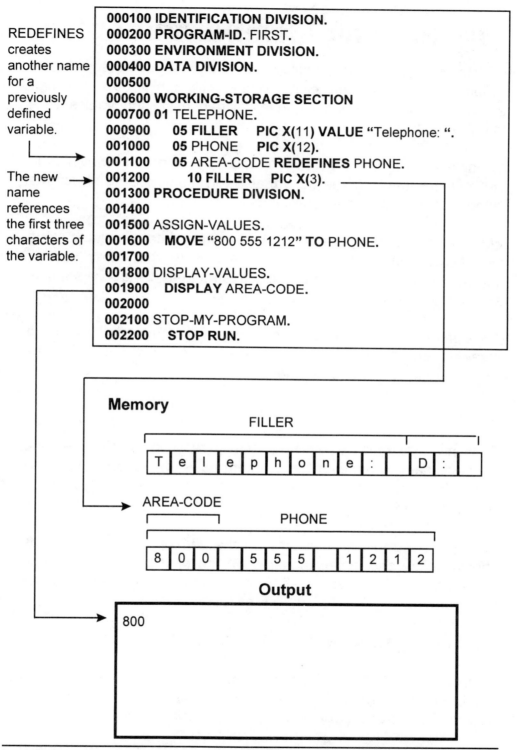

```
000100 IDENTIFICATION DIVISION.
000200 PROGRAM-ID. FIRST.
000300 ENVIRONMENT DIVISION.
000400 DATA DIVISION.
000500
000600 WORKING-STORAGE SECTION
000700 01 TELEPHONE.
000900     05 FILLER     PIC X(11) VALUE "Telephone: ".
001000     05 PHONE      PIC X(12).
001100     05 AREA-CODE REDEFINES PHONE.
001200         10 FILLER     PIC X(3).
001300 PROCEDURE DIVISION.
001400
001500 ASSIGN-VALUES.
001600     MOVE "800 555 1212" TO PHONE.
001700
001800 DISPLAY-VALUES.
001900     DISPLAY AREA-CODE.
002000
002100 STOP-MY-PROGRAM.
002200     STOP RUN.
```

Memory

FILLER

| T | e | l | e | p | h | o | n | e | : | | D | : | |

AREA-CODE

PHONE

| 8 | 0 | 0 | | 5 | 5 | 5 | | 1 | 2 | 1 | 2 |

Output

800

Identifying Member Variables

COBOL programs typically contain several data structures some of which use the same variable name to identify similar data. This can easily become confusing especially when assigning values to a variable.

Variable names define at level 01 must be unique. However, you can use the same name for variables in multiple data structures without causing a compiler problem.

For example, a program could contain two data structures. One identifies information about students and the other similar information about the faculty. Each structure contains variables FNAME and LNAME.

The compiler will display an error if the program attempts to assign a value to the FNAME variable because the compiler does not know which FNAME to use to store the value.

MOVE "Bob" TO FNAME.

The only way to avoid an error message is to specify the data structure name whenever the program uses the variable. You can identify data structure by using the **OF** clause or the **IN** clause. Both work the same way.

The *OF* clause follows the name of the variable in a sentence as shown below and in the example on the next page. This clearly gives the compiler direction as to which variable you want to use in the operation.

MOVE "Bob" TO FNAME OF STUDENT.

You don't need to specify the name of the data structure if the name of the variable is unique throughout your program. The compiler will have no trouble identifying which variable.

The compiler can become confused when the same variable name is used in multiple data structures.

```
000100 IDENTIFICATION DIVISION.
000200 PROGRAM-ID. FIRST.
000300 ENVIRONMENT DIVISION.
000400 DATA DIVISION.
000500 WORKING-STORAGE SECTION
000600 01 STUDENT.
000700     05 FNAME     PIC X(10) VALUE SPACES.
000800     05 FILLER    PIC X(1)  VALUE SPACES.
000900     05 LNAME     PIC X(20) VALUE SPACES.
001000
001100 01 FACULTY.
001200     05 FNAME     PIC X(10)  VALUE SPACES.
001300     05 FILLER    PIC X(1)   VALUE SPACES.
001400     05 LNAME     PIC X(20) VALUE SPACES.
001500 PROCEDURE DIVISION.
001600 ASSIGN-VALUES.
001700     MOVE "Bob" TO FNAME OF STUDENT.
001800     MOVE "Jones" TO LNAME OF FACULTY.
001900 STOP-MY-PROGRAM.
002000     STOP RUN.
```

Clarify which variable to reference by specifying the name of the data structure.

The OF clause is used to identify the name of the data structure.

```
000100 IDENTIFICATION DIVISION.
000200 PROGRAM-ID. FIRST.
000300 ENVIRONMENT DIVISION.
000400 DATA DIVISION.
000500
000600 WORKING-STORAGE SECTION
000700 01 STUDENT.
000800     05 FNAME     PIC X(10) VALUE SPACES.
000900     05 FILLER    PIC X(1)  VALUE SPACES.
001000     05 LNAME     PIC X(20) VALUE SPACES.
001100
001200 01 FACULTY.
001300     05 FNAME     PIC X(10) VALUE SPACES.
001400     05 FILLER    PIC X(1)  VALUE SPACES.
001500     05 LNAME     PIC X(20) VALUE SPACES.
001600 PROCEDURE DIVISION.
001700
001800 ASSIGN-VALUES.
001900     MOVE "Bob" TO FNAME IN STUDENT.
002000     MOVE "Jones" TO LNAME IN FACULTY.
002100 STOP-MY-PROGRAM.
002200     STOP RUN.
```

You can use the IN clause or the OF clause to specify the name of the data structure.

Creating an Array

A variable is the name assigned to a storage space in memory. A data structure is a name given to a group of related variables. In each of these cases, the name of the variable refers to one value.

Applications commonly refer to many instances of the same kind of information. For example, FNAME and LNAME in the STUDENT data structure contains the name of a single student. However, the program needs to access the names of many students.

The solution to this problem is to create an array of data. An *array* is a variable that uses a single name to reference more than one location in memory. Each memory location is identified by a number called an *index number* of the array and is called an *element* of the array.

You create an array by using the OCCURS clause when defining the variable in the Working-Storage Section of the Data Division. The OCCURS clause specifies the number of elements of the array to create as shown on the next page.

You define the array using the same technique used to define a variable and a data structure except the OCCURS clause follows the PIC clause in the definition. In this example, 10 elements of the array iare created.

You cannot use the OCCURS clause for variables defined at levels 01, 66, 77, or 88. You'll encounter a compiler error if you attempt to use the OCCURS clause beyond the level 02 through level 80 range.

Although arrays are typically defined as part of a data structure, you can define an array when you define any variable as long as the variable is defined at an acceptable level.

An array is an efficient method of manipulating several elements of similar data from within your program.

The index
number
specifies the
number of
elements of the
array.

An array is
created by
using the
OCCURS
clause.

```
000100 IDENTIFICATION DIVISION.
000200 PROGRAM-ID. FIRST.
000300 ENVIRONMENT DIVISION.
000400 DATA DIVISION.
000500
000600 WORKING-STORAGE SECTION
000700 01 STUDENT.
000800     05 FNAME    PIC X(10) OCCURS 5 TIMES.
000900     05 FILLER   PIC X(1)  OCCURS 5 TIMES.
001000     05 LNAME    PIC X(20) OCCURS 5 TIMES.
001100
001200 PROCEDURE DIVISION.
001300
001400 STOP-MY-PROGRAM.
001500     STOP RUN.
```

5 elements are defined. An element is used like a variable is used
in the program.

An array can
be defined
using variables
that are not
members of a
data structure.

```
000100 IDENTIFICATION DIVISION.
000200 PROGRAM-ID. FIRST.
000300 ENVIRONMENT DIVISION.
000400 DATA DIVISION.
000500
000600 WORKING-STORAGE SECTION
000700 01 CREATE-VARIABLES.
000800     05 FNAME    PIC X(10) OCCURS 5 TIMES.
000900     05 FILLER   PIC X(1)  OCCURS 5 TIMES.
001000     05 LNAME    PIC X(20) OCCURS 5 TIMES.
001100
001200 PROCEDURE DIVISION.
001300
001400 STOP-MY-PROGRAM.
001500     STOP RUN.
```

Facts You Should Know...

The **OCCURS** clause cannot be used in levels 01, 66, 77,
and 88. You use this clause in levels 02 through 80.

Accessing an Array

An array is like having several variables that have the same name. Each variable associated with the array is called an *element* of the array and is identified by an *index number*.

On the previous page, you saw how the **OCCURS** clause is used to specify the maximum number of elements of an array by using the index number.

You can access any element of the array by referencing the index number within the parentheses as shown on the next page.

An array element can be used in the same way as a variable is used in your program. You can assign values to an array element. You can display the value of an array element. And you can manipulate values of an array element.

The first element of the array is one that is different than the way array elements are numbered in other languages such as C where the first element is zero.

The index number of the array is a numeric value that can be represented by a numeric variable. You'll see the importance of this later in this chapter when you use the value of the index number to have your program efficiently access elements of the array.

Programmers commonly assign related values to the same index number of different arrays. This makes it easier to work with sets of data.

For example, you'd create two arrays called FNAME and LNAME and each will have 10 elements that permit you to store 10 names. The first element of FNAME and LNAME should contain the first and last name of the first person; the second elements contain the second name, and so on.

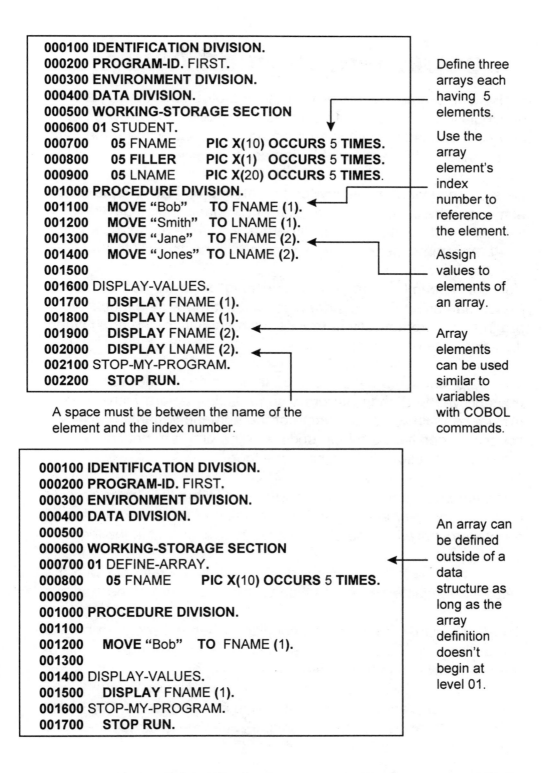

```
000100 IDENTIFICATION DIVISION.
000200 PROGRAM-ID. FIRST.
000300 ENVIRONMENT DIVISION.
000400 DATA DIVISION.
000500 WORKING-STORAGE SECTION
000600 01 STUDENT.
000700    05 FNAME     PIC X(10) OCCURS 5 TIMES.
000800    05 FILLER    PIC X(1)  OCCURS 5 TIMES.
000900    05 LNAME     PIC X(20) OCCURS 5 TIMES.
001000 PROCEDURE DIVISION.
001100    MOVE "Bob"    TO FNAME (1).
001200    MOVE "Smith"  TO LNAME (1).
001300    MOVE "Jane"   TO FNAME (2).
001400    MOVE "Jones"  TO LNAME (2).
001500
001600 DISPLAY-VALUES.
001700    DISPLAY FNAME (1).
001800    DISPLAY LNAME (1).
001900    DISPLAY FNAME (2).
002000    DISPLAY LNAME (2).
002100 STOP-MY-PROGRAM.
002200    STOP RUN.
```

Define three arrays each having 5 elements.

Use the array element's index number to reference the element.

Assign values to elements of an array.

Array elements can be used similar to variables with COBOL commands.

A space must be between the name of the element and the index number.

```
000100 IDENTIFICATION DIVISION.
000200 PROGRAM-ID. FIRST.
000300 ENVIRONMENT DIVISION.
000400 DATA DIVISION.
000500
000600 WORKING-STORAGE SECTION
000700 01 DEFINE-ARRAY.
000800    05 FNAME     PIC X(10) OCCURS 5 TIMES.
000900
001000 PROCEDURE DIVISION.
001100
001200    MOVE "Bob"    TO  FNAME (1).
001300
001400 DISPLAY-VALUES.
001500    DISPLAY FNAME (1).
001600 STOP-MY-PROGRAM.
001700    STOP RUN.
```

An array can be defined outside of a data structure as long as the array definition doesn't begin at level 01.

Looping through an Array

COBOL programs are frequently required to perform the same data manipulation on a series of variables or variables that are members of a data structure. Such a routine can be cumbersome if the data is assigned to different variable names.

Let's say you want to display the first names of three people. Each name can be assigned to a different variable such as FNAME1, FNAME2, and FNAME3. Your program would need to use three **DISPLAY** commands to show each name on the screen.

You can streamline the code by defining an array of first names rather than using three separate variables, then write a loop in your program to automatically reference each element of the array when displaying the names.

The *loop* shown on the next page increments the value of a numeric variable, then performs some action before incrementing the value again. Once the value of the numeric variable reaches a specified condition, the loop ends and the program continues with the sentence following the end of the loop.

The numeric variable that is incremented in the loop is commonly called the *counter* and is used as the value of the index number of array elements when the elements are accessed within the loop.

On the next page the loop assigns the **COUNTER** variable with the value 1, then increments the value by 1 for each turn of the loop.

The *UNTIL* clause specifies the condition when the program breaks out of the loop. In this example, the loop ends when the value of the *COUNTER* variable is greater than 2.

The **COUNTER** variable is used as the index number for the FNAME and LNAME arrays. This technique enables you to use one command to manipulate all the elements of the array.

Increment the COUNTER variable by 1 each time around the loop.

Initialize the COUNTER variable with the value 1.

COUNTER is the numeric variable that is increment each time the program completes one cycle around the loop.

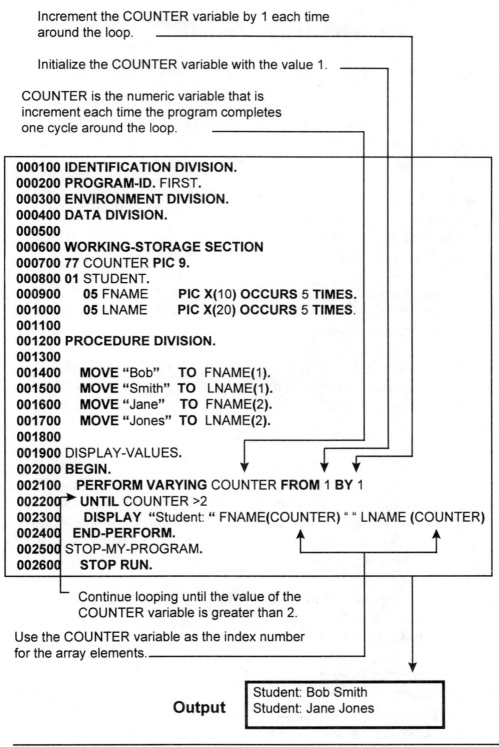

```
000100 IDENTIFICATION DIVISION.
000200 PROGRAM-ID. FIRST.
000300 ENVIRONMENT DIVISION.
000400 DATA DIVISION.
000500
000600 WORKING-STORAGE SECTION
000700 77 COUNTER PIC 9.
000800 01 STUDENT.
000900     05 FNAME      PIC X(10) OCCURS 5 TIMES.
001000     05 LNAME      PIC X(20) OCCURS 5 TIMES.
001100
001200 PROCEDURE DIVISION.
001300
001400     MOVE "Bob"    TO  FNAME(1).
001500     MOVE "Smith"  TO  LNAME(1).
001600     MOVE "Jane"   TO  FNAME(2).
001700     MOVE "Jones"  TO  LNAME(2).
001800
001900 DISPLAY-VALUES.
002000 BEGIN.
002100    PERFORM VARYING COUNTER FROM 1 BY 1
002200      UNTIL COUNTER >2
002300        DISPLAY "Student: " FNAME(COUNTER) " " LNAME (COUNTER)
002400      END-PERFORM.
002500 STOP-MY-PROGRAM.
002600     STOP RUN.
```

Continue looping until the value of the COUNTER variable is greater than 2.

Use the COUNTER variable as the index number for the array elements.

Output

```
Student: Bob Smith
Student: Jane Jones
```

Assigning Values
to an Array from the Keyboard

One of the most common routines found in a COBOL problem is to use a loop when capturing data from the keyboard and assigning the data to an array.

The *ACCEPT* command takes data entered at the keyboard and assigns the value to a variable, a member variable of a structure, or an element of an array. This technique is illustrated in the example on the next page.

You can use the **ACCEPT** command once within a loop to assign a value to each array element by using the **COUNTER** variable as the index number of the array element.

Within the loop in the example shown on the next page you'll see four sentences that tell the compiler to do something. The first displays a message on the screen prompting the user to enter a first name.

Following this sentence, the compiler is told to read data from the keyboard and assign them to the element of the FNAME array. The element is identified by the value of the **COUNTER** variable. The first time through the loop, the **COUNTER** variable's value is 1. Therefore, the first element of the FNAME array is being used to store the person's first name.

Again the compiler is told to prompt the user to enter a last name. The data is also read from the keyboard and assigned to the first array element of the LNAME array.

The compiler returns to the top of the loop, then increments the value of the **COUNTER** by 1. Next, the compiler determines if the condition to exist the loop is met. If not, then the process continues using the second element of the FNAME and LNAME arrays.

Increment the COUNTER variable by 1 each time around the loop. ────────────────

Initialize the COUNTER variable with the value 1. ──────

COUNTER is the numeric variable that is increment each time the program completes one cycle around the loop. ──

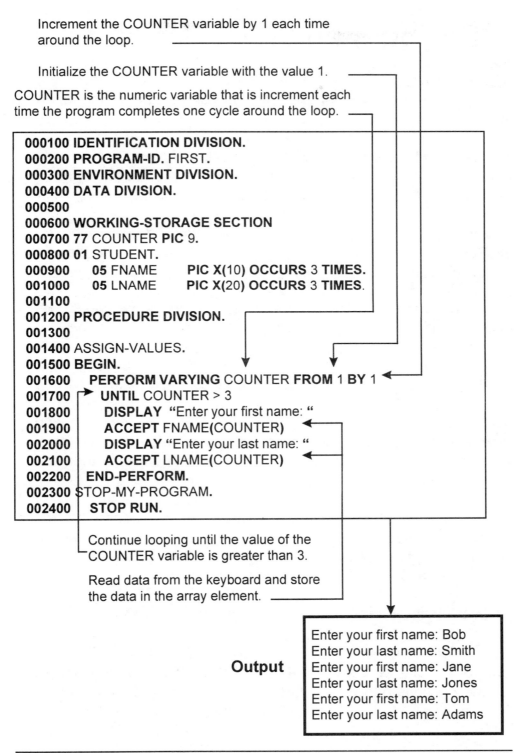

```
000100 IDENTIFICATION DIVISION.
000200 PROGRAM-ID. FIRST.
000300 ENVIRONMENT DIVISION.
000400 DATA DIVISION.
000500
000600 WORKING-STORAGE SECTION
000700 77 COUNTER PIC 9.
000800 01 STUDENT.
000900    05 FNAME    PIC X(10) OCCURS 3 TIMES.
001000    05 LNAME    PIC X(20) OCCURS 3 TIMES.
001100
001200 PROCEDURE DIVISION.
001300
001400 ASSIGN-VALUES.
001500 BEGIN.
001600    PERFORM VARYING COUNTER FROM 1 BY 1
001700      UNTIL COUNTER > 3
001800       DISPLAY  "Enter your first name: "
001900       ACCEPT FNAME(COUNTER)
002000       DISPLAY "Enter your last name: "
002100       ACCEPT LNAME(COUNTER)
002200    END-PERFORM.
002300 STOP-MY-PROGRAM.
002400    STOP RUN.
```

Continue looping until the value of the COUNTER variable is greater than 3.

Read data from the keyboard and store the data in the array element. ──────────

Output

```
Enter your first name: Bob
Enter your last name: Smith
Enter your first name: Jane
Enter your last name: Jones
Enter your first name: Tom
Enter your last name: Adams
```

Defining an Index Variable

An array can have many elements. Each element is identified by a number called an index number that is also referred to simply as an index.

You've seen in previous pages that the value of a numeric variable is used to store the index number when arrays are used within a loop. This variable is sometimes called an *index variable*.

Any numeric variable can be used as an index variable, although COBOL offers two ways to better define the index variable then as a numeric variable.

An index variable can be defined at level 77 in the Working-Storage Section of the Data Division by using the *USAGE INDEX* clause as shown here.

77 COUNTER USAGE INDEX.

The index variable is defined outside of the array definition and leaves it up to the compiler to determine the value and format of the index variable. An index variable defined using this method can be used with any array defined in the program.

The other method of defining an index variable requires that the index variable be defined as part of the array definition as in this example. The *INDEXED BY* clause limits the use of the index variable to the array specified in the sentence.

FNAME **PIC X(10) OCCURS** 3 **TIMES INDEXED BY COUNTER.**

Values of an index variable can be modified using either the **VARYING** or the **SET** clauses. The **VARYING** clauses are illustrated on the previous pages. The **SET** clause is used on the next page. You can't use **MOVE** or **COMPUTE** commands with an index variable.

```
000100 IDENTIFICATION DIVISION.
000200 PROGRAM-ID. FIRST.
000300 ENVIRONMENT DIVISION.
000400 DATA DIVISION.
000500 WORKING-STORAGE SECTION
000600 77 COUNTER USAGE INDEX. ◄─────────────────┐
000700 01 STUDENT.                               │
000800    05 NAME      PIC X(10) OCCURS 3 TIMES.  │
000900                                            │
001000 PROCEDURE DIVISION.                        │
001100                                            │
001200 BEGIN.                                     │
001300   PERFORM VARYING COUNTER FROM 1 BY 1      │
001400     UNTIL COUNTER > 3                      │
001500      DISPLAY "Enter your name: "           │
001600      ACCEPT NAME(COUNTER)                  │
001700   END-PERFORM.                             │
001800 STOP-MY-PROGRAM.                           │
001900   STOP RUN.                                │
```

Define an index variable separately from the array and you can use it with any array.

Define an index variable when defining an array and use it only with that array.

```
000100 IDENTIFICATION DIVISION.                   │
000200 PROGRAM-ID. FIRST.                         │
000300 ENVIRONMENT DIVISION.                      │
000400 DATA DIVISION.                             │
000500                                            │
000600 WORKING-STORAGE SECTION                    │
000800 01 STUDENT.                                ▼
000900    05 NAME  PIC X(10) OCCURS 3 TIMES INDEXED BY COUNTER.
001000
001100 PROCEDURE DIVISION.
001200   SET COUNTER TO 1.
001300 BEGIN.
001400   PERFORM VARYING COUNTER FROM 1 BY 1
001500    UNTIL COUNTER > 3
001600   DISPLAY "Enter your name: "
001700   ACCEPT NAME(COUNTER)
001800 END-PERFORM.
001900 STOP-MY-PROGRAM.
002000   STOP RUN.
```

Working with
Program Control

- Flow Control
- PERFORM
- PERFORM UNTIL
- PERFORM VARYING UNTIL
- GO TO
- GO TO DEPENDING ON
- IF and IF...ELSE Statements
- Nested IF Statement
- Create a Relational Expression
- GREATER THAN
- LESS THAN
- NOT GREATER THAN
- NOT LESS THAN
- GREATER THAN OR EQUAL TO
- LESS THAN OR EQUAL TO
- AND OR Operators
- CLASS
- EVALUATE

Flow Control

A COBOL program executes sentences sequentially. The program begins with the first sentence in the Procedure Division. This assumes all the necessary variables are previously defined in the Data Division.

After the first sentence, the program moves to the second sentence and continues stepping through the Procedure Division until the program terminates with the **STOP RUN** command.

The process by which each sentence is executed sequentially is called the *flow of the program*. The natural flow of a COBOL program begins with all the sentences in the Identification, Division, then with sentences in the Environment Division, Data Division and ending with sentences in the Procedure Division. The flow continues through each division without interruption.

However, you can change the flow of the program by using one of several flow control commands. You'll learn how to use these commands throughout this chapter.

PERFORM

The **PERFORM** command is used to temporally change the flow to another paragraph in the Procedure Division of the program.

The program jumps to the specified paragraph, then executes tsentences sequentially in the paragraph and returns to the sentence below the **PERFORM** command when the paragraph end is encountered. This is illustrated in the example on the next page.

The **PERFORM** command closely resembles a subroutine common to other programming languages although they are not exactly the same because there is no RETURN statement or END SUB statement used to terminate the end of the paragraph. The program determines the end of the paragraph when it encounters the beginning of another paragraph.

```
000100 IDENTIFICATION DIVISION.
000200 PROGRAM-ID. FIRST.
000300 ENVIRONMENT DIVISION.
000400 DATA DIVISION.
000500
000600 PROCEDURE DIVISION.
000700
000800 FIRST-PARAGRAPH.
000900     PERFORM WELCOME.
001000     PERFORM GOODBYE.
001100     PERFORM STOP-MY-PROGRAM.
001200
001300 WELCOME.
001400     DISPLAY "Welcome to COBOL.".
001500
001600 GOODBYE.
001700     DISPLAY "Take care now.".
001800
001900 STOP-MY-PROGRAM.
002000     STOP RUN.
```

Change the flow of the program to the WELCOME paragraph.

Jump to the GOODBYE paragraph.

Return to line 001000 when the beginning of the next paragraph is encountered.

Return to line 001100 when the beginning of the next paragraph is encountered.

```
000100 IDENTIFICATION DIVISION.
000200 PROGRAM-ID. FIRST.
000300 ENVIRONMENT DIVISION.
000400 DATA DIVISION.
000500
000600 WORKING-STORAGE SECTION.
000700 01 SUM-TOTAL  PIC 9(4) VALUE ZEROES.
000800 PROCEDURE DIVISION.
000900
001000 FIRST-PARAGRAPH.
001100     PERFORM INCREASE-BY-ONE 8 TIMES.
001200     PERFORM STOP-MY-PROGRAM.
001300
001400 INCREASE-BY-ONE.
001500     COMPUTE SUM-TOTAL = SUM-TOTAL + 1.
001600
001700 STOP-MY-PROGRAM.
001800     STOP RUN.
```

Define a numeric variable and initialize it with zeros.

Jump to the INCREASE-BY-ONE paragraph 8 times.

Jump to the STOP-MY-PROGRAM paragraph.

Increase the variable by one eight times, then return to line 001200.

PERFORM UNTIL

The **PERFORM** command can continue to call a paragraph until a specified condition is met by using the **UNTIL** phrase with the **PERFORM** command.

The condition is expressed in a *relational expression* which compares one value with another value. You'll learn how to create a variety of relational expressions later in this chapter.

There are four parts of a **PERFORM UNTIL** combination. First is the name of the command (**PERFORM**) followed by the paragraph to be called. Next is the **UNTIL** phrase followed by the relational expression.

> PERFORM GRAPH-1 **UNTIL** X > Y

As long as the value of variable X isn't greater than the value of variable Y, the **PERFORM** command continues to call the paragraph. Once the relational expression is true, then the program skips to the sentence following the **PERFORM** command.

PERFORM VARYING UNTIL

A paragraph can be called a specific number of times by using the **TIMES** phrase as shown previously in this chapter or by the use of the **VARYING** phrase.

The **VARYING** phrase is usually combined with the **FROM** phrase to specify the number of times the paragraph is to be called. The **VARYING** phrase specifies a variable name whose value is incremented each time the paragraph is called. The range of values used to increment the variable is specified in the **FROM** phrase. This is shown on the next page.

The **VARYING** phrase enables you to use the incremental value in the called paragraph while the **TIMES** phrase simply calls the paragraph a specified number of times.

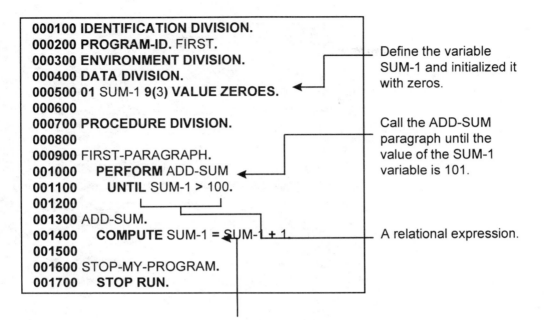

```
000100 IDENTIFICATION DIVISION.
000200 PROGRAM-ID. FIRST.
000300 ENVIRONMENT DIVISION.
000400 DATA DIVISION.
000500 01 SUM-1 9(3) VALUE ZEROES.
000600
000700 PROCEDURE DIVISION.
000800
000900 FIRST-PARAGRAPH.
001000    PERFORM ADD-SUM
001100      UNTIL SUM-1 > 100.
001200
001300 ADD-SUM.
001400    COMPUTE SUM-1 = SUM-1 + 1.
001500
001600 STOP-MY-PROGRAM.
001700    STOP RUN.
```

Define the variable SUM-1 and initialized it with zeros.

Call the ADD-SUM paragraph until the value of the SUM-1 variable is 101.

A relational expression.

The value of SUM-1 is incremented by 1 each time the paragraph is called.

Call the MULTIPLY-PRODUCT paragraph.

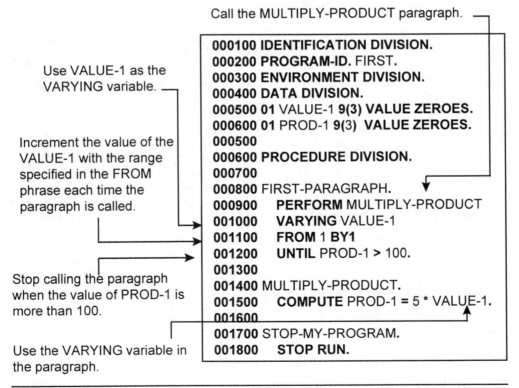

Use VALUE-1 as the VARYING variable.

Increment the value of the VALUE-1 with the range specified in the FROM phrase each time the paragraph is called.

```
000100 IDENTIFICATION DIVISION.
000200 PROGRAM-ID. FIRST.
000300 ENVIRONMENT DIVISION.
000400 DATA DIVISION.
000500 01 VALUE-1 9(3) VALUE ZEROES.
000600 01 PROD-1 9(3) VALUE ZEROES.
000500
000600 PROCEDURE DIVISION.
000700
000800 FIRST-PARAGRAPH.
000900    PERFORM MULTIPLY-PRODUCT
001000    VARYING VALUE-1
001100    FROM 1 BY1
001200    UNTIL PROD-1 > 100.
001300
001400 MULTIPLY-PRODUCT.
001500    COMPUTE PROD-1 = 5 * VALUE-1.
001600
001700 STOP-MY-PROGRAM.
001800    STOP RUN.
```

Stop calling the paragraph when the value of PROD-1 is more than 100.

Use the VARYING variable in the paragraph.

GO TO

Another way to tell the program to execute commands in a different paragraph is to use the **GO TO** command. The **GO TO** command is very similar to the **PERFORM** command illustrated on the previous pages. However, there is one important difference.

The **PERFORM** command tells the program to jump to a specific paragraph in the Procedure Division of the program. Once the program detects the beginning of the next paragraph, control returns to the next sentence below the **PERFORM** command.

In contrast, the **GO TO** command does not return control to the sentence following the **GO TO** command. Instead, the program continues executing sentences into the next paragraph.

You must be careful whenever you use a **GO TO** command in your program because you take control over the natural order in which paragraphs are executed.

Let's say you have three paragraphs called FIRST-PARAGRAPH, SECOND-PARAGRAPH, and THIRD-PARAGRAPH. A **GO TO** command is used to skip the first paragraph and begin executing the program with the second paragraph.

The program will execute the second paragraph and the third paragraph because the program did not encounter another flow control command such as the **GO TO** or **PERFORM** command.

Many COBOL programmers avoid using the **GO TO** command because it is easy to lose track of the flow of the program in very large programs.

Instead they use the **PERFORM** command because the flow of the program automatically returns to the paragraph containing the **PERFORM** command.

The GO TO command redirects the flow to the WELCOME paragraph.

The PERFORM commands won't be executed.

The flow continues to the next paragraph without returning to line 001000.

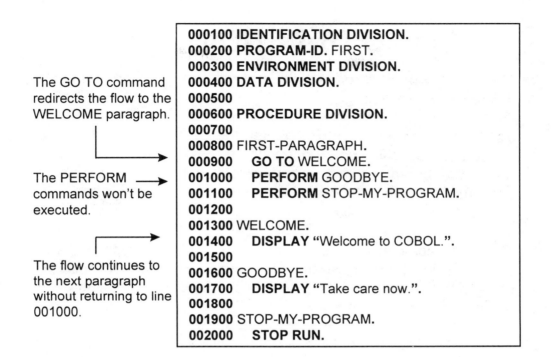

```
000100 IDENTIFICATION DIVISION.
000200 PROGRAM-ID. FIRST.
000300 ENVIRONMENT DIVISION.
000400 DATA DIVISION.
000500
000600 PROCEDURE DIVISION.
000700
000800 FIRST-PARAGRAPH.
000900     GO TO WELCOME.
001000     PERFORM GOODBYE.
001100     PERFORM STOP-MY-PROGRAM.
001200
001300 WELCOME.
001400     DISPLAY "Welcome to COBOL.".
001500
001600 GOODBYE.
001700     DISPLAY "Take care now.".
001800
001900 STOP-MY-PROGRAM.
002000     STOP RUN.
```

This program creates an endless loop.

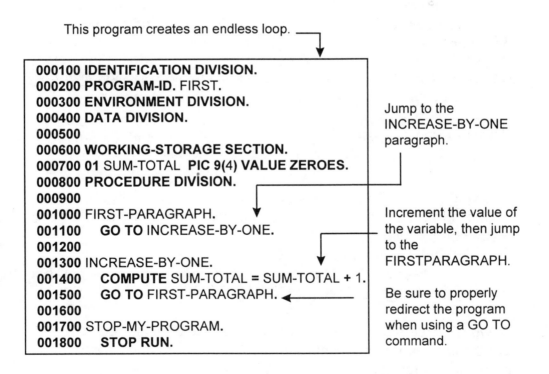

```
000100 IDENTIFICATION DIVISION.
000200 PROGRAM-ID. FIRST.
000300 ENVIRONMENT DIVISION.
000400 DATA DIVISION.
000500
000600 WORKING-STORAGE SECTION.
000700 01 SUM-TOTAL  PIC 9(4) VALUE ZEROES.
000800 PROCEDURE DIVISION.
000900
001000 FIRST-PARAGRAPH.
001100     GO TO INCREASE-BY-ONE.
001200
001300 INCREASE-BY-ONE.
001400     COMPUTE SUM-TOTAL = SUM-TOTAL + 1.
001500     GO TO FIRST-PARAGRAPH.
001600
001700 STOP-MY-PROGRAM.
001800     STOP RUN.
```

Jump to the INCREASE-BY-ONE paragraph.

Increment the value of the variable, then jump to the FIRSTPARAGRAPH.

Be sure to properly redirect the program when using a GO TO command.

GO TO DEPENDING ON

The **GO TO** command redirects the natural flow of the program to a different part of the program.

As you saw previously in this chapter, the **GO TO** command directs the flow to a specified paragraph in the Procedure Division. Sentences within the paragraph are executed sequentially and execution continues through to succeeding paragraphs until the **STOP RUN** command is encountered.

The **GO TO** command can chose one of several paragraphs to jump to by using the **DEPENDING ON** clause. The list of possible paragraphs are named in the **GO TO** command by separating each name with a space as shown here:

GO TO NAME-1 NAME-2 NAME-3 **DEPENDING ON** VAR-1

The **DEPENDING ON** clause specifies a numeric variable whose value identifies the position number of the paragraph to use in the **GO TO** command.

If the value of VAR-1 is 1, then the first paragraph is called. If the value is 2, then the second paragraph is called and so on. However, if the value of the variable does not correspond to the position of a paragraph named in the **GO TO** command, then the **GO TO** command is ignored.

The value of VAR-1 can be assigned using the **MOVE** command, by initializing the variable or by assigning a value to the variable as a result of a calculation.

The value must be stored in the variable before the value can be used by the **GO TO** command.

A word of caution. Most programmers avoid using **GO TO** and **DEPENDING ON** because improper use of this command can lead to bugs in an application.

Create a
numeric
variable the
value of which
will determine
which
paragraph is
called by the
GO TO
command.

```
000100 IDENTIFICATION DIVISION.
000200 PROGRAM-ID. FIRST.
000300 ENVIRONMENT DIVISION.
000400 DATA DIVISION.
000500
000600 WORKING-STORAGE SECTION.
000700 01 PICK PIC 9 VALUE IS 1.
000800 PROCEDURE DIVISION.
000900
001000 ASSIGN-VALUES.
001100  MOVE 2 TO PICK.
001200
001300 FIRST-PARAGRAPH.
001400   GO TO WELCOME GOODBYE DEPENDING ON PICK.
001500
001600 WELCOME.
001700   DISPLAY "Welcome to COBOL.".
001800
001900 GOODBYE.
002000   DISPLAY "Take care now.".
002100 STOP-MY-PROGRAM.
002200    STOP RUN.
```

Jump to the
second
paragraph
because the
value of PICK
is 2.

No paragraph
is called
because the
value of PICK
is greater than
the number of
paragraphs
specified.

If the value of
PICK is 1, then
the first
paragraph is
called. If the
value of PICK
is 2, then the
second
paragraph is
called.

```
000100 IDENTIFICATION DIVISION.
000200 PROGRAM-ID. FIRST.
000300 ENVIRONMENT DIVISION.
000400 DATA DIVISION.
000500
000600 WORKING-STORAGE SECTION.
000700 01 PICK PIC 9 VALUE 1.
000800 PROCEDURE DIVISION.
000900
001000 ASSIGN-VALUES.
001100   MOVE 3 TO PICK.
001200
001300 FIRST-PARAGRAPH.
001400   GO TO WELCOME GOODBYE DEPENDING ON PICK..
001500
001600 WELCOME.
001700   DISPLAY "Welcome to COBOL.".
001800
001900 GOODBYE.
002000   DISPLAY "Take care now.".
002100 STOP-MY-PROGRAM.
002200    STOP RUN.
```

IF and IF...ELSE Statements

Programs make decisions by comparing values, then determining if the comparison is true or false. You've seen this occur on the previous page when the **DEPENDING ON** clause forces the program to evaluate the value of a numeric variable.

The program compares the value of the variable specified in the **DEPENDING ON** clause with the position of paragraphs identified in the **GO TO** command. If the value matches a position, then the paragraph at that position is called. If the value does not match a position, then no paragraph is called.

The **DEPENDING ON** clause enables the program to make a decision. However, the condition on which to make this decision is very narrow and won't meet the needs of most applications.

An alternative to the **DEPENDING ON** clause is the **IF** statement. The **IF** *statement* has the same effect on the program as it does in English. If a condition is true, then do something. If a condition is not true, then don't do it.

The sentences that are executed if the condition is true are contained within the **IF** statement's block. The block begins with the IF statement and ends with the **END-IF** phrase.

The condition is specified as a relational expression such as COLOR = "blue". **IF** the value of the COLOR variable is "blue", then the sentences within the **IF** statement's block are executed, otherwise the sentence following the **END-IF** phrase is executed.

Later in this chapter you'll see the various techniques you can use to create a relational expression that are all called conditional expressions.

The **IF** statement can use the **ELSE** clause to provide an alternate group of sentences to use if the condition is false. Examples are shown on the next page.

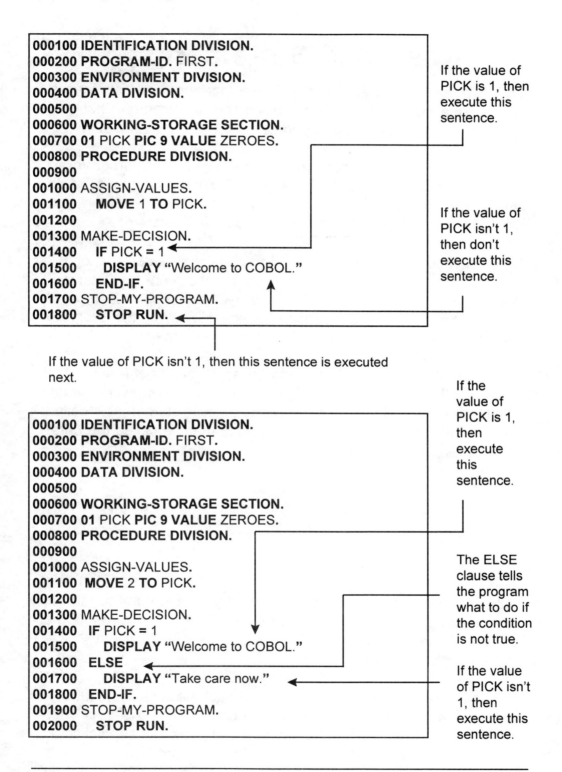

```
000100 IDENTIFICATION DIVISION.
000200 PROGRAM-ID. FIRST.
000300 ENVIRONMENT DIVISION.
000400 DATA DIVISION.
000500
000600 WORKING-STORAGE SECTION.
000700 01 PICK PIC 9 VALUE ZEROES.
000800 PROCEDURE DIVISION.
000900
001000 ASSIGN-VALUES.
001100     MOVE 1 TO PICK.
001200
001300 MAKE-DECISION.
001400     IF PICK = 1
001500        DISPLAY "Welcome to COBOL."
001600     END-IF.
001700 STOP-MY-PROGRAM.
001800     STOP RUN.
```

If the value of PICK is 1, then execute this sentence.

If the value of PICK isn't 1, then don't execute this sentence.

If the value of PICK isn't 1, then this sentence is executed next.

If the value of PICK is 1, then execute this sentence.

```
000100 IDENTIFICATION DIVISION.
000200 PROGRAM-ID. FIRST.
000300 ENVIRONMENT DIVISION.
000400 DATA DIVISION.
000500
000600 WORKING-STORAGE SECTION.
000700 01 PICK PIC 9 VALUE ZEROES.
000800 PROCEDURE DIVISION.
000900
001000 ASSIGN-VALUES.
001100  MOVE 2 TO PICK.
001200
001300 MAKE-DECISION.
001400   IF PICK = 1
001500      DISPLAY "Welcome to COBOL."
001600   ELSE
001700      DISPLAY "Take care now."
001800   END-IF.
001900 STOP-MY-PROGRAM.
002000     STOP RUN.
```

The ELSE clause tells the program what to do if the condition is not true.

If the value of PICK isn't 1, then execute this sentence.

Working with Program Control

Nested IF Statements

You can force a program to execute one or more sentences whenever a condition is true by using the IF statement that you learned about on the previous page.

Any number of IF statements can be used in a program to selectively execute groups of sentences. There is technically no limit to the number of IF statements you can use, although if you use too many, your code becomes unreadable to humans.

Some situations require your program to consider a decision only if another condition is true. For example, the first IF statement determines whether the person is a female. If so, the next IF statement determines if she is pregnant. However, the program shouldn't ask if she is pregnant if the person is a male.

A solution to this problem is to write an IF statement within the block of another IF statement. This is called a *nested IF statement*. The IF statement within the block of the other IF statement is called the *inner IF statement*. The outside IF statement is called the *outer IF statement*. Here's how it looks in code:

```
IF PERSON = "female"
    IF PREGNANT = "yes"
        do something
    END-IF.
END-IF.
```

Notice the inner IF statement is not executed if the condition in the outer IF statement isn't true. The program skips over the rest of the outer IF statement block and continues executing with the line following the last END-IF phrase.

Program examples on the other page illustrates the technique of writing a nested IF statement into your program. As you'll see throughout the rest of the chapter, you can construct sophisticated condition expressions for use with the IF statement.

```
000100 IDENTIFICATION DIVISION.
000200 PROGRAM-ID. FIRST.
000300 ENVIRONMENT DIVISION.
000400 DATA DIVISION.
000500
000600 WORKING-STORAGE SECTION.
000700 01 PICK-1 PIC 9 VALUE ZEROES.
000800 01 PICK-2 PIC 9 VALUE ZEROES.
000800 PROCEDURE DIVISION.
000900
001000 ASSIGN-VALUES.
001100    MOVE 1 TO PICK-1.
001200    MOVE 1 TO PICK-2.
001300
001400 MAKE-DECISION.
001500    IF PICK-1 = 1
001600       DISPLAY "Welcome to COBOL."
001700       IF PICK-2 = 1
001800          DISPLAY "DISPLAY "Take care now."
001900       END-IF.
002000    END-IF.
002100 STOP-MY-PROGRAM.
002200    STOP RUN.
```

The condition in the inner IF statement won't be evaluated unless the condition in the outer IF statement is true.

An IF statement can be enclosed within another IF statement block. This is called a nested IF statement.

```
000100 IDENTIFICATION DIVISION.
000200 PROGRAM-ID. FIRST.
000300 ENVIRONMENT DIVISION.
000400 DATA DIVISION.
000500 WORKING-STORAGE SECTION.
000600 01 PICK-1 PIC 9 VALUE ZEROES.
000700 01 PICK-2 PIC 9 VALUE ZEROES.
000800 PROCEDURE DIVISION.
000900
001000 ASSIGN-VALUES.
001100    MOVE 1 TO PICK-1.
001200    MOVE 3 TO PICK-2.
001300 MAKE-DECISION.
001400    IF PICK-1 = 1
001500       DISPLAY "Welcome to COBOL.".
001600       IF PICK-2 = 1
001700          DISPLAY "DISPLAY "Take care now.".
001800       END-IF.
001900    END-IF.
002000 STOP-MY-PROGRAM.
002100    STOP RUN.
```

Too many nested IF statements can make your code unreadable except for the computer.

The sentence in the inner IF statement won't be executed because the condition is false.

Creating a Relational Expression

A *relational* is an expression that compares two values to each other and is used with commands such as an IF statement. You'll learn about other commands that use a relational expression throughout this book.

The expression is called a relational expression because the results of the expression is either true or false. PICK-1 = 1 is a relational expression used in an example of the IF statement on the previous pages.

In this example, the equal operator, called a *relational operator*, directs the computer to compare the value stored in the PICK-1 variable with the literal value 1. There are only two possible results to this expression. Either both values are the same or they're not the same.

A relational expression can be as simple as the one just described or a complex expression that contains two or more relational expressions. You'll learn more about how to create complex relational expressions later in this chapter.

The simplest and probably the most common relational expression that you'll use is one that determines if two values are equal.

You can write this expression in one of two ways by either using relational operator words or symbol. EQUAL TO is the relational operator word and the equal symbol (=) is the symbol version of the same operator. Both are evaluated the same way.

Another commonly used relational operator is the NOT operator such as NOT EQUAL TO or NOT = . The NOT operator reverses the result of the expression. It says, if the expression isn't true, then execute the block of code.

```
000100 IDENTIFICATION DIVISION.
000200 PROGRAM-ID. FIRST.
000300 ENVIRONMENT DIVISION.
000400 DATA DIVISION.
000500
000600 WORKING-STORAGE SECTION.
000700 01 PICK-1 PIC 9 VALUE ZEROES.
000800 PROCEDURE DIVISION.
000900
001000 ASSIGN-VALUES.
001100    MOVE 1 TO PICK-1.
001200
001300 MAKE-DECISION.
001400    IF PICK-1 = 1
001500       DISPLAY "Welcome to COBOL."
001600    END-IF.
001700 STOP-MY-PROGRAM.
001800    STOP RUN.
```

A relational expression must evaluate to either a true or false. The equals (=) operator compares two values and returns a true if both are the same, otherwise a false is returned.

The equal operator can be written in words as EQUAL TO or by using the symbol (=).

```
000100 IDENTIFICATION DIVISION.
000200 PROGRAM-ID. FIRST.
000300 ENVIRONMENT DIVISION.
000400 DATA DIVISION.
000500
000600 WORKING-STORAGE SECTION.
000700 01 PICK-1 PIC 9 VALUE ZEROES.
000800 PROCEDURE DIVISION.
000900
001000 ASSIGN-VALUES.
001100  MOVE 3 TO PICK-1.
001200
001300 MAKE-DECISION.
001400    IF PICK-1 NOT EQUAL TO 1
001500       DISPLAY "Goodbye for now.".
001600    END-IF.
001700 STOP-MY-PROGRAM.
001800    STOP RUN.
```

The condition must not be true before the code within the IF statement is executed.

The value of PICK-1 must not equal 1 before the message is displayed on the screen.

GREATER THAN

A relational expression uses a relational operator to compare two values. You learned about the equal relational operator and the **NOT** relational operator on the previous page.

Another relational operator you'll use frequently in your programs is the greater than operator. The *greater than* operator is used to determine if the value on the left side of the operator has a higher value than the operator on the right side of the operator.

If the value on the left is greater than the value on the right, the relational expression is true.

Unlike other programming languages, COBOL enables the use of several forms of the greater than operator. These are illustrated on the next page.

You'll find the symbol form of the greater than operator (>) used in most programs because this is easier to read, takes up less space on the line, and requires little typing. However, all forms have exactly the same effect in your program.

LESS THAN

Values can also be compared to determine if one value is less than another value by using the *less than* operator. A relational expression that uses the less than operator is true if the value on the left side of the less than operator is of a smaller value than the value on the right side of the less than operator.

There are two forms of the less than operator. These are using the words **IS LESS THAN** and using the less than symbol (<). Most programmers use the symbol.

```
000100 IDENTIFICATION DIVISION.
000200 PROGRAM-ID. FIRST.
000300 ENVIRONMENT DIVISION.
000400 DATA DIVISION.
000500
000600 WORKING-STORAGE SECTION.
000700 01 PICK-1 PIC 9 VALUE ZEROES.
000800 PROCEDURE DIVISION.
000900
001000 ASSIGN-VALUES.
001100     MOVE 1 TO PICK-1.
001200
001300 MAKE-DECISION.
001400     IF PICK-1 > 12
001500         DISPLAY "Welcome to COBOL."
001600     END-IF.
001700     IF PICK-1 < 13
001800         DISPLAY "Goodbye now."
001900     END-IF.
002000 STOP-MY-PROGRAM.
002100     STOP RUN.
```

The greater than operator compares the value on both sides of the operator.

If the value on the left is greater than the value on the right, then the expression is true.

This message will be displayed.

The less than operator is used to determine if the value on the left is smaller than the value on the right.

This message will not be displayed.

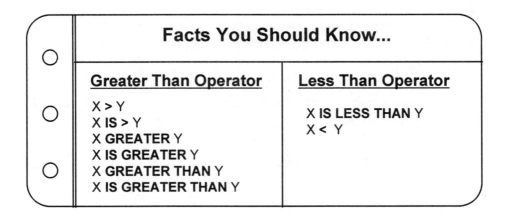

Facts You Should Know...

Greater Than Operator	Less Than Operator
X > Y X IS > Y X GREATER Y X IS GREATER Y X GREATER THAN Y X IS GREATER THAN Y	X IS LESS THAN Y X < Y

NOT GREATER THAN

The greater than relational operator compares values on both sides of the operator to determine if the left value is greater than the right value.

If this condition is true, then the expression is true. You can reverse the logic by using the **NOT** operator. The **NOT** operator in conjunction with the greater than operator asks the question, is the value on the left not greater than the value on the right?

There are only two conditions when an expression using the **NOT** greater than operator is true:

if the value on the left is smaller than the value on the right

or

if the value on the left is equal to the value on the right.

There are several forms of the **NOT** greater than operator that are listed on the next page. All work exactly the same way, although the symbol (*NOT* >) for the operator is used most frequently in programs.

NOT LESS THAN

The **NOT** operator is also used to reverse the logic of the less than operator. It asks the questions, is the value on the left not less than the value on the right.

There are only two conditions when an expression using the **NOT** less than operator is true:

if the value on the left is greater than the value on the right

or

if the value on the left is equal to the value on the right.

```
000100 IDENTIFICATION DIVISION.
000200 PROGRAM-ID. FIRST.
000300 ENVIRONMENT DIVISION.
000400 DATA DIVISION.
000500
000600 WORKING-STORAGE SECTION.
000700 01 PICK-1 PIC 9 VALUE ZEROES.
000800 PROCEDURE DIVISION.
000900
001000 ASSIGN-VALUES.
001100     MOVE 1 TO PICK-1.
001200
001300 MAKE-DECISION.
001400     IF PICK-1 NOT > 12
001500         DISPLAY "Welcome to COBOL."
001600     END-IF.
001700     IF PICK-1 NOT < 13
001800         DISPLAY "Goodbye now."
001900     END-IF.
002000 STOP-MY-PROGRAM.
002100     STOP RUN.
```

The NOT operator reverses the logic of the greater than operator.

If the value on the left is not greater than the value on the right, then the expression is true.

This message will not be displayed.

If the value on the left is not less than the value on the right, then the expression is true.

This message will be displayed.

Facts You Should Know...

Greater Than Operator	Less Than Operator
X NOT > Y	X < Y
X IS NOT > Y	X IS NOT LESS THAN Y
X NOT GREATER Y	
X IS NOT GREATER Y	
X NOT GREATER THAN Y	
X IS NOT GREATER THAN Y	

GREATER THAN OR EQUAL TO

On the previous page you've seen an example where you can use the greater than operator to determine if the value on the left of the operator is larger than the value to the right of the operator.

Some COBOL applications require you to execute sentences if the left value is greater than or equal to the right value. You must use both the greater than and the equal to operators to evaluate such an relational expression.

There are two ways to write these operators in an expression. You can use words or symbols as shown here.

X **IS GREATER THAN OR EQUAL TO** Y

X >= Y

Using the word form of the operator requires you to join two operators together using the logical *OR* operator. You'll recognized from examples used in previous pages that **IS GREATER THAN** is a relational operator and so is **EQUAL TO**. Both can be used independently of any other relational operator.

OR is a logical operator you can use to combine expressions. You'll learn more about the **OR** operator later in this chapter.

LESS THAN OR EQUAL TO

The equal operator is also used with the less than operator whenever you need to determine if the value on the left of the less then operator is less than or equal to the value on the right.

You'll see examples of the less than and equal to operators used in examples on the next page.

```
000100 IDENTIFICATION DIVISION.
000200 PROGRAM-ID. FIRST.
000300 ENVIRONMENT DIVISION.
000400 DATA DIVISION.
000500
000600 WORKING-STORAGE SECTION.
000700 01 PICK-1 PIC 9 VALUE ZEROES.
000800 PROCEDURE DIVISION.
000900
001000 ASSIGN-VALUES.
001100     MOVE 1 TO PICK-1.
001200
001300 MAKE-DECISION.
001400     IF PICK-1 IS GREATER THAN OR EQUAL T0 1
001500        DISPLAY "Welcome to COBOL."
001600     END-IF.
001700     IF PICK-1 >= 3
001800        DISPLAY "Goodbye now."
001900     END-IF.
002000     IF PICK-1 IS LESS THAN OR EQUAL T0 6
002100        DISPLAY "Welcome to COBOL again."
002200     END-IF.
002300     IF PICK-1 <= 9
002400        DISPLAY "Goodbye now again.".
002500     END-IF.
002600 STOP-MY-PROGRAM.
002700     STOP RUN.
```

The symbol for the greater than or equal to has the same effect as if the word form of the operator is used.

Is the value stored in PICK-1 smaller or equal to 6?

Many programmers use the symbol for the less than or equal to operator.

Output

```
Welcome to COBOL.
Welcome to COBOL again.
Goodbye now again.
```

AND OR Operators

You can incorporate more than one relational expression in a conditional statement such as the IF statement by using either the AND or the OR operator.

The AND and OR operators are called *logical operators* because they only evaluate true or false values.

The AND operator joins two relational expressions as shown here:

$$X = Y \text{ AND } X > Z$$

This example consist of three expressions. The first expression determines if X and Y are equal. The second expression determines if X is greater than Z. The third expression determines if both the first and second expressions are true.

Only if the first and second expressions are true will the entire (third expression) be true. Both conditions must be met. If one of the expressions is false, then the entire expression is false.

The OR operator functions similar as to the AND operator except the entire expression is true if either the first or second expressions are true. The entire expression is false only if both the first and second expressions are false.

You can create compound expressions that use multiple AND or OR operators or a combination of these operators as illustrated in the example on the next page.

Evaluating a compound expression can be confusing for some programmers because it is not clear where to begin the evaluation. Avoid confusion and evaluate a compound expression from left to right which is the way the expression will be evaluated when your program is running.

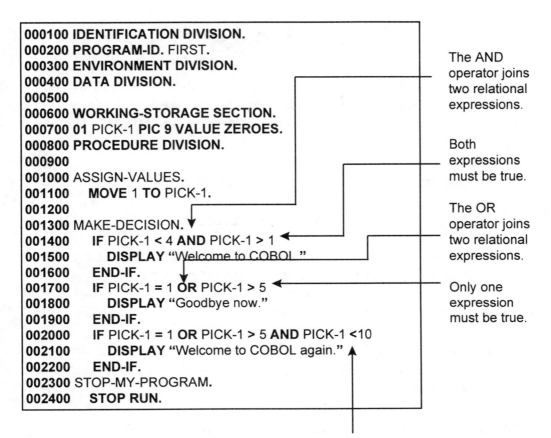

```
000100 IDENTIFICATION DIVISION.
000200 PROGRAM-ID. FIRST.
000300 ENVIRONMENT DIVISION.
000400 DATA DIVISION.
000500
000600 WORKING-STORAGE SECTION.
000700 01 PICK-1 PIC 9 VALUE ZEROES.
000800 PROCEDURE DIVISION.
000900
001000 ASSIGN-VALUES.
001100    MOVE 1 TO PICK-1.
001200
001300 MAKE-DECISION.
001400    IF PICK-1 < 4 AND PICK-1 > 1
001500       DISPLAY "Welcome to COBOL."
001600    END-IF.
001700    IF PICK-1 = 1 OR PICK-1 > 5
001800       DISPLAY "Goodbye now."
001900    END-IF.
002000    IF PICK-1 = 1 OR PICK-1 > 5 AND PICK-1 <10
002100       DISPLAY "Welcome to COBOL again."
002200    END-IF.
002300 STOP-MY-PROGRAM.
002400    STOP RUN.
```

The AND operator joins two relational expressions.

Both expressions must be true.

The OR operator joins two relational expressions.

Only one expression must be true.

Compound expressions are evaluated from left to right. First the equal, then the greater than, and finally the less than expressions.

Facts You Should Know...

You can use parentheses in a compound expression to force the order in which expressions are evaluated. Expressions within parentheses are evaluated before expressions outside of the parentheses.

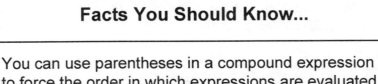

IF PICK-1 = 1 OR PICK-1 > 5 AND (PICK-1 <10)

CLASS

A variable is either a string variable or a numeric variable that is illustrated in Chapter 2. These are called *data types*. Variables can also be classified by the kind of value stored in the variable. This is called a *classification*.

There are standard classifications used in COBOL. These are Numeric, Alphabetic, Alphabetic-upper, Alphabetic-lower, Positive, and Negative. Each is the name of a classification.

You can examine the classification of a variable by using the classification name in a relational expression such as:

X IS ALPHABETIC-UPPER

This expression can be used in any statement that evaluates a relational expression. You've seen this used in an **IF** statement throughout this chapter.

In this example, the expression is asking the question, does the value stored in variable X contain an uppercase alphabetical character? The result of evaluating this expression is either true or false.

You can create your own classification of values by using the **CLASS** clause to define a class such as the Special-Names paragraph of the Configuration Section in the Environment Division.

A **CLASS** must be identified by a name and followed by values that are members of the class. An example of this is shown on the next page.

You can use the name of the user-defined class just as you would use the name of a COBOL class in a relational expression. The expression evaluates true if the value of the variable is a member of your class definition, otherwise the expression is false.

```
000100 IDENTIFICATION DIVISION.
000200 PROGRAM-ID. FIRST.
000300 ENVIRONMENT DIVISION.
000400 CONFIGURATION SECTION.
000500 SPECIAL-NAMES.
000600    CLASS FRIEND "Bob" "Mary" "Joe".
000700 DATA DIVISION.
000800
000900 WORKING-STORAGE SECTION.
001000 01 PICK-1 PIC 9 VALUE ZEROES.
001100 01 PICK-2 PIC X(4) VALUE SPACES.
001200 01 VISITOR PIC X(5) VALUE SPACES.
001300 PROCEDURE DIVISION.
001400
001500 ASSIGN-VALUES.
001600    MOVE 1 TO PICK-1.
001700    MOVE "X" TO PICK-2.
001800    MOVE "Tom" TO VISITOR.
001900
002000 MAKE-DECISION.
002100    IF PICK-1 IS NUMERIC
002200       DISPLAY "Welcome to COBOL."
002300    END-IF.
002400    IF PICK-1 IS ALPHABETIC
002500       DISPLAY "Goodbye now."
002600    END-IF.
002700    IF PICK-2 IS ALPHABETIC-LOWER
002800       DISPLAY "Welcome to COBOL again."
002900    END-IF.
003000    IF VISITOR IS FRIEND
003100       DISPLAY "Come on in."
003200    END-IF.
003300 STOP-MY-PROGRAM.
003400    STOP RUN.
```

Define a user-defined class called FRIEND. These are members of the FRIEND class.

Is the value of PICK-1 a numeric value?

Is the value of PICK-1 an alphabetical character?

Is the value of PICK-1 a lowercase character?

Is the value of VISITOR a member of the class FRIEND?

COBOL Standard Classes

IS NUMERIC	Is this a numeric value?
IS ALPHABETIC	Is this a character of the alphabet?
IS ALPHABETIC-UPPER	Is this a lowercase character?
IS ALPHABETIC-LOWER	Is this an uppercase character?
IS POSITIVE	Is this a positive number?
IS NEGATIVE	Is this a negative number?

EVALUATE

You've seen throughout this chapter how you can change the flow of your program by comparing two values, then change direction based upon the outcome of the comparison.

Examples used throughout this chapter used an IF statement and a relational expression to make such a comparison. If the expression is true, then sentences with the IF statement block are executed, otherwise they are skipped.

You've also seen how more than one comparison can be made by using nested IF statements. A nested IF *statement* is an IF statement that contains one or more IF statements within the IF statement block.

Too many nested IF statements make a COBOL program confusing to read because of the levels of decisions crammed into a small area of your program.

An alternative to nested IF statements is the **EVALUATE** statement. The **EVALUATE** statement compares one value to many other values as shown here:

```
EVALUATE PICK-1
    WHEN 5
        DISPLAY 5
    WHEN 6
        DISPLAY 6
END-EVALUATE.
```

In this example, the value of the variable PICK-1 is compared to the value 5, then to the value 6. You can add any number of WHEN clauses to the **EVALUATE** statement.

Notice the **EVALUATE** statement is much easier to read than a series of IF statements or a nested IF statement.

```
000100 IDENTIFICATION DIVISION.
000200 PROGRAM-ID. FIRST.
000300 ENVIRONMENT DIVISION.
000700 DATA DIVISION.
000800
000900 WORKING-STORAGE SECTION.
001000 01 VISITOR PIC X(5) VALUE SPACES.
001100 PROCEDURE DIVISION.
001200
001300 ASSIGN-VALUES.
001400     MOVE "Tom" TO VISITOR.
001500
001600 MAKE-DECISION.
001700     EVALUATE VISITOR
0C1800         WHEN "Bob"
001900           DISPLAY "Hello Bob"
002000         WHEN "Mary"
002100           DISPLAY "Hello Mary"
002200         WHEN OTHER
002300           DISPLAY "I don't know you"
002400     END-EVALUATE.
002500 STOP-MY-PROGRAM.
002600     STOP RUN.
```

Compare the value stored in the variable VISITOR with values specified in the WHEN clauses.

Execute the sentence or sentences below the appropriate WHEN clause if the values are the same.

Execute this sentence if none of the values match.

```
000100 IDENTIFICATION DIVISION.
000200 PROGRAM-ID. FIRST.
000300 ENVIRONMENT DIVISION.
000400 DATA DIVISION.
000500
000600 WORKING-STORAGE SECTION.
000700 01 GRADE PIC 9(2) VALUE ZEROES.
00130800 PROCEDURE DIVISION.
000900
001000 ASSIGN-VALUES.
001100     MOVE 50 TO GRADE.
001200
001300 MAKE-DECISION.
001400     EVALUATE GRADE > 69
001500         WHEN TRUE
001600           DISPLAY "You passed."
001700         WHEN FALSE
001800           DISPLAY "You failed."
001900     END-EVALUATE.
002000 STOP-MY-PROGRAM.
002100     STOP RUN.
```

Any relational expression can be used with the EVALUATE statement.

If the expression is true, then execute this sentence.

If the expression is false, then execute this sentence.

Chapter
Five

Working with
Operators and Expressions

- Numeric Operators
- Addition
- Addition Verb
- Subtraction
- Subtraction Verb
- Multiplication
- Multiplication Verb
- Division
- Division Verb
- Precedence
- Reusing an Expression in an Array
- Reusing an Expression Using the PERFORM Command

Numeric Operators

Numeric operators are used to perform mathematical operations such as addition, subtraction, multiplication, and division. There are two ways you can write these operators in COBOL.

The first method is by using the traditional symbol of the operator in the mathematical expression such as +, -, *, /. The other way is to use the word to describe the operator that you'll learn about in this chapter.

Either method produces the same results. Many programmers prefer to use the symbol because it takes less room on the line, is easier to read, and cuts down on typing.

Addition

The *addition numeric operator* is the plus sign (+) and is used to add the value on the right of the plus sign to the value on the left of the plus sign. The sum of these values is typically assigned to a numeric variable by using the *equal operator* (=).

The sentence that contains the addition expression must begin with the **COMPUTE** command. The **COMPUTE** command tells the compiler that the rest of the sentence is a mathematical expression. You'll receive a compiler error if you fail to include the **COMPUTE** command before beginning the expression.

The values on either side of the operator are called *operands*. Operands can be literal values, names of variables, a combination of both, or the results of another expression.

The result of the expression can be rounded to the next whole number by using the **ROUNDED** phrase in the expression as is illustrated on the next page.

You can also tell the program what to do if the size of the results is too large for the variable as shown on the next page.

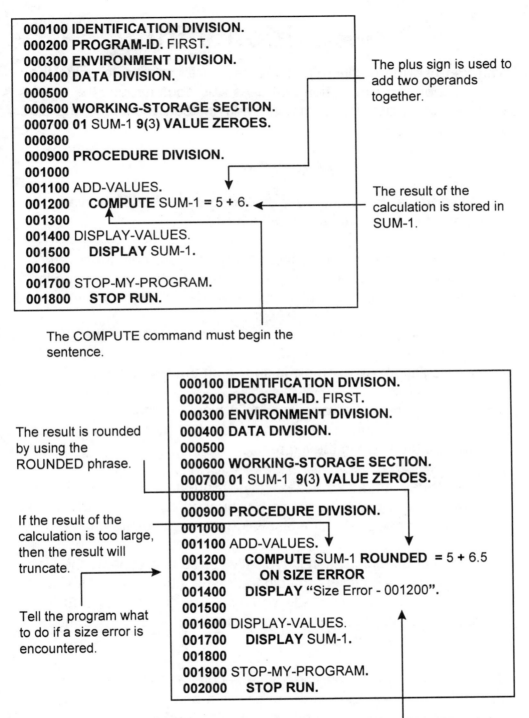

```
000100 IDENTIFICATION DIVISION.
000200 PROGRAM-ID. FIRST.
000300 ENVIRONMENT DIVISION.
000400 DATA DIVISION.
000500
000600 WORKING-STORAGE SECTION.
000700 01 SUM-1 9(3) VALUE ZEROES.
000800
000900 PROCEDURE DIVISION.
001000
001100 ADD-VALUES.
001200     COMPUTE SUM-1 = 5 + 6.
001300
001400 DISPLAY-VALUES.
001500     DISPLAY SUM-1.
001600
001700 STOP-MY-PROGRAM.
001800     STOP RUN.
```

The plus sign is used to add two operands together.

The result of the calculation is stored in SUM-1.

The COMPUTE command must begin the sentence.

```
000100 IDENTIFICATION DIVISION.
000200 PROGRAM-ID. FIRST.
000300 ENVIRONMENT DIVISION.
000400 DATA DIVISION.
000500
000600 WORKING-STORAGE SECTION.
000700 01 SUM-1  9(3) VALUE ZEROES.
000800
000900 PROCEDURE DIVISION.
001000
001100 ADD-VALUES.
001200     COMPUTE SUM-1 ROUNDED  = 5 + 6.5
001300         ON SIZE ERROR
001400     DISPLAY "Size Error - 001200".
001500
001600 DISPLAY-VALUES.
001700     DISPLAY SUM-1.
001800
001900 STOP-MY-PROGRAM.
002000     STOP RUN.
```

The result is rounded by using the ROUNDED phrase.

If the result of the calculation is too large, then the result will truncate.

Tell the program what to do if a size error is encountered.

Display this message when a size error is encountered.

Addition Verb

You can use the addition verb **ADD** as an alternative to using the addition sign. An expression that uses **ADD** does not use the equal sign nor the **COMPUTE** command and instead must use the **TO** keyword as shown here:

ADD 5.2 **TO** VAR-1.

In this example, the value 5.2 is added to the value of the variable VAR-1 and the sum is also stored in VAR-1.

The values on either side of the **TO** keyword are called *operands*. Operands can be literal values, names of variables, a combination of both, or the results of another expression.

If both operands are literal values, then you must use the **GIVING** phrase to specify the variable that will be used to store the results of the calculation. An example is shown on the next page.

The result of the calculation can be a whole number, a fractional value, or a mixed number that can be rounded up or down by using the **ROUNDED** phrase in the expression.

The **ROUNDED** phrase causes values greater than four to be rounded up and less than five to be rounded down. The **ROUNDED** phrase must appear after the last value in the calculation.

The result of the calculation is typically stored in a variable the size of which must be sufficient to hold the result, otherwise the value of the results will be truncated. You can use the **ON SIZE ERROR** phrase to tell the program what to do if a size error is encountered as shown on the next page.

The **ON SIZE ERROR** phrase can execute a command such as displaying an error on the screen or call a paragraph that does the same. Typically, such a paragraph will also terminate the program.

```
000100 IDENTIFICATION DIVISION.
000200 PROGRAM-ID. FIRST.
000300 ENVIRONMENT DIVISION.
000400 DATA DIVISION.
000500
000600 WORKING-STORAGE SECTION.
000700 01 SUM-1  9(3) VALUE ZEROES.
000800
000900 PROCEDURE DIVISION.
001000
001100 ADD-VALUES.
001200     ADD 5 TO SUM-1.
001300
001400 DISPLAY-VALUES.
001500     DISPLAY SUM-1.
001600
001700 STOP-MY-PROGRAM.
001800     STOP RUN.
```

The ADD verb is used to add two operands together.

The result of the calculation is stored in SUM-1.

The COMPUTE command must not begin the sentence.

```
000100 IDENTIFICATION DIVISION.
000200 PROGRAM-ID. FIRST.
000300 ENVIRONMENT DIVISION.
000400 DATA DIVISION.
000500
000600 WORKING-STORAGE SECTION.
000700 01 SUM-1 = 9(3) VALUE ZEROES.
000800 01 VAR-1   9(3) VALUE ZEROES.
000900 PROCEDURE DIVISION.
001000
001100 ADD-VALUES.
001200     ADD 6.5 TO VAR-1
001300     GIVING SUM-1
001400     ROUNDED
001500     ON SIZE ERROR
001600     DISPLAY "Size Error - 001200".
001700
001800 DISPLAY-VALUES.
001900     DISPLAY SUM-1.
002000
002100 STOP-MY-PROGRAM.
002200     STOP RUN.
```

The GIVING phrase identifies the variable used to store the result of the calculation.

The result is rounded by using the ROUNDED phrase.

Tell the program what to do if a size error is encountered.

Subtraction

The *subtraction numeric* operator is the minus sign (-) and is used to subtract the value on the left of the minus sign from the value on the right of the minus sign. The difference of these values is typically assigned to a numeric variable by using the equal operator (=).

The values on either side of the operator are called operands. *Operands* can be literal values, names of variables, a combination of both, or the results of another expression.

The sentence that contains the addition expression must begin with the **COMPUTE** command. The **COMPUTE** command tells the compiler that the rest of the sentence is a mathematical expression. You'll receive a compiler error if you fail to include the **COMPUTE** command before beginning the expression.

The result of the calculation can be a whole number, a fractional value, or a mixed number. You can have the program round the results of the expression up or down by using the **ROUNDED** phrase in the expression.

The **ROUNDED** phrase causes values greater than four to be rounded up and less than five to be rounded down. The **ROUNDED** phrase must appear immediately to the left of the equal sign as shown here:

COMPUTE RESULT-1 **ROUNDED** = VAR-1 - VAR-2.

The result of the calculation is typically stored in a variable. The size of the variable must be sufficient to hold the result, otherwise the value of the result will be truncated. The program will not stop running, but continue as if the full value was stored in the variable.

You can use the **ON SIZE ERROR** phrase to tell the program what to do if a size error is encountered. Include the commands you want executed when the error occurs as shown on the next page.

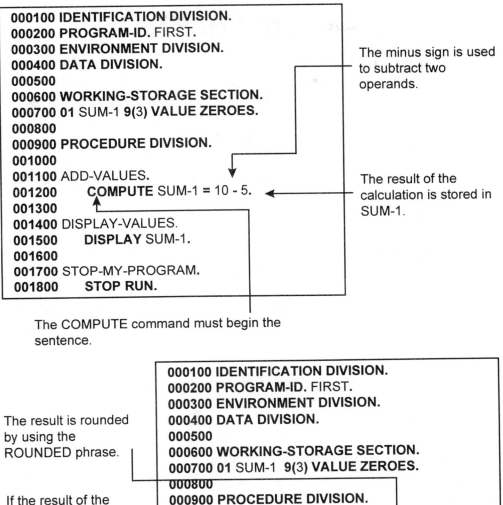

The minus sign is used to subtract two operands.

The result of the calculation is stored in SUM-1.

```
000100 IDENTIFICATION DIVISION.
000200 PROGRAM-ID. FIRST.
000300 ENVIRONMENT DIVISION.
000400 DATA DIVISION.
000500
000600 WORKING-STORAGE SECTION.
000700 01 SUM-1 9(3) VALUE ZEROES.
000800
000900 PROCEDURE DIVISION.
001000
001100 ADD-VALUES.
001200      COMPUTE SUM-1 = 10 - 5.
001300
001400 DISPLAY-VALUES.
001500      DISPLAY SUM-1.
001600
001700 STOP-MY-PROGRAM.
001800      STOP RUN.
```

The COMPUTE command must begin the sentence.

The result is rounded by using the ROUNDED phrase.

If the result of the calculation is too large, then the value of the result is truncated.

Tell the program what to do if a size error is encountered.

```
000100 IDENTIFICATION DIVISION.
000200 PROGRAM-ID. FIRST.
000300 ENVIRONMENT DIVISION.
000400 DATA DIVISION.
000500
000600 WORKING-STORAGE SECTION.
000700 01 SUM-1  9(3) VALUE ZEROES.
000800
000900 PROCEDURE DIVISION.
001000
001100 ADD-VALUES.
001200      COMPUTE SUM-1 ROUNDED = 10 - 6.5
001300        ON SIZE ERROR
001400        DISPLAY "Size Error - 001200".
001500
001600 DISPLAY-VALUES.
001700      DISPLAY SUM-1.
001800
001900 STOP-MY-PROGRAM.
002000      STOP RUN.
```

Display this message when a size error is encountered.

Working with Operators and Expressions

Subtraction Verb

You can use the subtraction verb **SUBTRACT** as an alternative to using the subtraction sign. An expression that uses **SUBTRACT** does not use the equal sign and must use the **FROM** keyword.

SUBTRACT 5.2 **FROM** VAR-1.

In this example, the value 5.2 is subtracted from the value of the variable VAR-1 and the difference is also stored in VAR-1.

The values on either side of the **FROM** keyword are called operands. *Operands* can be literal values, names of variables, a combination of both, or the results of another expression.

If both operands are literal values, then you must use the **GIVING** phrase to specify the variable that will be used to store the results of the calculation. An example is shown on the next page.

The result of the calculation can be a whole number, a fractional value, or a mixed number that can be rounded up or down by using the **ROUNDED** phrase in the expression.

The **ROUNDED** phrase causes values greater than four to be rounded up and less than five to be rounded down. The **ROUNDED** phrase must appear after the last value in the calculation.

The result of the calculation is typically stored in a variable the size of which must be sufficient to hold the result, otherwise the value of the result will be truncated. The program will not stop running, but continue as if the full value was stored in the variable. You can use the **ON SIZE ERROR** phrase to tell the program what to do if a size error is encountered as shown on the next page.

The **ON SIZE ERROR** phrase can execute a command such as displaying an error on the screen or call a paragraph that does the same. Typically, such a paragraph will also terminate the program.

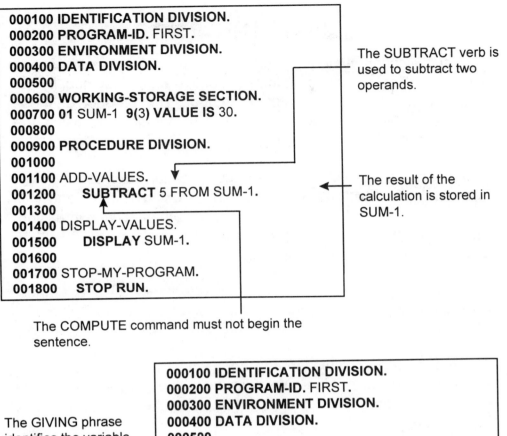

```
000100 IDENTIFICATION DIVISION.
000200 PROGRAM-ID. FIRST.
000300 ENVIRONMENT DIVISION.
000400 DATA DIVISION.
000500
000600 WORKING-STORAGE SECTION.
000700 01 SUM-1  9(3) VALUE IS 30.
000800
000900 PROCEDURE DIVISION.
001000
001100 ADD-VALUES.
001200      SUBTRACT 5 FROM SUM-1.
001300
001400 DISPLAY-VALUES.
001500      DISPLAY SUM-1.
001600
001700 STOP-MY-PROGRAM.
001800     STOP RUN.
```

The SUBTRACT verb is used to subtract two operands.

The result of the calculation is stored in SUM-1.

The COMPUTE command must not begin the sentence.

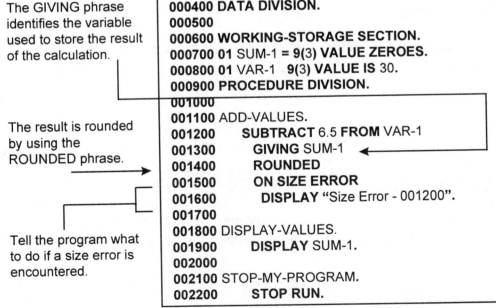

The GIVING phrase identifies the variable used to store the result of the calculation.

The result is rounded by using the ROUNDED phrase.

Tell the program what to do if a size error is encountered.

```
000100 IDENTIFICATION DIVISION.
000200 PROGRAM-ID. FIRST.
000300 ENVIRONMENT DIVISION.
000400 DATA DIVISION.
000500
000600 WORKING-STORAGE SECTION.
000700 01 SUM-1 = 9(3) VALUE ZEROES.
000800 01 VAR-1   9(3) VALUE IS 30.
000900 PROCEDURE DIVISION.
001000
001100 ADD-VALUES.
001200      SUBTRACT 6.5 FROM VAR-1
001300       GIVING SUM-1
001400       ROUNDED
001500       ON SIZE ERROR
001600        DISPLAY "Size Error - 001200".
001700
001800 DISPLAY-VALUES.
001900       DISPLAY SUM-1.
002000
002100 STOP-MY-PROGRAM.
002200      STOP RUN.
```

Multiplication

The *multiplication numeric* operator is the asterisk symbol (*) and is used to multiply the value on the right of the asterisk symbol by the value on the left of the asterisk symbol. The product of these values is typically assigned to a numeric variable by using the equal operator (=).

The sentence that contains the multiplication expression must begin with the **COMPUTE** command. The **COMPUTE** command tells the compiler the rest of the sentence is a mathematical expression. You'll receive a compiler error if you fail to include the **COMPUTE** command before beginning the expression.

The values on either side of the operator are called operands. *Operands* can be literal values, names of variables, a combination of both, or the results of another expression.

The result of the calculation can be a whole number, a fractional value, or a mixed number. You can have the program round the result of the expression up or down by using the **ROUNDED** phrase in the expression.

The **ROUNDED** phrase causes values greater than four to be rounded up and less than five to be rounded down. The **ROUNDED** phrase must appear immediately to the left of the equal sign as shown here:

COMPUTE RESULT-1 **ROUNDED** = VAR-1 * VAR-2.

The result of the calculation is typically stored in a variable. The size of the variable must be sufficient to hold the result, otherwise the value of the result will be truncated. The program will not stop running, but continue as if the full value was stored in the variable.

You can use the **ON SIZE ERROR** phrase to tell the program what to do if a size error is encountered. Include the commands you want executed when the error occurs as shown on the next page.

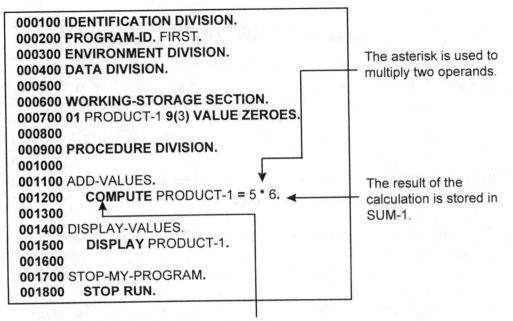

The asterisk is used to multiply two operands.

The result of the calculation is stored in SUM-1.

The COMPUTE command must begin the sentence.

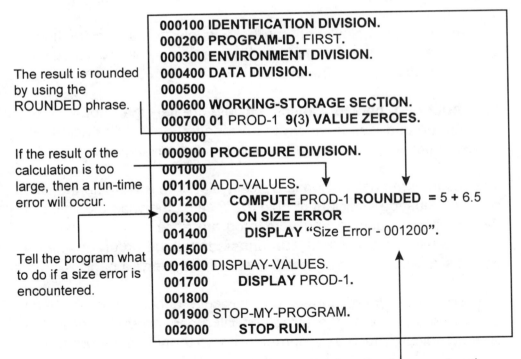

The result is rounded by using the ROUNDED phrase.

If the result of the calculation is too large, then a run-time error will occur.

Tell the program what to do if a size error is encountered.

Display this message when a size error is encountered.

Multiplication Verb

You can use the multiplication verb **MULTIPLY** as an alternative to using the multiplication sign. An expression that uses **MULTIPLY** does not use the equal sign and must use the **BY** keyword.

MULTIPLY 5.2 **BY** VAR-1.

In this example, the value 5.2 is multiplied by the value of the variable VAR-1 and the product is also stored in VAR-1.

The values on either side of the **BY** keyword are called operands. *Operands* can be literal values, names of variables, a combination of both, or the results of another expression.

If both operands are literal values, then you must use the **GIVING** phrase to specify the variable that will be used to store the results of the calculation. An example is shown on the next page.

The result of the calculation can be a whole number, a fractional value, or a mixed number that can be rounded up or down by using the **ROUNDED** phrase in the expression.

The **ROUNDED** phrase causes values greater than four to be rounded up and less than five to be rounded down. The **ROUNDED** phrase must appear after the last value in the calculation.

The result of the calculation is typically stored in a variable the size of which must be sufficient to hold the result, otherwise the value of the result will truncate and your program does not stop running. You can use the **ON SIZE ERROR** phrase to tell the program what to do if a size error is encountered as shown on the next page.

The **ON SIZE ERROR** phrase can execute a command such as displaying an error on the screen or call a paragraph that does the same. Typically, such a paragraph will also terminate the program.

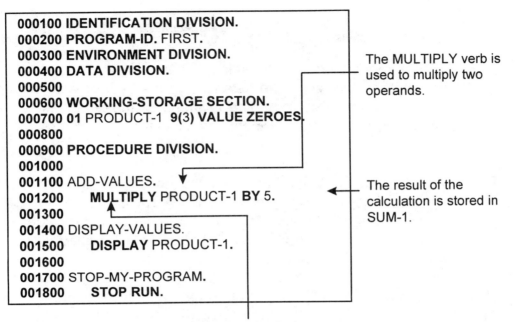

The MULTIPLY verb is used to multiply two operands.

```
000100 IDENTIFICATION DIVISION.
000200 PROGRAM-ID. FIRST.
000300 ENVIRONMENT DIVISION.
000400 DATA DIVISION.
000500
000600 WORKING-STORAGE SECTION.
000700 01 PRODUCT-1  9(3) VALUE ZEROES.
000800
000900 PROCEDURE DIVISION.
001000
001100 ADD-VALUES.
001200     MULTIPLY PRODUCT-1 BY 5.
001300
001400 DISPLAY-VALUES.
001500     DISPLAY PRODUCT-1.
001600
001700 STOP-MY-PROGRAM.
001800     STOP RUN.
```

The result of the calculation is stored in SUM-1.

The COMPUTE command must not begin the sentence.

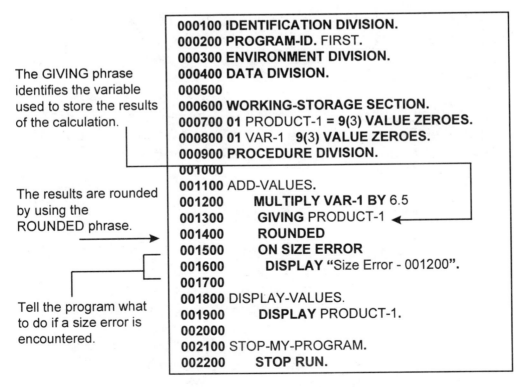

The GIVING phrase identifies the variable used to store the results of the calculation.

The results are rounded by using the ROUNDED phrase.

Tell the program what to do if a size error is encountered.

```
000100 IDENTIFICATION DIVISION.
000200 PROGRAM-ID. FIRST.
000300 ENVIRONMENT DIVISION.
000400 DATA DIVISION.
000500
000600 WORKING-STORAGE SECTION.
000700 01 PRODUCT-1 = 9(3) VALUE ZEROES.
000800 01 VAR-1   9(3) VALUE ZEROES.
000900 PROCEDURE DIVISION.
001000
001100 ADD-VALUES.
001200     MULTIPLY VAR-1 BY 6.5
001300     GIVING PRODUCT-1
001400     ROUNDED
001500     ON SIZE ERROR
001600       DISPLAY "Size Error - 001200".
001700
001800 DISPLAY-VALUES.
001900     DISPLAY PRODUCT-1.
002000
002100 STOP-MY-PROGRAM.
002200     STOP RUN.
```

Division

The *division numeric* operator is the slash symbol (/) and is used to divide the value on the left of the asterisk symbol by the value on the right of the asterisk symbol. The dividend of these values is typically assigned to a numeric variable by using the equal operator (=).

The sentence that contains the multiplication expression must begin with the **COMPUTE** command. The **COMPUTE** command tells the compiler the rest of the sentence if a mathematical expression. You'll receive a compiler error is you fail to include the **COMPUTE** command before beginning the expression.

The values on either side of the operator are called operands. *Operands* can be literal values, names of variables, a combination of both, or the results of another expression.

The result of the calculation can be a whole number, a fractional value, or a mixed number. You can have the program round the results of the expression up or down by using the **ROUNDED** phrase in the expression.

The **ROUNDED** phrase causes values greater than four to be rounded up and less than five to be rounded down. The **ROUNDED** phrase must appear immediately to the left of the equals sign as shown here:

COMPUTE RESULT-1 **ROUNDED** = VAR-1 / VAR-2.

The result of the calculation is typically stored in a variable. The size of the variable must be sufficient to hold the result, otherwise the value of the result will be truncated. The program will not stop running, but continue as if the full value was stored in the variable.

You can use the **ON SIZE ERROR** phrase to tell the program what to do if a size error is encountered. Include the commands you want executed when the error occurs as shown on the next page.

```
000100 IDENTIFICATION DIVISION.
000200 PROGRAM-ID. FIRST.
000300 ENVIRONMENT DIVISION.
000400 DATA DIVISION.
000500
000600 WORKING-STORAGE SECTION.
000700 01 DIV-1 9(3) VALUE ZEROES.
000800
000900 PROCEDURE DIVISION.
001000
001100 ADD-VALUES.
001200     COMPUTE DIV-1 = 6 / 3.
001300
001400 DISPLAY-VALUES.
001500     DISPLAY DIV-1.
001600
001700 STOP-MY-PROGRAM.
001800     STOP RUN.
```

The slash is used to divide two operands.

The result of the calculation is stored in SUM-1.

The COMPUTE command must begin the sentence.

The result is rounded by using the ROUNDED phrase.

If the result of the calculation is too large, then a run-time error will occur.

Tell the program what to do if a size error is encountered.

```
000100 IDENTIFICATION DIVISION.
000200 PROGRAM-ID. FIRST.
000300 ENVIRONMENT DIVISION.
000400 DATA DIVISION.
000500
000600 WORKING-STORAGE SECTION.
000700 01 DIV-1  9(3) VALUE ZEROES.
000800
000900 PROCEDURE DIVISION.
001000
001100 ADD-VALUES.
001200     COMPUTE DIV-1 ROUNDED = 5 / 2
001300         ON SIZE ERROR
001400         DISPLAY "Size Error - 001200".
001500
001600 DISPLAY-VALUES.
001700     DISPLAY DIV-1.
001800
001900 STOP-MY-PROGRAM.
002000     STOP RUN.
```

Display this message when a size error is encountered.

Division Verb

You can use the division verb **DIVIDE** as an alternative to using the division sign. An expression that uses **DIVIDE** does not use the equals sign and instead must us the **INTO** keyword as shown here:

DIVIDE 5.2 **INTO** VAR-1.

In this example, the value 5.2 is divided into the value of the variable VAR-1 and the dividend is also stored in VAR-1. Remainders can be stored in a separate variable using the phrase **REMAINDER** to identify the variable as shown on the next page.

The values on either side of the *INTO* keyword are called operands. *Operands* can be literal values, names of variables, a combination of both, or the result of another expression.

If both operands are literal values, then you must use the **GIVING** phrase to specify the variable that is used to store the results.

The results of the calculation can be a whole number, a fractional value, or a mixed number that can be rounded up or down by using the **ROUNDED** phrase in the expression.

The **ROUNDED** phrase causes values greater than four to be rounded up and less than five to be rounded down. The **ROUNDED** phrase must appear after the last value in the calculation.

The result of the calculation is typically stored in a variable the size of which must be sufficient to hold the result, otherwise the value of the result will be truncated. You can use the **ON SIZE ERROR** phrase to tell the program what to do if a size error is encountered as shown on the next page.

The **ON SIZE ERROR** phrase can execute a command such as displaying an error on the screen or call a paragraph that does the same. Typically such a paragraph will also terminate the program.

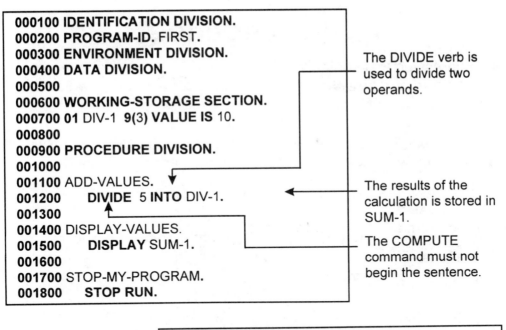

The DIVIDE verb is used to divide two operands.

```
000100 IDENTIFICATION DIVISION.
000200 PROGRAM-ID. FIRST.
000300 ENVIRONMENT DIVISION.
000400 DATA DIVISION.
000500
000600 WORKING-STORAGE SECTION.
000700 01 DIV-1  9(3) VALUE IS 10.
000800
000900 PROCEDURE DIVISION.
001000
001100 ADD-VALUES.
001200     DIVIDE 5 INTO DIV-1.
001300
001400 DISPLAY-VALUES.
001500     DISPLAY SUM-1.
001600
001700 STOP-MY-PROGRAM.
001800     STOP RUN.
```

The results of the calculation is stored in SUM-1.

The COMPUTE command must not begin the sentence.

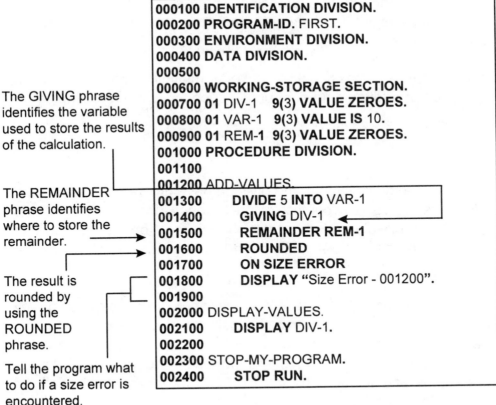

The GIVING phrase identifies the variable used to store the results of the calculation.

The REMAINDER phrase identifies where to store the remainder.

```
000100 IDENTIFICATION DIVISION.
000200 PROGRAM-ID. FIRST.
000300 ENVIRONMENT DIVISION.
000400 DATA DIVISION.
000500
000600 WORKING-STORAGE SECTION.
000700 01 DIV-1   9(3) VALUE ZEROES.
000800 01 VAR-1   9(3) VALUE IS 10.
000900 01 REM-1   9(3) VALUE ZEROES.
001000 PROCEDURE DIVISION.
001100
001200 ADD-VALUES.
001300     DIVIDE 5 INTO VAR-1
001400       GIVING DIV-1
001500       REMAINDER REM-1
001600       ROUNDED
001700       ON SIZE ERROR
001800       DISPLAY "Size Error - 001200".
001900
002000 DISPLAY-VALUES.
002100     DISPLAY DIV-1.
002200
002300 STOP-MY-PROGRAM.
002400     STOP RUN.
```

The result is rounded by using the ROUNDED phrase.

Tell the program what to do if a size error is encountered.

Precedence

An expression that contains more than one mathematical operation could arrive at different result depending on the order in which the operations are performed.

For example, is the results of this expression 13 or 25? The answer depends on whether you multiply 5 * 2 first or add 2 + 3 first.

$$Z = 5 * 2 + 3$$

The program follows a set of rules that specify the order of operations. This is called the *precedence* and sometimes referred to as the *precedence table*.

Division and multiplication are performed before addition and subtract in a compound expression. The result of the expression in the previous example is 13 since the program will multiply before adding values.

A *compound expression* can have a multiplication and division operation or addition and subtraction such as in these examples.

$$Z = 10 * 6 / 2$$
$$Z = 10 + 5 - 2$$

You'll notice multiplication and division have the same precedence. Whenever there is a conflict of precedence, the program follows the left to right rule and calculates the left-most operation first. The same holds true when addition and subtraction are used in the same expression.

You can change the order of precedence in an expression by enclosing an operation within the parentheses. Operations within parentheses are performed before operations outside of the parentheses. The inner-most parentheses are evaluated first if operations are nested. The left to right rule is also followed if an expression contains multiple parentheses.

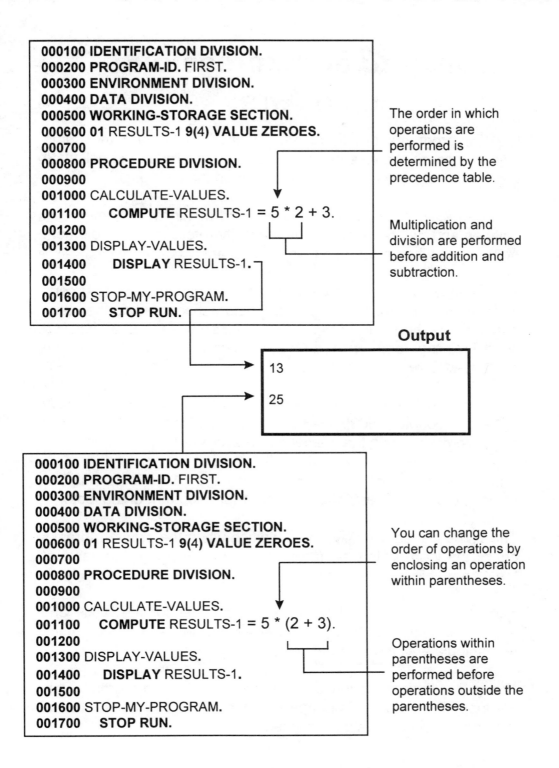

```
000100 IDENTIFICATION DIVISION.
000200 PROGRAM-ID. FIRST.
000300 ENVIRONMENT DIVISION.
000400 DATA DIVISION.
000500 WORKING-STORAGE SECTION.
000600 01 RESULTS-1 9(4) VALUE ZEROES.
000700
000800 PROCEDURE DIVISION.
000900
001000 CALCULATE-VALUES.
001100    COMPUTE RESULTS-1 = 5 * 2 + 3.
001200
001300 DISPLAY-VALUES.
001400    DISPLAY RESULTS-1.
001500
001600 STOP-MY-PROGRAM.
001700    STOP RUN.
```

The order in which operations are performed is determined by the precedence table.

Multiplication and division are performed before addition and subtraction.

Output

```
13
25
```

```
000100 IDENTIFICATION DIVISION.
000200 PROGRAM-ID. FIRST.
000300 ENVIRONMENT DIVISION.
000400 DATA DIVISION.
000500 WORKING-STORAGE SECTION.
000600 01 RESULTS-1 9(4) VALUE ZEROES.
000700
000800 PROCEDURE DIVISION.
000900
001000 CALCULATE-VALUES.
001100    COMPUTE RESULTS-1 = 5 * (2 + 3).
001200
001300 DISPLAY-VALUES.
001400    DISPLAY RESULTS-1.
001500
001600 STOP-MY-PROGRAM.
001700    STOP RUN.
```

You can change the order of operations by enclosing an operation within parentheses.

Operations within parentheses are performed before operations outside the parentheses.

Reusing an Expression
in an Array

COBOL programs are frequently required to perform the same calculations on a series of values such as are routine to calculate gross and net salary, which is illustrated on the next page.

You can streamline the code by defining an array of names and salaries and write a loop to automatically reference each element of the array when performing the calculation.

A *loop* shown on the next page increments the value of a numeric variable, then performs some action before incrementing the value again. Once the value of the numeric variable reaches a specified condition, the loop ends and the program continues with the sentence following the end of the loop.

The numeric variable that is incremented in the loop is commonly called the *counter* and is used as the value of the index number of array elements when the elements are accessed within the loop.

The example on the next page assigns the CT variable with the value 1, then increments the value by 1 for each turn of the loop.

The **UNTIL** clause specifies the condition when the program breaks out of the loop. In this example, the loop ends when the value of the CT variable is greater than 2.

The CT variable is used as the index number for the NAME and SALARY arrays. This technique enables you to use one command to manipulate all the elements of the array.

Notice that the calculation is expressed once in the program within the loop. The values of the operand change as the index value of the array elements are incremented.

CT is the numeric variable that is incremented each time the program completes one cycle around the loop.

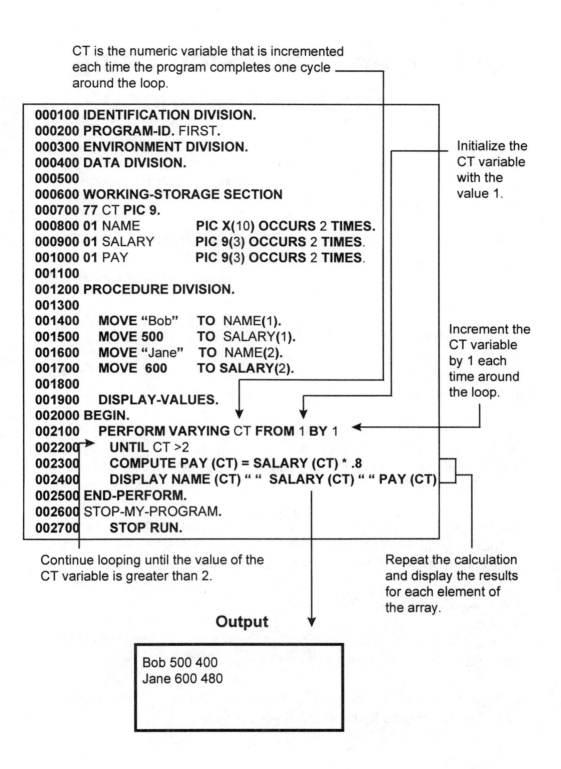

Initialize the CT variable with the value 1.

Increment the CT variable by 1 each time around the loop.

```
000100 IDENTIFICATION DIVISION.
000200 PROGRAM-ID. FIRST.
000300 ENVIRONMENT DIVISION.
000400 DATA DIVISION.
000500
000600 WORKING-STORAGE SECTION
000700 77 CT PIC 9.
000800 01 NAME        PIC X(10) OCCURS 2 TIMES.
000900 01 SALARY      PIC 9(3) OCCURS 2 TIMES.
001000 01 PAY         PIC 9(3) OCCURS 2 TIMES.
001100
001200 PROCEDURE DIVISION.
001300
001400    MOVE "Bob"    TO  NAME(1).
001500    MOVE 500      TO  SALARY(1).
001600    MOVE "Jane"   TO  NAME(2).
001700    MOVE 600      TO  SALARY(2).
001800
001900    DISPLAY-VALUES.
002000 BEGIN.
002100    PERFORM VARYING CT FROM 1 BY 1
002200       UNTIL CT >2
002300       COMPUTE PAY (CT) = SALARY (CT) * .8
002400       DISPLAY NAME (CT) " "  SALARY (CT) " " PAY (CT)
002500 END-PERFORM.
002600 STOP-MY-PROGRAM.
002700    STOP RUN.
```

Continue looping until the value of the CT variable is greater than 2.

Repeat the calculation and display the results for each element of the array.

Output

Bob 500 400
Jane 600 480

Reusing an Expression Using the PERFORM Command

You can write a mathematical expression that needs to be performed frequently in your program in its own paragraph, then use the **PERFORM** command to call the paragraph whenever you need to perform the calculation.

Values of the operands in the expression can be stored in variables that are reassigned values in your program before the program calls the paragraph containing the calculation. This is illustrated on the next page.

When the program encounters the **PERFORM** command, it jumps to the specified paragraph, then executes the sentences sequentially in the paragraph and returns to the sentence below the **PERFORM** command when the end of the paragraph is encountered.

You use the **PERFORM** command anywhere in your program to call the paragraph that contains the paragraph. This is the primary advantage over using a loop to reuse mathematical expressions in your program.

The loop requires the calculation to be performed a specified number of times. The **PERFORM** command lets you call upon the calculation as many times as it is necessary in the program.

Here are guidelines to follow:

Use a calculation within a loop whenever you need to include a calculation in the processing of a series of data.

Use a calculation within a paragraph whenever you need to calculate sporadically throughout your program.

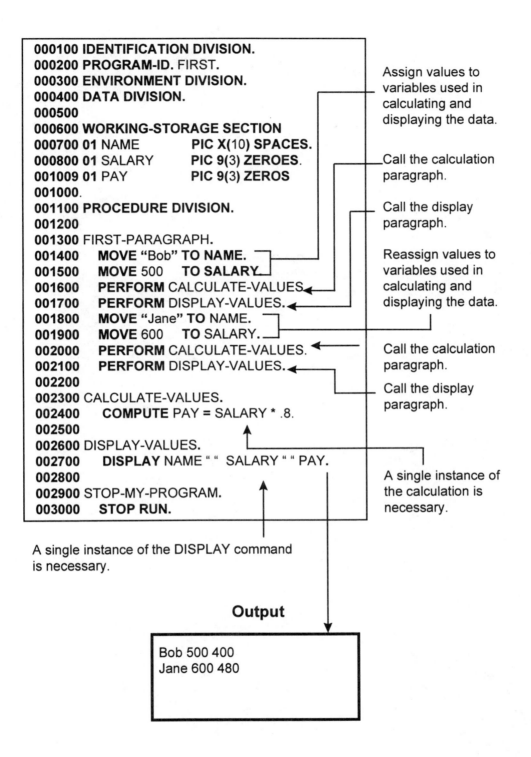

```
000100 IDENTIFICATION DIVISION.
000200 PROGRAM-ID. FIRST.
000300 ENVIRONMENT DIVISION.
000400 DATA DIVISION.
000500
000600 WORKING-STORAGE SECTION
000700 01 NAME        PIC X(10) SPACES.
000800 01 SALARY      PIC 9(3) ZEROES.
001009 01 PAY         PIC 9(3) ZEROS
001000 .
001100 PROCEDURE DIVISION.
001200
001300 FIRST-PARAGRAPH.
001400     MOVE "Bob" TO NAME.
001500     MOVE 500   TO SALARY.
001600     PERFORM CALCULATE-VALUES.
001700     PERFORM DISPLAY-VALUES.
001800     MOVE "Jane" TO NAME.
001900     MOVE 600   TO SALARY.
002000     PERFORM CALCULATE-VALUES.
002100     PERFORM DISPLAY-VALUES.
002200
002300 CALCULATE-VALUES.
002400     COMPUTE PAY = SALARY * .8.
002500
002600 DISPLAY-VALUES.
002700     DISPLAY NAME " " SALARY " " PAY.
002800
002900 STOP-MY-PROGRAM.
003000     STOP RUN.
```

Assign values to variables used in calculating and displaying the data.

Call the calculation paragraph.

Call the display paragraph.

Reassign values to variables used in calculating and displaying the data.

Call the calculation paragraph.

Call the display paragraph.

A single instance of the calculation is necessary.

A single instance of the DISPLAY command is necessary.

Output

```
Bob 500 400
Jane 600 480
```

Working with
Data Input and Screens

- ACCEPT and DISPLAY
- Displaying a Menu
- Reading a Selection from a Menu
- Processing a Menu Selection
- Handling Selection Errors
- Creating a Menu Tree
- Data Entry Screen
- Data Display Screen

ACCEPT and DISPLAY

Many applications developed using COBOL interact with the user via the screen and the keyboard. The application displays a message on the screen prompting the user to enter information using the keyboard. This information is then processed and may be stored in a file or cause other information to be displayed on the screen.

The simplest way to show a prompt on the screen is to use the **DISPLAY** command. The **DISPLAY** command copies numbers or characters entered into your code on to the screen.

Information shown by the **DISPLAY** command is placed on the screen at the current cursor location. Later in this chapter you'll see how to specify the screen position to use when displaying information.

The **DISPLAY** command can show the value stored in a variable, a literal numeric value, and a literal alphanumeric value. The variable name is used in the **DISPLAY** command whenever you want the value of the variable shown on the screen.

The value you want to display must appear to the left of the **DISPLAY** command in the sentence. Literal alphanumeric values must appear within double quotations. Literal numeric values must not be enclosed with quotations.

More than one value can be displayed using the same **DISPLAY** command by placing them to the left of the **DISPLAY** command and separating each with a space. This is illustrated on the next page.

The **ACCEPT** command reads characters from the keyboard and assigns this value to a variable specified to the left of the **ACCEPT** command. The variable can then be used to process the information.

```
000100 IDENTIFICATION DIVISION.
000200 PROGRAM-ID. FIRST.
000300 ENVIRONMENT DIVISION.
000400 DATA DIVISION.
000500
000600 WORKING-STORAGE SECTION.
000700 01 NAME-1    PIC X(10) VALUE SPACES.
000800
000900 PROCEDURE DIVISION.
001000
001100 DISPLAY-VALUES.
001200    DISPLAY "Enter your name: ".
001300    ACCEPT NAME-1.
001400    DISPLAY NAME-1.
001500
001600 STOP-MY-PROGRAM.
001700    STOP RUN.
```

Prompt the user to enter his or her name.

Read the name entered at the keyboard into the variable NAME-1.

Display the name entered at the keyboard.

```
Enter your name:
Bob
Bob
Enter your name:
Bob
Bob, your number is 10
```

Output

```
000100 IDENTIFICATION DIVISION.
000200 PROGRAM-ID. FIRST.
000300 ENVIRONMENT DIVISION.
000400 DATA DIVISION.
000500
000600 WORKING-STORAGE SECTION.
000700 01 NAME-1    PIC X(10) VALUE SPACES.
000800 01 MESG-1    PIC X(10) VALUE SPACES.
000900
001000 PROCEDURE DIVISION.
001100    MOVE "Enter your name: " TO MESG-1.
001200
001300 DISPLAY-VALUES.
001400    DISPLAY MESG-1.
001500    ACCEPT NAME-1.
001600    DISPLAY NAME-1 ", your number is " 10.
001700
001800 STOP-MY-PROGRAM.
001900    STOP RUN.
```

Assign the prompt message to a variable.

Display the prompt.

Read the name from the keyboard.

Display the name, an alphanumeric literal, and a numeric literal on the same line.

Displaying a Menu

Applications typically interact with users through the use of menus. A menu lists a series of options on the screen, then prompts you to make a selection.

Menus come in various styles; however, nearly all of them offer the same components. There are a list of menu options, a unique identified for each option, and a prompt to tell the user what to do when the menu is displayed.

Each option must be listed using terms familiar to the user. Avoid using unfamiliar abbreviations and too many words to describe the option. The fewer words used in a menu, the less cluttered the menu becomes, and the menu is easy for the user to read.

A menu is displayed using the LINE and COL commands as illustrated on the next page. The LINE command is followed by a line number. The line number refers to one of the 25 lines on the screen.

The COL command specifies the column on the line where the first character is to be displayed. There are 80 columns on the screen. Each column can display one character.

A simple menu which is shown on the next page will have each menu option appear on different lines, but begin at the same column position. This gives a uniform appearance to the menu when it is shown on the screen.

Menu options should identify with a single character or number that reduces the keystrokes required to respond to the menu. As you'll see later in this chapter, the single character response will be compared to available options when the selection is processed by the program.

Always be sure one of those options enables the user to exit the application.

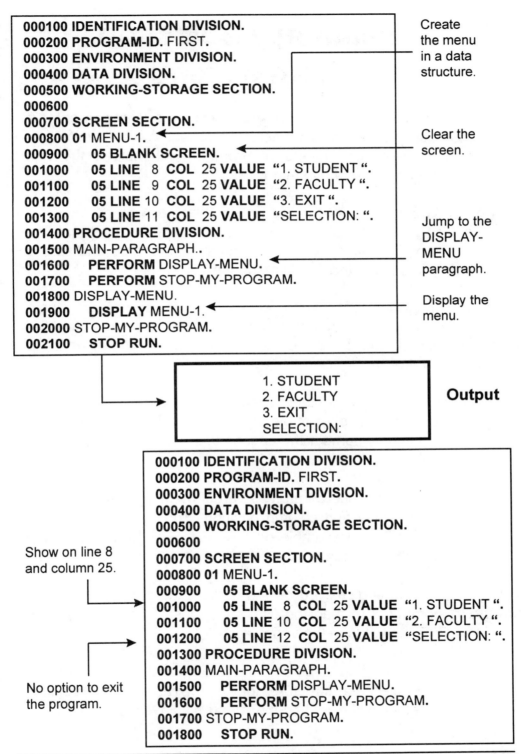

```
000100 IDENTIFICATION DIVISION.
000200 PROGRAM-ID. FIRST.
000300 ENVIRONMENT DIVISION.
000400 DATA DIVISION.
000500 WORKING-STORAGE SECTION.
000600
000700 SCREEN SECTION.
000800 01 MENU-1.
000900    05 BLANK SCREEN.
001000    05 LINE  8 COL 25 VALUE "1. STUDENT ".
001100    05 LINE  9 COL 25 VALUE "2. FACULTY ".
001200    05 LINE 10 COL 25 VALUE "3. EXIT ".
001300    05 LINE 11 COL 25 VALUE "SELECTION: ".
001400 PROCEDURE DIVISION.
001500 MAIN-PARAGRAPH..
001600    PERFORM DISPLAY-MENU.
001700    PERFORM STOP-MY-PROGRAM.
001800 DISPLAY-MENU.
001900    DISPLAY MENU-1.
002000 STOP-MY-PROGRAM.
002100    STOP RUN.
```

Create the menu in a data structure.

Clear the screen.

Jump to the DISPLAY-MENU paragraph.

Display the menu.

```
1. STUDENT
2. FACULTY
3. EXIT
SELECTION:
```

Output

```
000100 IDENTIFICATION DIVISION.
000200 PROGRAM-ID. FIRST.
000300 ENVIRONMENT DIVISION.
000400 DATA DIVISION.
000500 WORKING-STORAGE SECTION.
000600
000700 SCREEN SECTION.
000800 01 MENU-1.
000900    05 BLANK SCREEN.
001000    05 LINE  8 COL 25 VALUE "1. STUDENT ".
001100    05 LINE 10 COL 25 VALUE "2. FACULTY ".
001200    05 LINE 12 COL 25 VALUE "SELECTION: ".
001300 PROCEDURE DIVISION.
001400 MAIN-PARAGRAPH.
001500    PERFORM DISPLAY-MENU.
001600    PERFORM STOP-MY-PROGRAM.
001700 STOP-MY-PROGRAM.
001800    STOP RUN.
```

Show on line 8 and column 25.

No option to exit the program.

Reading a Selection
from a Menu

A menu displays a list of options from which the user can enter a selection using the keyboard. There are various ways in which you can read the selection into your program. The example on the next page illustrates one of these methods.

The user's selection is stored in a variable that can be used for processing the selection that you'll see later in this chapter. The variable is defined at a level 77 as whatever data type and size is necessary to contain the user's response.

Many menu-drive applications require the user to enter a single keystroke to select an option from the menu. The unique identifier for the option can be either an alphanumeric character or a numerical value.

The choice of which to use is subjective. Some programmers prefer to use the first letter of the option description as the identifier while others simply number the options sequentially. Either method is acceptable.

The variable is also incorporated as part of the menu data structure and assigned a row and column position. You'll notice the USING phrase is used in the example on the next page to associate the variable with the structure.

Once the menu is displayed on the screen, the program uses the ACCEPT command to read the user's response from the keyboard and assigns the value to the variable.

The program places the cursor at the line and column position specified in the data structure for the variable. This provides continuity between the text of the menu displayed on the screen and the entry of the selection.

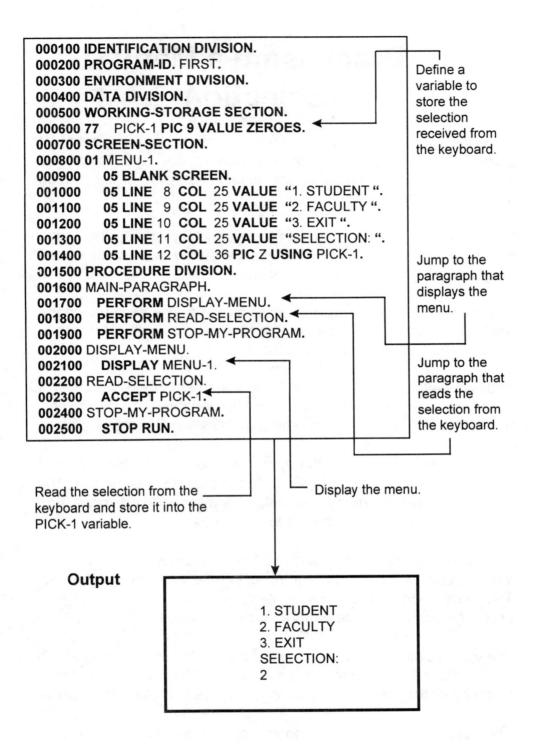

```
000100 IDENTIFICATION DIVISION.
000200 PROGRAM-ID. FIRST.
000300 ENVIRONMENT DIVISION.
000400 DATA DIVISION.
000500 WORKING-STORAGE SECTION.
000600 77   PICK-1 PIC 9 VALUE ZEROES.
000700 SCREEN-SECTION.
000800 01 MENU-1.
000900     05 BLANK SCREEN.
001000     05 LINE  8 COL 25 VALUE "1. STUDENT ".
001100     05 LINE  9 COL 25 VALUE "2. FACULTY ".
001200     05 LINE 10 COL 25 VALUE "3. EXIT ".
001300     05 LINE 11 COL 25 VALUE "SELECTION: ".
001400     05 LINE 12 COL 36 PIC Z USING PICK-1.
001500 PROCEDURE DIVISION.
001600 MAIN-PARAGRAPH.
001700     PERFORM DISPLAY-MENU.
001800     PERFORM READ-SELECTION.
001900     PERFORM STOP-MY-PROGRAM.
002000 DISPLAY-MENU.
002100     DISPLAY MENU-1.
002200 READ-SELECTION.
002300     ACCEPT PICK-1.
002400 STOP-MY-PROGRAM.
002500     STOP RUN.
```

Define a variable to store the selection received from the keyboard.

Jump to the paragraph that displays the menu.

Jump to the paragraph that reads the selection from the keyboard.

Read the selection from the keyboard and store it into the PICK-1 variable.

Display the menu.

Output

```
1. STUDENT
2. FACULTY
3. EXIT
SELECTION:
2
```

Processing a Menu Selection

Once the user makes a selection from the menu, the program must process the entry. The value assigned to the variable by the **ACCEPT** command relates to the unique identifier of the option displayed on the screen.

Processing the user's request occurs by comparing the value stored in the variable with values associated with each of the unique identifiers for each menu option.

The comparison can be made in several ways. The example on the next page uses the **IF** statement for the comparison. Each menu option must have its own **IF** statement.

Another way is to use the **EVALUATE** statement where a series of values are compared to the value of the variable. You can review how to use the **EVALUATE** statement by revisiting Chapter 4.

The **IF** statement block or the appropriate **EVALUATE** block should contain sentences that will respond to the user's selection. In the example shown on the opposite page, a message is displayed on the screen, then the program ends.

This is to illustrate how to respond to a menu selection. Typically, the sentence will call a paragraph using the **PERFORM** command. The paragraph would contain more complex code to display another menu or execute a more involved process.

Many applications redisplay the menu once the appropriate action is taken in response to the user's selection. The menu is displayed again by calling the paragraph containing the **DISPLAY** command.

The user is then given the opportunity to make another selection one of which is to exit the program.

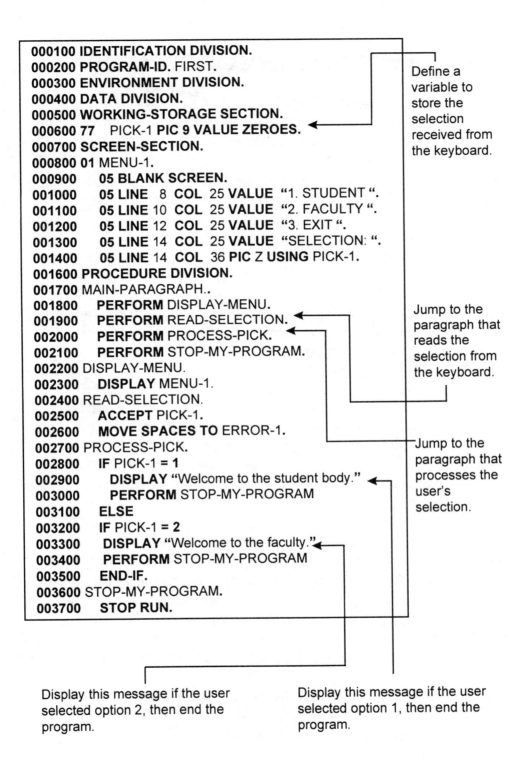

```
000100 IDENTIFICATION DIVISION.
000200 PROGRAM-ID. FIRST.
000300 ENVIRONMENT DIVISION.
000400 DATA DIVISION.
000500 WORKING-STORAGE SECTION.
000600 77   PICK-1 PIC 9 VALUE ZEROES.
000700 SCREEN-SECTION.
000800 01 MENU-1.
000900     05 BLANK SCREEN.
001000     05 LINE  8  COL  25 VALUE "1. STUDENT ".
001100     05 LINE 10  COL  25 VALUE "2. FACULTY ".
001200     05 LINE 12  COL  25 VALUE "3. EXIT ".
001300     05 LINE 14  COL  25 VALUE "SELECTION: ".
001400     05 LINE 14  COL  36 PIC Z USING PICK-1.
001600 PROCEDURE DIVISION.
001700   MAIN-PARAGRAPH..
001800     PERFORM DISPLAY-MENU.
001900     PERFORM READ-SELECTION.
002000     PERFORM PROCESS-PICK.
002100     PERFORM STOP-MY-PROGRAM.
002200 DISPLAY-MENU.
002300     DISPLAY MENU-1.
002400 READ-SELECTION.
002500     ACCEPT PICK-1.
002600     MOVE SPACES TO ERROR-1.
002700 PROCESS-PICK.
002800     IF PICK-1 = 1
002900       DISPLAY "Welcome to the student body."
003000       PERFORM STOP-MY-PROGRAM
003100     ELSE
003200     IF PICK-1 = 2
003300       DISPLAY "Welcome to the faculty."
003400       PERFORM STOP-MY-PROGRAM
003500     END-IF.
003600 STOP-MY-PROGRAM.
003700     STOP RUN.
```

Define a variable to store the selection received from the keyboard.

Jump to the paragraph that reads the selection from the keyboard.

Jump to the paragraph that processes the user's selection.

Display this message if the user selected option 2, then end the program.

Display this message if the user selected option 1, then end the program.

Handling Selection Errors

The assumption most of us make is that the user will correctly respond to a menu. That is, the user will enter only keystrokes that correspond to a valid menu option identifier.

The reality is users will make mistakes and it is up to the program to properly react to those mistakes by giving the user the opportunity to enter a correct selection.

There are a number of ways to create a routine to handle errors. One of those is illustrated on the next page.

The routine begins by defining a variable assigned the range of acceptable selections. The variable is defined at level 88 and in this example is assigned the range of values from 1 through 3 that corresponds to the unique identifier used for the options on the menu.

There is also a variable defined at level 77 to contain the error message that will be displayed on the screen when an error is detected. The variable is also incorporated in the menu data structure and given a line and column position at which the error message is displayed.

After the **ACCEPT** command stores the keystroke into the variable, the program calls the paragraph that processes the selection. If a match occurs, then the program displays a message and ends the program.

If there isn't a match, the program calls the ERROR-DETECTED paragraph and continues calling it until a valid option is entered.

The ERROR-DETECTED paragraph assigns an error message to the error variable, then displays the menu data structure, reads the keystroke, and processes the user's response.

```
000100 IDENTIFICATION DIVISION.
000200 PROGRAM-ID. FIRST.
000300 ENVIRONMENT DIVISION.
000400 DATA DIVISION.
000500 WORKING-STORAGE SECTION.
000600 77    PICK-1 PIC 9 VALUE ZEROES.
000700      88 PICKV      VALUES 1 THRU 3.
000800 77 ERROR-1    PIC X(30).
000900 SCREEN-SECTION.
001000 01 MENU-1.
001100     05 BLANK SCREEN.
001200     05 LINE  8 COL  25 VALUE "1. STUDENT ".
001300     05 LINE 10 COL  25 VALUE "2. FACULTY ".
001400     05 LINE 12 COL  25 VALUE "3. EXIT ".
001500     05 LINE 14 COL  25 VALUE "SELECTION: ".
001600     05 LINE 14 COL  36 PIC Z USING PICK-1.
001700     05 LINE 16 COL  25 PIC X(30) FROM ERROR-1.
001800 PROCEDURE DIVISION.
001900 MAIN-PARAGRAPH.
002000     PERFORM DISPLAY-MENU.
002100     PERFORM READ-SELECTION.
002200     PERFORM PROCESS-PICK.
002300     PERFORM ERROR-DETECTED UNTIL PICKV.
002400     PERFORM STOP-MY-PROGRAM.
002500 DISPLAY-MENU.
002600     DISPLAY MENU-1.
002700 READ-SELECTION.
002800     ACCEPT PICK-1.
002900     MOVE SPACES TO ERROR-1.
003000 ERROR-DETECTED.
003100     MOVE "INVALID SELECTION" TO ERROR-1.
003200     PERFORM DISPLAY-MENU.
003300     PERFORM READ-SELECTION.
003400     PERFORM PROCESS-PICK.
003500 PROCESS-PICK.
003600     IF PICK-1 = 1
003700        DISPLAY "Welcome to the student body."
003800        PERFORM STOP-MY-PROGRAM
003900     ELSE
004000     IF PICK-1 = 2
004100        DISPLAY "Welcome to the faculty."
004200        PERFORM STOP-MY-PROGRAM
004300     END-IF.
004400 STOP-MY-PROGRAM.
004500     STOP RUN.
```

Define a variable to store the selection received from the keyboard.

Define the range of acceptable values.

Define the variable for the error message.

Jump to the paragraph that processes the user's selection.

Jump to the paragraph that handles the error until the selection is valid.

Copy the error message to the error variable that is displayed when the menu is displayed again.

Read and process the user's selection.

Creating a Menu Tree

Some applications are designed to minimize choices available on a menu to options relative to the current situation. For example, you wouldn't expect to see student activity as a menu option if the user of the application is a faculty member.

A series of menus can be logically organized and displayed at the appropriate time by creating a menu tree. A *menu tree* resembles branches of a tree. The application begins with a main menu containing high level choices such as Student, Faculty, Exit as shown in the example on the next page.

Depending on the response from the user, another menu is displayed containing options relative to the original choice. In this example, the main menu is divided into two branches. Each branch can also be divided into one or more menus.

A menu tree is sometimes referred to as a drilled down menu. Each branch is considered a drill down further into a menu path.

The best approach to creating a menu tree is to lay out the tree using paper and pencil, PowerPoint, or some other tool that enables you to graphically depict the link among the branches.

Each menu should contain only identities that logically fit with the question at hand. For example, there is no need to place the course offerings option on the main menu since this only pertains to some of the users of the application.

Instead you'd want to categorize the user of the application on the main menu, then branch off to an appropriate menu of interest to the group of users.

Each menu branch must be defined as its down data structure, then displayed and processed as you would any menu. Be sure an option exist to display the previous menu and to exit the program.

```
000100 IDENTIFICATION DIVISION.
000200 PROGRAM-ID. FIRST.
000300 ENVIRONMENT DIVISION.
000400 DATA DIVISION.
000500 WORKING-STORAGE SECTION.
000600 77   PICK-1 PIC 9 VALUE ZEROES.
000700 SCREEN-SECTION.
000800 01 MENU-1.
000900    05 BLANK SCREEN.
001000    05 LINE  8  COL  25 VALUE  "1. STUDENT ".
001100    05 LINE 10  COL  25 VALUE  "2. FACULTY ".
001200    05 LINE 12  COL  25 VALUE  "3. EXIT ".
001300    05 LINE 14  COL  25 VALUE  "SELECTION: ".
001400    05 LINE 14  COL  36 PIC Z USING PICK-1.
001500 01 MENU-2.
001600    05 BLANK SCREEN.
001700    05 LINE  8  COL  25 VALUE  "1. COURSES".
001800    05 LINE 10  COL  25 VALUE  "2. ACTIVITIES".
001900    05 LINE 12  COL  25 VALUE  "3. MAIN MENU".
002000    05 LINE 14  COL  25 VALUE  "SELECTION: ".
002100    05 LINE 14  COL  36 PIC Z USING PICK-1.
002200 PROCEDURE DIVISION.
002300 MAIN-PARAGRAPH.
002400    PERFORM DISPLAY-MENU.
002500    PERFORM READ-SELECTION.
002600    PERFORM PROCESS-PICK.
002700    PERFORM STOP-MY-PROGRAM.
002800 DISPLAY-MENU.
002900    DISPLAY MENU-1.
003000 READ-SELECTION.
003100    ACCEPT PICK-1.
003200 PROCESS-PICK.
003300    IF PICK-1 = 1
003400      DISPLAY MENU-2
003500      PERFORM STOP-MY-PROGRAM
003600    ELSE
003700    IF PICK-1 = 2
003800      DISPLAY "Welcome to the faculty."
003900      PERFORM STOP-MY-PROGRAM
004000    END-IF.
004100 STOP-MY-PROGRAM.
004200    STOP RUN.
```

Define a variable to store the selection received from the keyboard.

Define the first menu.

Define the second menu.

Display the first menu, then read and process the selection.

If the first menu option is selected, then display the second menu.

Each menu must have its own processing paragraph. None is shown here for MENU-2 because of space limitation, but it resembles the code for PROCESS-PICK.

Data Entry Screen

Many applications are required to gather information from the user through the use of a data entry screen. A *data entry screen* typically displays text on the screen and labels for places to enter the data.

A *label* is like any text except it is strategically located on the screen to identify where the user can enter data into the application. *Data*, as you'll recall from Chapter 2, is information required by the program such as a person's name and address.

Text and labels can be positioned anywhere on the screen by using the **LINE** and **COL** phrases. The **LINE** phrase specifies which of the 25 lines on the screen defined to place the characters. The **COL** phrase indicates the column position on the line where the first character of the text or label begins.

A data entry screen also displays areas on the display where the user enters data. Typically, these locations are alongside of the labels.

Variables are defined to store data entered by the user. These variables and the text and labels of the data entry screen are defined in a data structure as shown in the example on the next page.

The program uses the **DISPLAY** command followed by the name of the data structure to show the data entry screen. Likewise, the **ACCEPT** command is used with the name of the data structure to read each data element and store them in the appropriate variable.

The cursor is placed at the location of the first variable on the screen. After the user enters the date and presses the **Enter** key, the cursor moves to the next variable position. This process continues until all the information is entered into the screen. Some applications skip variables by pressing the TAB key.

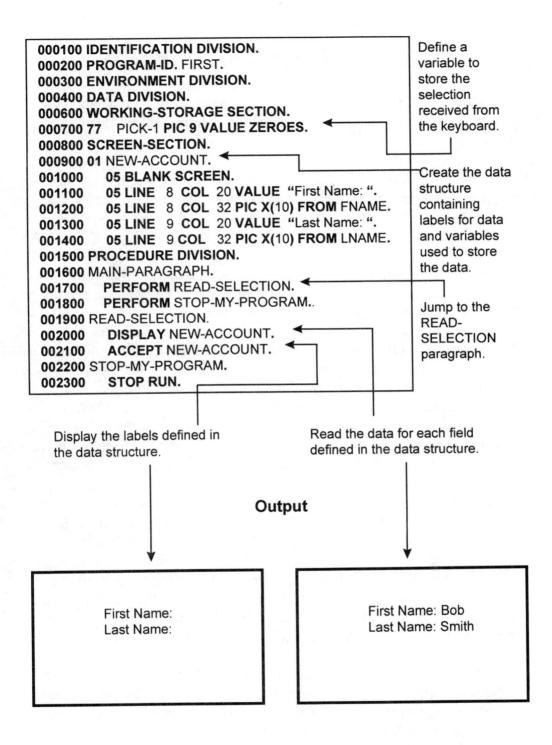

```
000100 IDENTIFICATION DIVISION.
000200 PROGRAM-ID. FIRST.
000300 ENVIRONMENT DIVISION.
000400 DATA DIVISION.
000600 WORKING-STORAGE SECTION.
000700 77   PICK-1 PIC 9 VALUE ZEROES.
000800 SCREEN-SECTION.
000900 01 NEW-ACCOUNT.
001000     05 BLANK SCREEN.
001100     05 LINE  8 COL 20 VALUE "First Name: ".
001200     05 LINE  8 COL 32 PIC X(10) FROM FNAME.
001300     05 LINE  9 COL 20 VALUE "Last Name: ".
001400     05 LINE  9 COL  32 PIC X(10) FROM LNAME.
001500 PROCEDURE DIVISION.
001600 MAIN-PARAGRAPH.
001700     PERFORM READ-SELECTION.
001800     PERFORM STOP-MY-PROGRAM..
001900 READ-SELECTION.
002000     DISPLAY NEW-ACCOUNT.
002100     ACCEPT NEW-ACCOUNT.
002200 STOP-MY-PROGRAM.
002300     STOP RUN.
```

Define a variable to store the selection received from the keyboard.

Create the data structure containing labels for data and variables used to store the data.

Jump to the READ-SELECTION paragraph.

Display the labels defined in the data structure.

Read the data for each field defined in the data structure.

Output

```
First Name:
Last Name:
```

```
First Name: Bob
Last Name: Smith
```

Data Display Screen

A COBOL application can display data from a variety of sources including data entry, program assigned data, and information retrieved from a file.

Data received from whatever source is typically stored in a variable to enable the data to be processed by the program. This data can be displayed at specific locations on the screen by creating a data display screen.

A *data display screen* does nothing more than show the contents of a group of variables on the screen along side labels that identify the information to the user of the application.

The example on the next page illustrates the basic concepts used to build a data display screen for your application. You can easily enhance this application by using various features presented throughout this book such as making the application menu driven.

Three variables are defined at level 01 to contain the student's name and grade. A data structure is also defined and contains information used to create the screen.

Reference is made to the variables within the data structure. It is here where you decide where to position the data on the screen.

When doing so, keep in mind how the labels and data will appear. For example, you want to keep the label and relative data on the same line. The last character in the label should be separated on the screen from the data by at least 1 space.

In this application, the program assigns data to the variables. In your application, the data also could have been assigned after being copied from a file and processed by your program. Notice the **Display** command only references the name of the data structure and not each member of the data structure.

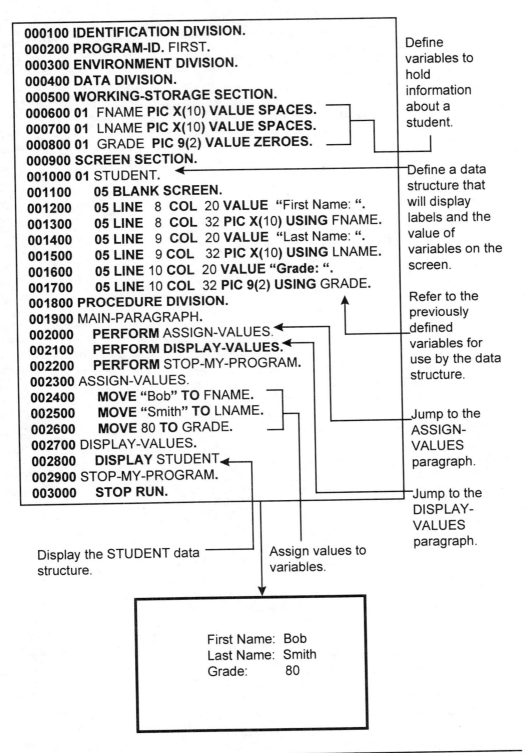

```
000100 IDENTIFICATION DIVISION.
000200 PROGRAM-ID. FIRST.
000300 ENVIRONMENT DIVISION.
000400 DATA DIVISION.
000500 WORKING-STORAGE SECTION.
000600 01  FNAME PIC X(10) VALUE SPACES.
000700 01  LNAME PIC X(10) VALUE SPACES.
000800 01  GRADE  PIC 9(2) VALUE ZEROES.
000900 SCREEN SECTION.
001000 01 STUDENT.
001100     05 BLANK SCREEN.
001200     05 LINE  8 COL 20 VALUE  "First Name: ".
001300     05 LINE  8 COL 32 PIC X(10) USING FNAME.
001400     05 LINE  9 COL 20 VALUE  "Last Name: ".
001500     05 LINE  9 COL 32 PIC X(10) USING LNAME.
001600     05 LINE 10 COL 20 VALUE "Grade: ".
001700     05 LINE 10 COL 32 PIC 9(2) USING GRADE.
001800 PROCEDURE DIVISION.
001900 MAIN-PARAGRAPH.
002000     PERFORM ASSIGN-VALUES.
002100     PERFORM DISPLAY-VALUES.
002200     PERFORM STOP-MY-PROGRAM.
002300 ASSIGN-VALUES.
002400     MOVE "Bob" TO FNAME.
002500     MOVE "Smith" TO LNAME.
002600     MOVE 80 TO GRADE.
002700 DISPLAY-VALUES.
002800     DISPLAY STUDENT
002900 STOP-MY-PROGRAM.
003000     STOP RUN.
```

Define variables to hold information about a student.

Define a data structure that will display labels and the value of variables on the screen.

Refer to the previously defined variables for use by the data structure.

Jump to the ASSIGN-VALUES paragraph.

Jump to the DISPLAY-VALUES paragraph.

Display the STUDENT data structure.

Assign values to variables.

```
First Name:  Bob
Last Name:   Smith
Grade:       80
```

Chapter Seven

Working with Other Programs

- Module Programming
- Calling Another Program
- Passing Data to the Called Program
- Passing Data Back to the Calling Program
- Returning Control Back to a Calling Program

Module Programming

Programs used throughout this book are short in length and can easily be stored into a single source code file. However, these programs are for illustrative purposes. COBOL applications are created from smaller programs that are called components.

A *component* is a smaller program that does one thing such as processing information although there is nothing preventing the component from doing more than one task. The concept of building an application from components is called *module programming*.

Large applications are divided into components also called *modules* each of which can be assigned to a programmer to develop.

Each module is tested independently of the other modules. This is called *unit testing*. Once the bugs have been removed from each module, the modules are assembled into an application that then undergoes an application test called *system testing*.

Modules are known by different names depending on the computer languages. These include functions, procedures, or subroutines. All are lines of code maintained separately from any application. Some modules accept data from the application and some modules return processed data to the application.

COBOL does not have functions, procedures or subroutines as they are known in other languages. Instead, the same general concept is achieved by creating smaller programs that perform unique routines that can be called from within another program.

The diagram on the next page illustrates the organization of a typical COBOL application. Notice how the application is divided into functional modules. Each of these become a program called by other programs in the application.

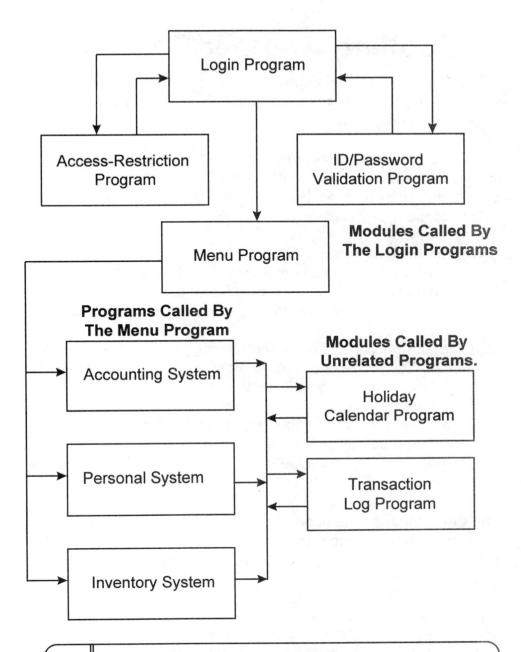

Login Program

Access-Restriction Program

ID/Password Validation Program

Menu Program

Modules Called By The Login Programs

Programs Called By The Menu Program

Accounting System

Modules Called By Unrelated Programs.

Holiday Calendar Program

Personal System

Transaction Log Program

Inventory System

Facts You Should Know...

○ Larger applications are divided into smaller programs
○ called modules each of which is callable from other
modules as shown above.

Calling Another Program

A COBOL application is composed of several small programs each of which typically performs a specific task such as validating data entered at the keyboard.

These programs are called *modules*. Modules can be designed to meet the needs of a particular application for instance processing payroll data can also be used for different applications such as data validations or calculations.

Some Information Systems departments develop a series modules that can be used in a variety of applications built for the company. This reduces the time and cost of creating a new application because the code in the modules is already written and tested.

Modules can be called from within a program by using the **CALL** command. The **Call** command is very similar to the **PERFORM** command that is illustrated in Chapter 4.

The **PERFORM** command temporarily jumps the flow of the program to another paragraph within the same source code file. The paragraph name must appear to the right of the **PERFORM** command.

The **CALL** command temporarily jumps the flow of the program to another program. A program accessing another program is called the *calling program* and the program being accessed is called the *called program*.

The name of the called program must appear within double quotations to the right of the **CALL** command. You don't need to include the file extension in the file name of the called program. However, the called program must be available in the environment.

An example of how to use the **CALL** command in your program is shown on the next page.

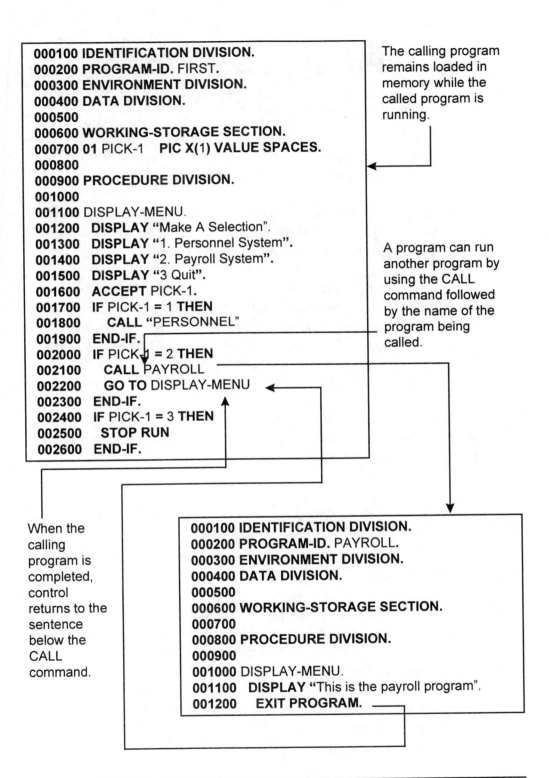

```
000100 IDENTIFICATION DIVISION.
000200 PROGRAM-ID. FIRST.
000300 ENVIRONMENT DIVISION.
000400 DATA DIVISION.
000500
000600 WORKING-STORAGE SECTION.
000700 01 PICK-1    PIC X(1) VALUE SPACES.
000800
000900 PROCEDURE DIVISION.
001000
001100 DISPLAY-MENU.
001200    DISPLAY "Make A Selection".
001300    DISPLAY "1. Personnel System".
001400    DISPLAY "2. Payroll System".
001500    DISPLAY "3 Quit".
001600    ACCEPT PICK-1.
001700    IF PICK-1 = 1 THEN
001800       CALL "PERSONNEL"
001900    END-IF.
002000    IF PICK-1 = 2 THEN
002100       CALL PAYROLL
002200       GO TO DISPLAY-MENU
002300    END-IF.
002400    IF PICK-1 = 3 THEN
002500    STOP RUN
002600    END-IF.
```

The calling program remains loaded in memory while the called program is running.

A program can run another program by using the CALL command followed by the name of the program being called.

When the calling program is completed, control returns to the sentence below the CALL command.

```
000100 IDENTIFICATION DIVISION.
000200 PROGRAM-ID. PAYROLL.
000300 ENVIRONMENT DIVISION.
000400 DATA DIVISION.
000500
000600 WORKING-STORAGE SECTION.
000700
000800 PROCEDURE DIVISION.
000900
001000 DISPLAY-MENU.
001100    DISPLAY "This is the payroll program".
001200    EXIT PROGRAM.
```

Passing Data to the Called Program

Some modules are designed to accept information from the calling program that is then processed in some way.

For example, a module can be designed to validate a person's login. The calling program sends the called program the person's login ID and password. This is called *passing data*.

The validation module validates the data. If the login information is invalid, the validation module displays the necessary warning messages on the screen. Typically, the user is asked to re-enter login information again. After the third failure, the validation module exits the application. However, if the login information is valid, the module returns control back to the calling program.

Notice that the validation module can be used by many applications. Only one module needs to be corrected if there are any changes to the validation process.

You can pass data to a called program by including the **USING** phrase in the **CALL** command. The **USING** phrase identifies variables defined in the calling program that are passed to the called program. All variables passed to the called program must be defined in the calling program.

The example on the next page illustrates how to pass information to a called program. The calling program treats the called program as a paragraph except the called program only has access to variables defined in the **USING** phrase.

Only variables required for the called program to process data should be included in the **USING** phrase. You need to define the variables passed to the called program in the called program.

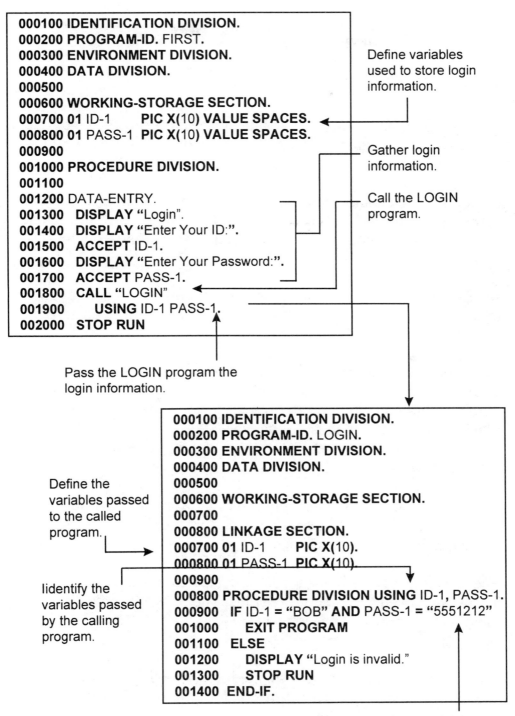

```
000100 IDENTIFICATION DIVISION.
000200 PROGRAM-ID. FIRST.
000300 ENVIRONMENT DIVISION.
000400 DATA DIVISION.
000500
000600 WORKING-STORAGE SECTION.
000700 01 ID-1    PIC X(10) VALUE SPACES.
000800 01 PASS-1  PIC X(10) VALUE SPACES.
000900
001000 PROCEDURE DIVISION.
001100
001200 DATA-ENTRY.
001300   DISPLAY "Login".
001400   DISPLAY "Enter Your ID:".
001500   ACCEPT ID-1.
001600   DISPLAY "Enter Your Password:".
001700   ACCEPT PASS-1.
001800   CALL "LOGIN"
001900      USING ID-1 PASS-1.
002000   STOP RUN
```

Define variables used to store login information.

Gather login information.

Call the LOGIN program.

Pass the LOGIN program the login information.

Define the variables passed to the called program.

Iidentify the variables passed by the calling program.

```
000100 IDENTIFICATION DIVISION.
000200 PROGRAM-ID. LOGIN.
000300 ENVIRONMENT DIVISION.
000400 DATA DIVISION.
000500
000600 WORKING-STORAGE SECTION.
000700
000800 LINKAGE SECTION.
000700 01 ID-1    PIC X(10).
000800 01 PASS-1  PIC X(10).
000900
000800 PROCEDURE DIVISION USING ID-1, PASS-1.
000900   IF ID-1 = "BOB" AND PASS-1 = "5551212"
001000     EXIT PROGRAM
001100   ELSE
001200     DISPLAY "Login is invalid."
001300     STOP RUN
001400   END-IF.
```

Compare the login information against valid values.

Passing Data Back to the Calling Program

A called program is a module that typically performs a specific function that sometimes requires information to be supplied by the calling program.

Earlier in this chapter, you saw how to pass information to the called program by including the **USING** phrase with the **CALL** command. The **USING** phrase identifies variables that are available for use by the called program.

A called program can simply process data, then return control back to the calling program as is the case in a program used to print payroll checks.

However, a called program might process data, then return data back to the calling program for future processing. For example, a called program could perform data validation. The calling program provides the data that is to be validated. The called program attempts to validate the data, then returns the result of the validation process back to the calling program.

Data is returned to the calling program by assigning the data to a variable identified in the **USING** phrase. This technique is illustrated in the example on the next page.

The calling program passes two variables to the called program. These are called NAME and GREETING. The NAME variable contains information required by the called program to formulate the greeting.

The GREETING variable is assigned the greeting by the called program that is displayed when control is returned to the calling program.

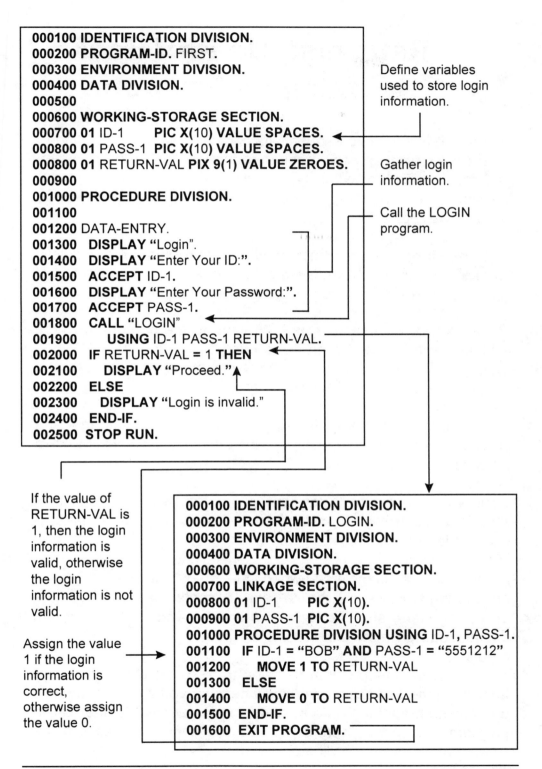

```
000100 IDENTIFICATION DIVISION.
000200 PROGRAM-ID. FIRST.
000300 ENVIRONMENT DIVISION.
000400 DATA DIVISION.
000500
000600 WORKING-STORAGE SECTION.
000700 01 ID-1     PIC X(10) VALUE SPACES.
000800 01 PASS-1  PIC X(10) VALUE SPACES.
000800 01 RETURN-VAL PIX 9(1) VALUE ZEROES.
000900
001000 PROCEDURE DIVISION.
001100
001200 DATA-ENTRY.
001300    DISPLAY "Login".
001400    DISPLAY "Enter Your ID:".
001500    ACCEPT ID-1.
001600    DISPLAY "Enter Your Password:".
001700    ACCEPT PASS-1.
001800    CALL "LOGIN"
001900       USING ID-1 PASS-1 RETURN-VAL.
002000    IF RETURN-VAL = 1 THEN
002100       DISPLAY "Proceed."
002200    ELSE
002300       DISPLAY "Login is invalid."
002400    END-IF.
002500    STOP RUN.
```

Define variables used to store login information.

Gather login information.

Call the LOGIN program.

If the value of RETURN-VAL is 1, then the login information is valid, otherwise the login information is not valid.

Assign the value 1 if the login information is correct, otherwise assign the value 0.

```
000100 IDENTIFICATION DIVISION.
000200 PROGRAM-ID. LOGIN.
000300 ENVIRONMENT DIVISION.
000400 DATA DIVISION.
000600 WORKING-STORAGE SECTION.
000700 LINKAGE SECTION.
000800 01 ID-1     PIC X(10).
000900 01 PASS-1  PIC X(10).
001000 PROCEDURE DIVISION USING ID-1, PASS-1.
001100    IF ID-1 = "BOB" AND PASS-1 = "5551212"
001200       MOVE 1 TO RETURN-VAL
001300    ELSE
001400       MOVE 0 TO RETURN-VAL
001500    END-IF.
001600    EXIT PROGRAM.
```

Returning Control Back to a Calling Program

A program is executed sequentially beginning with the first line of code in the file, then flows through to the last line of the program. You can change the flow using techniques described in Chapter 4. You can also change the flow by calling another program as you've seen in this chapter.

The called program is treated as a paragraph in the calling program. A paragraph is a segment of code within a program that is identified by a name such as DISPLAY-VALUES.

The **PERFORM** command is used to jump to the paragraph where the code within the paragraph is executed sequentially. Control returns to the line below the **PERFORM** command once the name of a new paragraph is encountered.

The **CALL** command is similar to the **PERFORM** command in that it changes the flow to another program that is considered a paragraph.

Control doesn't return to the calling program when the end of a paragraph is reached. Instead, the calling program runs until completion.

A program is completed when the **STOP RUN** sentence is encountered. However, the **STOP RUN** sentence ends both the called program and the calling program. The called program doesn't return control to the calling program.

You can avoid this problem by using the **EXIT PROGRAM** sentence in place of the **STOP RUN** sentence whenever you want to terminate the called program. This sentence only terminates the called program and returns control back to the sentence following the **CALL** command in the calling program.

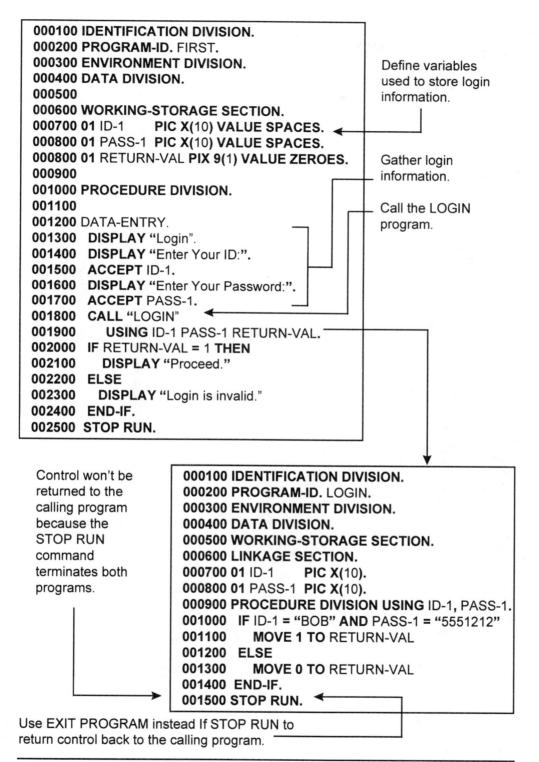

```
000100 IDENTIFICATION DIVISION.
000200 PROGRAM-ID. FIRST.
000300 ENVIRONMENT DIVISION.
000400 DATA DIVISION.
000500
000600 WORKING-STORAGE SECTION.
000700 01 ID-1     PIC X(10) VALUE SPACES.
000800 01 PASS-1  PIC X(10) VALUE SPACES.
000800 01 RETURN-VAL PIX 9(1) VALUE ZEROES.
000900
001000 PROCEDURE DIVISION.
001100
001200 DATA-ENTRY.
001300    DISPLAY "Login".
001400    DISPLAY "Enter Your ID:".
001500    ACCEPT ID-1.
001600    DISPLAY "Enter Your Password:".
001700    ACCEPT PASS-1.
001800    CALL "LOGIN"
001900       USING ID-1 PASS-1 RETURN-VAL.
002000    IF RETURN-VAL = 1 THEN
002100       DISPLAY "Proceed."
002200    ELSE
002300       DISPLAY "Login is invalid."
002400    END-IF.
002500  STOP RUN.
```

Define variables used to store login information.

Gather login information.

Call the LOGIN program.

Control won't be returned to the calling program because the STOP RUN command terminates both programs.

```
000100 IDENTIFICATION DIVISION.
000200 PROGRAM-ID. LOGIN.
000300 ENVIRONMENT DIVISION.
000400 DATA DIVISION.
000500 WORKING-STORAGE SECTION.
000600 LINKAGE SECTION.
000700 01 ID-1     PIC X(10).
000800 01 PASS-1  PIC X(10).
000900 PROCEDURE DIVISION USING ID-1, PASS-1.
001000    IF ID-1 = "BOB" AND PASS-1 = "5551212"
001100       MOVE 1 TO RETURN-VAL
001200    ELSE
001300       MOVE 0 TO RETURN-VAL
001400    END-IF.
001500 STOP RUN.
```

Use EXIT PROGRAM instead If STOP RUN to return control back to the calling program.

Chapter Eight

Working with Files

- What Is a file?
- What Is a record?
- What Is a field?
- Fixed Length and Delimited Files
- What is an index?
- Defining a Logical File
- Defining a Physical File
- Opening and Closing a File
- Creating a Sequential File
- Writing a Record to a Sequential File
- Reading a Record from a Sequential File
- Rewriting a Record from a Sequential File
- Looping through a File
- Creating a Relative File
- Writing a Record to a Relative File
- Reading a Record Sequentially from a Relative File
- Reading a Record Relatively from a Relative File
- Rewriting a Record to a Relative File
- Deleting a Record from a Relative File
- Creating an Indexed File
- Adding Records to an Index File
- Reading Records Using an Indexed File
- Rewriting Records in an Index File
- Deleting Records in an Index File
- Using Alternate Keys

What Is a File?

A file is the logical and physical group of information stored usually on a permanent medium such as on a tape or disk. Most of the information used by an application is contained in a file that is accessed by a program.

Information stored in a file is stored in two ways - logically and physically. Logical storage is the organization of the information in the file. Physical storage is how the information is placed on the tape or disk.

Application programmers need to know the logical organization of data in the file so they can write programs to access the information. Systems programmers who build and modify the operating system need to know the physical organization of information in a file.

All information is stored sequentially in the file. That is, each character of data is stored in the order in which the information is written to the file. This is illustrated on the next page.

Although conceptually we store data as a series of characters in a file, each character is stored in binary code that consists of zeroes and ones.

A character is represented by a combination of eight zeroes and ones each called a bit and collectively called a byte. A byte can be interpreted using one of two methods either by using the EBCDIC or the ASCII code.

Mainframe computers typically use the EBCDIC code and PCs and workstations use the ASCII code to encode a character.

Programmers rarely use either the EBCDIC or the ASCII code since the compiler automatically translates bytes to characters.

Conceptual Storage of Data On a File

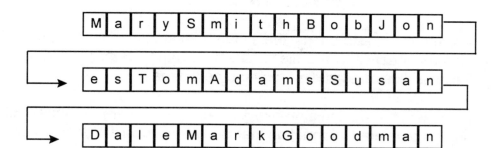

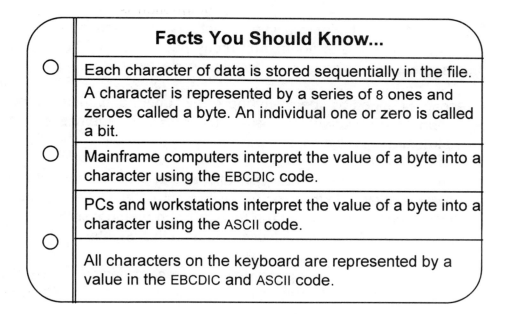

Facts You Should Know...

○ Each character of data is stored sequentially in the file.

A character is represented by a series of 8 ones and zeroes called a byte. An individual one or zero is called a bit.

○ Mainframe computers interpret the value of a byte into a character using the EBCDIC code.

PCs and workstations interpret the value of a byte into a character using the ASCII code.

○ All characters on the keyboard are represented by a value in the EBCDIC and ASCII code.

Logical Storage of Data On a File

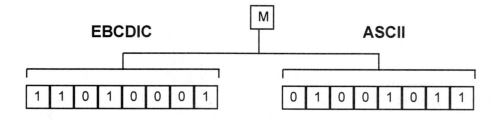

What Is a Record?

Information is stored as the binary representation of characters stored sequentially in a file. Characters remain unorganized in the file as is illustrated at the top of the next page.

However, information stored in a file can be logically organized into groups of related information that is called a *record*. For example, a person's name and address are related information.

Typically, a file contains multiple collections of related information such as the name and address of many people. Each set of data represents a person as a record within the file.

A record is defined by specifying the kind of information used in the collection of information. This is similar to defining members of a data structure that was shown in Chapter 3.

This includes the name, data type, and size of the members of the record as is shown on the next page. The sum of the sizes of each member is called the size of the record. Each member of a record is called a *field* that will be discussed later in this chapter.

The example on the next page defines a record having a size 12 character. Every 13th character in the file is the beginning of a new record.

A *record definition* reserves space in the record where data can be stored by a program. However, not all the spaces need to be filled with data. If there isn't data to fill the space, then the space is left blank and can be used when the record is modified.

The example at the bottom of the next page shows the conceptual storage of a fixed length record. A fixed-length record is one where character positions in the record are filled with the space character if no data is stored in the position. Later in this chapter you'll learn about a delimited record where no character position is left empty.

A series Of Characters in a File

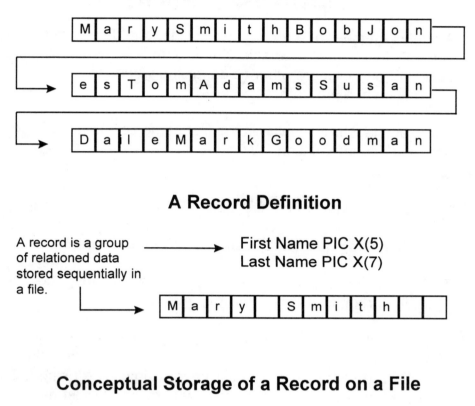

| M | a | r | y | S | m | i | t | h | B | o | b | J | o | n |

| e | s | T | o | m | A | d | a | m | s | S | u | s | a | n |

| D | a | l | e | M | a | r | k | G | o | o | d | m | a | n |

A Record Definition

A record is a group of relationed data stored sequentially in a file.

First Name PIC X(5)
Last Name PIC X(7)

| M | a | r | y | | S | m | i | t | h | | |

Conceptual Storage of a Record on a File

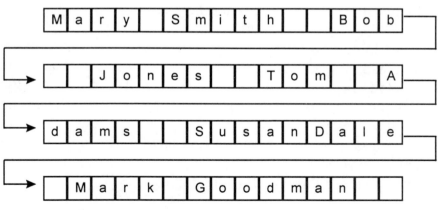

| M | a | r | y | | S | m | i | t | h | | B | o | b |

| | J | o | n | e | s | | T | o | m | | A |

| d | a | m | s | | S | u | s | a | n | D | a | l | e |

| | M | a | r | k | | G | o | o | d | m | a | n | |

What Is a Field?

A *field* is member of a record and consist of a data item such as a person's first name. The value of a field must be combined with the values of one or more other fields for the values to become useful information to a program.

For example, Bob is a value in the first name field. It doesn't provide any useful information. Who is Bob? Which Bob is being referenced?

However, the value of the first name field becomes important when it is combined with the value of the last name field such as Bob Smith. Of course, the next question is, Which Bob Smith?

The values of additional fields are required to fully identify Bob Smith. Important fields are Street, City, and State.

A field is defined similarly to the definition of a variable that is illustrated in Chapter 2. A field must have a unique name that is not a COBOL reserve word. It must have a data type using the X to represent characters and 9 to represent digits. It must have a size that is shown on the top of the next page.

Keep in mind a field is a logical organization of information stored in a file. If you could peer into a file on the tape or disk, you wouldn't be able to see any markers that identify the beginning or the end of a field if data was stored in a fixed length file.

Data is stored as a string of characters. The only way a program knows how to regroup those characters into meaningful pieces of information is through the field definition.

If the field definition in the program is inaccurate, then data read from the file by the program will be erroneous. For example, if the first name field is defined as 6 characters on the next page, then the value of the first field is Mary S instead of Mary.

A Field Definition

Each data item in a record definition is called a field. ⟶ First-Name PIC X(5)
Last-Name PIC X(7)

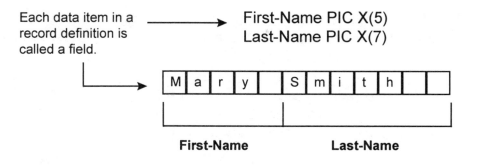

First-Name   **Last-Name**

Conceptual Storage of Fields On a File

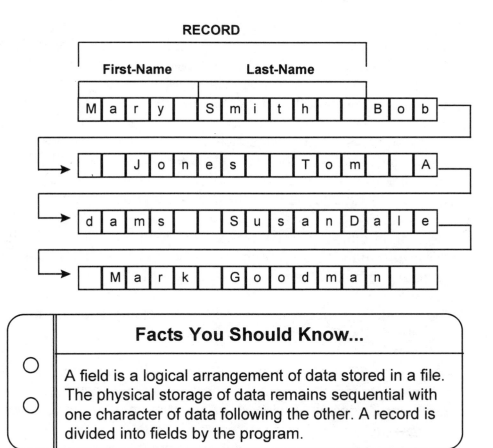

Facts You Should Know...

A field is a logical arrangement of data stored in a file. The physical storage of data remains sequential with one character of data following the other. A record is divided into fields by the program.

Fixed Length and Delimited Files

Information is organized in a file as fields and records. A field is a piece of data that has little meaning until the field is associated with other fields to form a record.

Fields and records are used to form a logical organization of data. There is no physical record in a file. The physical file only contains a series of characters represented in binary code.

Fields and records are recognized by the program based on a known algorithm. An *algorithm* is a way of doing something. In this case, the algorithm is the way of identifying fields and records in a file.

There are two common algorithms used to recognize fields and records. These are fixed length and delimited algorithms. Files are typically called a fixed length file or a delimited file depending on which method is used to identify the fields and records.

Fixed length is used to describe a file where fields are a fixed-length as illustrated in the first example on the next page. The First-Name field is five characters long. The Last-Name field is five characters long and the Grade field is two characters long.

Information stored in a field of a fixed length file can have fewer characters than the size of the field, but not more characters than the field can hold, otherwise data will be lost.

The length of a record is determined by adding together the sizes of all the fields. Each record is a fixed length.

A *delimited file* contains fields and records that use markers, called delimiters, to identify where they begin. The most common is called the comma delimited file where a comma separates fields; a carriage return separates records; double quotations delimit character fields; and numeric fields are not enclosed.

A Record Definition

```
First-Name PIC X(5)
Last-Name PIC X(5)
GRADE     9(2)
```

Fixed-Length Record

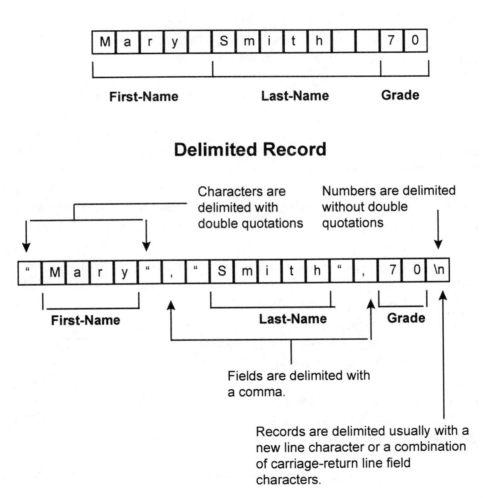

Delimited Record

Characters are delimited with double quotations

Numbers are delimited without double quotations

First-Name

Last-Name

Grade

Fields are delimited with a comma.

Records are delimited usually with a new line character or a combination of carriage-return line field characters.

What Is an Index?

A large amount of information can be stored in a file in the form of fields and records. Many applications are required to find a specific record in a file quickly.

This task could be slow and cumbersome even for a computer if the program has to read each record sequentially, then compare the search criteria to a field in the file to see if they match.

A faster method of searching for a record in a file is to use an indexed file. An *indexed file* is searched by using an index rather than examining every record in the file.

An *index* is similar to an index of a book except the index is a file created and maintained automatically by the program.

Information in a book is contained on pages. Important words on the pages are copied and stored in a list along with the number of the page. This list is called the index of the book. Finding information in a book is fast when you use the index since the index contains only important words and related page numbers.

Information in a file is contained in records. Each record is assigned a number based on the record's position in the file. The first record is 1, the second is 2, and so on.

The value of at least one field is used to identify the record. This field is called the *primary key* such as a person's ID number.

An index contains the value of the key field and the number of the related record. This is illustrated at the top of the next page. Notice the size of the index is shorter than the size of the file.

The index is searched, then if a match occurs the position number is used to find the record in the file.

Index

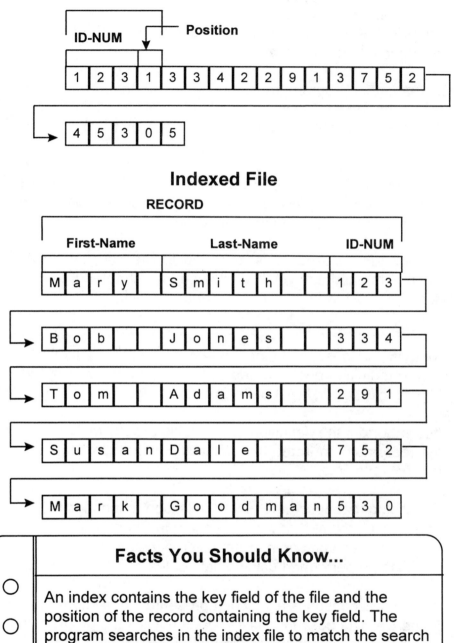

Indexed File

RECORD

Facts You Should Know...

○ An index contains the key field of the file and the
○ position of the record containing the key field. The
   program searches in the index file to match the search
   value entered by the user into the program.

Defining a Logical File

A file contains a series of characters as illustrated earlier in this chapter. The file itself does not organize the information stored in the file into fields and records.

Instead, the program must define the data organization that is called the logical file definition. The logical file definition begins in the File Section of the Data Division. as shown on the next page.

The definition starts at a special level number identified as **FD** that is the abbreviation for file descriptor. The *file descriptor* must begin in Area A and be followed by a variable used to store the name of the physical file that must begin in Area B.

The physical file name is assigned to the variable by using the **OPEN** command that you'll see later in this chapter. Beneath the file descriptor is the label records clause that identifies that the file is labeled.

Next is the description of the record contained in the file. The record definition begins at the 01 level with the name of the record. This is followed by a list of fields at the 05 level.

It is important the definition of the fields exactly match the layout of the record stored in the file, otherwise information could be stored in the wrong field.

You'll also that notice the record definition resembles the definition of a data structure that was presented in Chapter 3. Many of the same routines you can perform using a member of a data structure can also be performed using a field of the complete record.

The file description is a logical representation of information stored in the file. The description itself does not link the program to the file. Instead, it describes the format of the data the program is expected to find in the file.

FD is a special level number called a file descriptor

The file descriptor must appear in Area A.

```
000100 IDENTIFICATION DIVISION.
000200 PROGRAM-ID. FIRST.
000300 ENVIRONMENT DIVISION.
000400 DATA DIVISION.
000500
000600 FILE SECTION.
000700 FD   CONTACTS
000800        LABEL RECORDS ARE STANDARD.
000900 01 CONTACT-RECORD.
001000      05 FNAME       PIC X(10).
001100      05 LNAME       PIC X(10).
001200      05 STREET      PIC X(30).
001300      05 CITY        PIC X(30).
001400      05 STATE       PIC X(2).
001500      05 ZIP         PIC X(10).
001600      05 PHONE       PIC X(12).
001700
001800 WORKING-STORAGE SECTION.
001900
002000 PROCEDURE DIVISION.
002100
002200  STOP RUN.
```

The variable contains the actual name of the file as it must appear in Area B.

The name of the record begins at level 01.

Fields within the record are defined in a similar manner to the way variables are defined

Facts You Should Know...

○ The variable used to reference the file in the program must be assigned to a physical file as is illustrated later in this chapter.

○ The variable name used to reference the file is not really a variable. Instead, it is called a *file identifier*.

You cannot use the **MOVE** command to assign a value to the variable used as the file identifier.

○ The record definition in the program must exactly match the record definition in the file, otherwise data will be read incorrectly from the file.

Defining a Physical File

A logical file is the conceptual organization of data into informative pieces called fields that are grouped together to form a record. The logical definition of a file is only meaningful as the information is read into memory from the file by the program.

Before this can happen, the program must have information about the physical file. The *physical file* is the locally of the data on a disk or on tape.

Every file used by your program is identified by a name. The name of the file typically has no more than eight characters followed by a period and a three-character file extension. However, the convention used for naming files is dependent upon restrictions imposed by the operating system.

The physical file is defined in the File Control paragraph of the Input-Output section within the Environment Division as shown in the example on the next page.

The file definition begins with the **SELECT** command that is followed by the name of the variable used throughout the program to refer to the file name.

The **ASSIGN** command is used to assign the name of the file to the variable. You cannot use the **MOVE** command to store a value to this variable.

The file name must be within double quotations and will appear as the name appears to the operating system. Be sure to include the full path with the file name if the operating system isn't able to locate the file.

The physical file definition must also identify how records are organized in the file. As you'll see later in this chapter, records can be organized in several different ways, one of which is Sequential as shown on the next page.

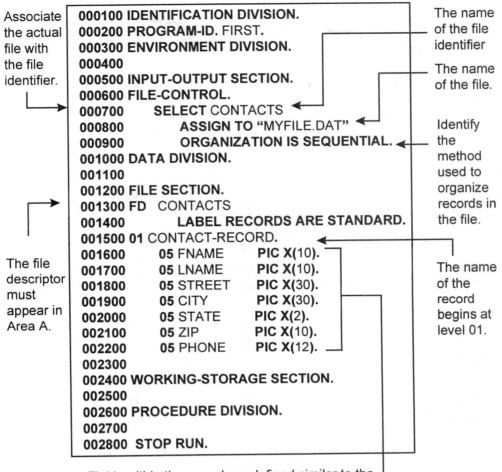

Associate the actual file with the file identifier.

The file descriptor must appear in Area A.

```
000100 IDENTIFICATION DIVISION.
000200 PROGRAM-ID. FIRST.
000300 ENVIRONMENT DIVISION.
000400
000500 INPUT-OUTPUT SECTION.
000600 FILE-CONTROL.
000700       SELECT CONTACTS
000800          ASSIGN TO "MYFILE.DAT"
000900          ORGANIZATION IS SEQUENTIAL.
001000 DATA DIVISION.
001100
001200 FILE SECTION.
001300 FD  CONTACTS
001400          LABEL RECORDS ARE STANDARD.
001500 01 CONTACT-RECORD.
001600       05 FNAME     PIC X(10).
001700       05 LNAME     PIC X(10).
001800       05 STREET    PIC X(30).
001900       05 CITY      PIC X(30).
002000       05 STATE     PIC X(2).
002100       05 ZIP       PIC X(10).
002200       05 PHONE     PIC X(12).
002300
002400 WORKING-STORAGE SECTION.
002500
002600 PROCEDURE DIVISION.
002700
002800  STOP RUN.
```

The name of the file identifier

The name of the file.

Identify the method used to organize records in the file.

The name of the record begins at level 01.

Fields within the record are defined similar to the way variables are defined.

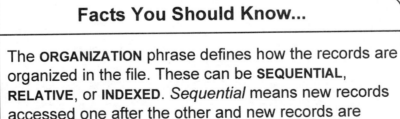

Facts You Should Know...

The **ORGANIZATION** phrase defines how the records are organized in the file. These can be **SEQUENTIAL**, **RELATIVE**, or **INDEXED**. *Sequential* means new records accessed one after the other and new records are appended to the end of the file. *Relative* means records are accessed by their position in the file. *Indexed* means the file is an indexed one and will be discussed later in this chapter.

Opening and Closing a File

The physical file definition tells the program where to find the physical file and how records are stored within the file. The logical file definition identifies the record layout and assigns field names and a record name to the data read from the file.

However, the program can't access the data within the file until the file is opened by using the **OPEN** command. The **OPEN** command requires two pieces of information. These are the file mode and the name of the file.

The file mode identifies how you want to use the file. There are four file modes. These are **OUTPUT**, **EXTEND**, **INPUT**, and **I-O**.

OUTPUT mode overwrites an existing file or creates a new file. **EXTEND** is similar to **OUTPUT** except information is appended to the end of the file rather than overwriting the entire file. **INPUT** opens the file so information can be read by the program. **I-O** enables the file to be used for both reading and writing data. You'll see how these are used later in this chapter.

The **OPEN** command also requires reference to the name of the file that needs to be opened. You must use the name of the variable that is assigned the file name in the physical file definition. You cannot use the file name itself.

Once a file is opened, the program can freely access information stored in the file as you'll learn in upcoming pages.

The file remains open until the program closes the file by using the **CLOSE** command. The **CLOSE** command can be used in two ways by either referencing the file name using the name of the variable or by using the **CLOSE** command without any reference to the file name. If you don't make reference to the file name, the last opened file will be closed. It is good programming style to always reference the file you want to close.

Associate the actual file with the file identifier.

```
000100 IDENTIFICATION DIVISION.
000200 PROGRAM-ID. FIRST.
000300 ENVIRONMENT DIVISION.
000400
000500 INPUT-OUTPUT SECTION.
000600 FILE-CONTROL.
000700      SELECT CONTACTS
000800          ASSIGN TO "MYFILE.DAT"
000900          ORGANIZATION IS SEQUENTIAL.
001000 DATA DIVISION.
001100
001200 FILE SECTION.
001300 FD   CONTACTS
001400          LABEL RECORDS ARE STANDARD.
001500 01 CONTACT-RECORD.
001600      05 FNAME      PIC X(10).
001700      05 LNAME      PIC X(10).
001800      05 STREET     PIC X(30).
001900      05 CITY       PIC X(30).
002000      05 STATE      PIC X(2).
002100      05 ZIP        PIC X(10).
002200      05 PHONE      PIC X(12).
002300
002400 WORKING-STORAGE SECTION.
002500
002600 PROCEDURE DIVISION.
002700
002700 OPEN-FILE.
002800    OPEN EXTEND CONTACTS.
002900
003000 CLOSE-FILE.
003100    CLOSE CONTACTS.
003000  STOP RUN.
```

The name of the file identifier

The name of the file.

Identify the method used to organize records in the file.

The name of the record begins at level 01.

Extend is the file mode used to create a new file or append records to the end of an existing file.

The file descriptor must appear in Area A.

Open the file before using the file.

The file identifier.

Facts You Should Know...

○ The file mode can be **OUTPUT**, **EXTEND**, **INPUT**, or **I-O**. **OUTPUT** creates a new file or overwrites an existing file. **EXTEND** creates a new file or appends records to an

○ existing file. **INPUT** enables data to be read from the file. The file must exist. **I-O** allows for reading and writing data.

Creating
a Sequential File

Information in a file can be organized in several ways. These are sequentially, indexed, and relative.

A *sequential file* contains information stored in the order in which the data is written to the file. That is, the first record written to the file is followed by the second record, and so forth.

The speed at which information is found in a sequential file is hindered by a large record size and a high volume of records stored in the file.

Information is accessed sequentially that requires the program to read records in order without being able to skip around the file. This means to find information in the 100th record, the program must read the 99 previous records first.

An *indexed file* organizes information similar to a book where records are like pages, the position of the record in the file is like a page number called a *record number*, and information is searched using an index.

An index is a field used to identify each record. Whenever the program needs to locate a particular record, it searches the index that contains the search value and record number, then uses the record number to quickly search the file for the complete record.

A *relative file* is one that can be accessed either sequentially or through the use of an index. You'll see how to create an indexed file and a relative file later in this chapter.

A sequential file is created by identifying how you want the data organized in the file in defining the physical file in the File Control paragraph of the Input-Output section in the Environment Division. This is illustrated on the next page.

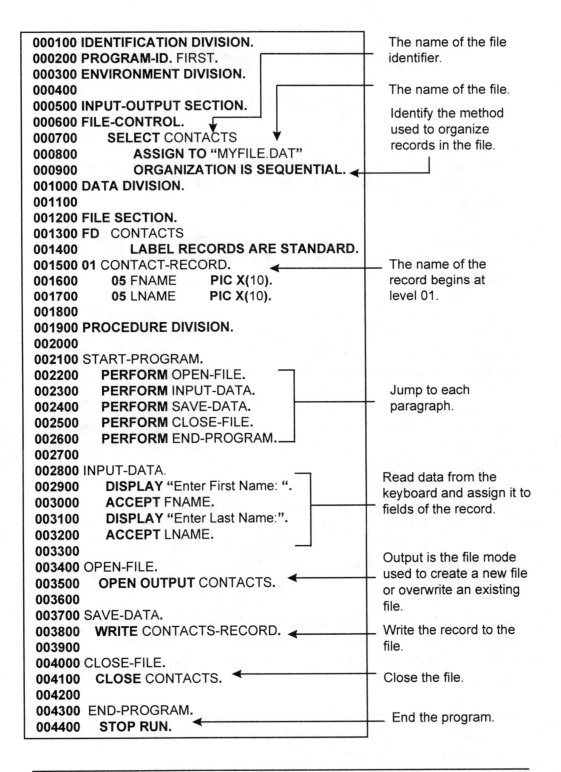

```
000100 IDENTIFICATION DIVISION.
000200 PROGRAM-ID. FIRST.
000300 ENVIRONMENT DIVISION.
000400
000500 INPUT-OUTPUT SECTION.
000600 FILE-CONTROL.
000700     SELECT CONTACTS
000800        ASSIGN TO "MYFILE.DAT"
000900        ORGANIZATION IS SEQUENTIAL.
001000 DATA DIVISION.
001100
001200 FILE SECTION.
001300 FD   CONTACTS
001400        LABEL RECORDS ARE STANDARD.
001500 01 CONTACT-RECORD.
001600     05 FNAME      PIC X(10).
001700     05 LNAME      PIC X(10).
001800
001900 PROCEDURE DIVISION.
002000
002100 START-PROGRAM.
002200     PERFORM OPEN-FILE.
002300     PERFORM INPUT-DATA.
002400     PERFORM SAVE-DATA.
002500     PERFORM CLOSE-FILE.
002600     PERFORM END-PROGRAM.
002700
002800 INPUT-DATA.
002900     DISPLAY "Enter First Name: ".
003000     ACCEPT FNAME.
003100     DISPLAY "Enter Last Name:".
003200     ACCEPT LNAME.
003300
003400 OPEN-FILE.
003500   OPEN OUTPUT CONTACTS.
003600
003700 SAVE-DATA.
003800   WRITE CONTACTS-RECORD.
003900
004000 CLOSE-FILE.
004100   CLOSE CONTACTS.
004200
004300 END-PROGRAM.
004400   STOP RUN.
```

The name of the file identifier.

The name of the file.

Identify the method used to organize records in the file.

The name of the record begins at level 01.

Jump to each paragraph.

Read data from the keyboard and assign it to fields of the record.

Output is the file mode used to create a new file or overwrite an existing file.

Write the record to the file.

Close the file.

End the program.

Writing a Record to a Sequential File

A sequential file is created by defining the physical file in the File Control paragraph of the Input-Output section in the Environment Division. This is where the name of the file is assigned to the variable used to reference the file throughout the program.

The description of the file must be defined in the File section of the Data Division. This is where the record is defined by creating fields as shown on the next page.

Field names are used similar to the way variables are used. You'll notice on the next page information read from the keyboard is assigned to the FNAME and LNAME fields using the **ACCEPT** command once the file is opened using the **Open** command.

The file is opened in the output mode that means any information saved to the file will overwrite information in the existing file. The program creates a new file if the file isn't found, the program creates a new file.

Information is written to the file by using the **WRITE** command followed by the name of the record. The value of all the fields are written to the file as a block of data defined by the size of the record and identified by the name given to the record in the file descriptor.

Be sure that all the fields have an initial value before saving the record to the file. Character variables can be initialized using spaces, and numeric fields can be initialized using zeroes as was shown in Chapter Two.

After writing the record to the file, use the **CLOSE** command to close the file. Once closed, the file is no longer available to the program unless it is opened again.

```
000100 IDENTIFICATION DIVISION.
000200 PROGRAM-ID. FIRST.
000300 ENVIRONMENT DIVISION.
000400
000500 INPUT-OUTPUT SECTION.
000600 FILE-CONTROL.
000700       SELECT CONTACTS
000800          ASSIGN TO "MYFILE.DAT"
000900          ORGANIZATION IS SEQUENTIAL.
001000 DATA DIVISION.
001100
001200 FILE SECTION.
001300 FD   CONTACTS
001400          LABEL RECORDS ARE STANDARD.
001500 01 CONTACT-RECORD.
001600       05 FNAME      PIC X(10).
001700       05 LNAME      PIC X(10).
001800
001900 PROCEDURE DIVISION.
002000
002100 START-PROGRAM.
002200       PERFORM OPEN-FILE.
002300       PERFORM INPUT-DATA.
002400       PERFORM SAVE-DATA.
002500       PERFORM CLOSE-FILE.
002600       PERFORM END-PROGRAM.
002700
002800 INPUT-DATA.
002900       DISPLAY "Enter First Name: ".
003000       ACCEPT FNAME.
003100       DISPLAY "Enter Last Name:".
003200       ACCEPT LNAME.
003300
003400 OPEN-FILE.
003500       OPEN EXTEND CONTACTS.
003600
003700 SAVE-DATA.
003800       WRITE CONTACTS-RECORD.
003900
004000 CLOSE-FILE.
004100       CLOSE CONTACTS.
004200
004300 END-PROGRAM.
004400       STOP RUN.
```

The name of the file identifier.

The name of the file.

Identify the method used to organize records in the file.

The name of the record begins at level 01.

Jump to each paragraph.

Read data from the keyboard and assign it to fields of the record.

Extend is the file mode used to create a new file or append records to the end of an existing file.

Appends the record to the end of the file.

Close the file.

End the program.

Reading a Record
from a Sequential File

A program can utilize information stored in a sequential file by reading data from the file into memory that is illustrated in the example on the next page.

The program must define the physical file in the Environment Division and associate the file name with a variable. The file must also be identified as a sequential file using the **ORGANIZATION** phrase.

The description of the file must define the record and each field in the Data Division of the program. The type and size of each field must correspond to the layout of records stored in the file, otherwise information will be misread from the file.

After the file is opened, information can be read from the file using the **READ** command. The **READ** command must be followed by the name of the file as defined in the file descriptor.

The next record in the file is assigned to the appropriate field name, then field names can be referenced by the program any time the program needs to access the value of the field. The example on the next page uses field names to display their values on the screen.

Each time the **READ** command is executed in the program, the next record in the field is assigned to field names overwriting the current values of the fields.

Data is only copied into memory whenever the **READ** command is executed by the program. The information remains unchanged in the file even if the program changes values of fields in memory.

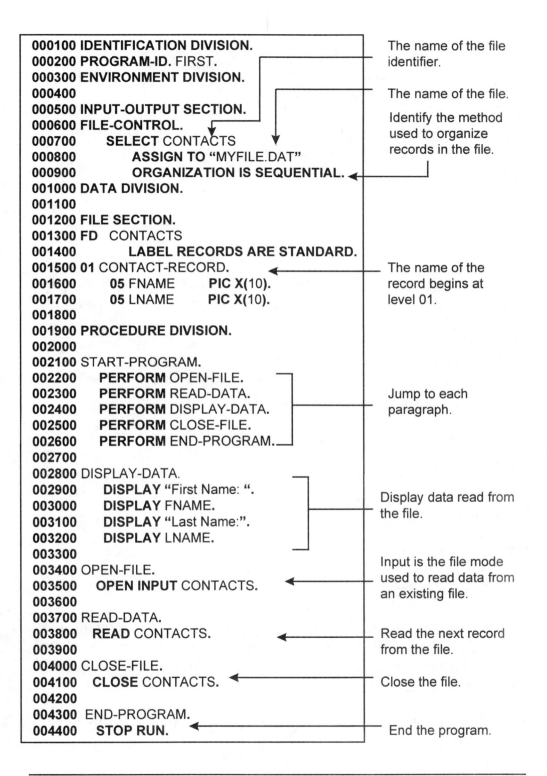

```
000100 IDENTIFICATION DIVISION.
000200 PROGRAM-ID. FIRST.
000300 ENVIRONMENT DIVISION.
000400
000500 INPUT-OUTPUT SECTION.
000600 FILE-CONTROL.
000700     SELECT CONTACTS
000800         ASSIGN TO "MYFILE.DAT"
000900         ORGANIZATION IS SEQUENTIAL.
001000 DATA DIVISION.
001100
001200 FILE SECTION.
001300 FD   CONTACTS
001400         LABEL RECORDS ARE STANDARD.
001500 01 CONTACT-RECORD.
001600     05 FNAME      PIC X(10).
001700     05 LNAME      PIC X(10).
001800
001900 PROCEDURE DIVISION.
002000
002100 START-PROGRAM.
002200     PERFORM OPEN-FILE.
002300     PERFORM READ-DATA.
002400     PERFORM DISPLAY-DATA.
002500     PERFORM CLOSE-FILE.
002600     PERFORM END-PROGRAM.
002700
002800 DISPLAY-DATA.
002900     DISPLAY "First Name: ".
003000     DISPLAY FNAME.
003100     DISPLAY "Last Name:".
003200     DISPLAY LNAME.
003300
003400 OPEN-FILE.
003500     OPEN INPUT CONTACTS.
003600
003700 READ-DATA.
003800     READ CONTACTS.
003900
004000 CLOSE-FILE.
004100     CLOSE CONTACTS.
004200
004300 END-PROGRAM.
004400     STOP RUN.
```

The name of the file identifier.

The name of the file.

Identify the method used to organize records in the file.

The name of the record begins at level 01.

Jump to each paragraph.

Display data read from the file.

Input is the file mode used to read data from an existing file.

Read the next record from the file.

Close the file.

End the program.

Rewriting a Record from a Sequential File

Records read from a sequential file can be modified by a program, then rewritten to the file overwriting the unmodified information by using the **REWRITE** command.

Information in a sequential file are accessed in the order in which records are written to the file. A program is unable to choose one record from any other within a sequential file.

This limitation plays an important role when rewriting information to a sequential file because the updated information must be rewritten to the same record in the file.

Many applications that rewrite a record in the sequential file do not move to another record between the time information is read from the file to the time data is rewritten to the file.

The example on the next page illustrates how to properly rewrite information to a record. Notice the application copies information from the file into fields. The value of the fields are modified by the program and the **REWRITE** command is used to write the record back to the file.

The **REWRITE** command uses the name of the record to copy information from fields in memory to the sequential file overwriting the existing data in the file.

Only information stored in the record is lost when replaced with updated information. All data in other records remain intact and untouched by the program until the next **READ** command is used to move to the next record in the file.

Make sure the record definition in the program matches the record layout of the file, otherwise data could be misread causing data to be lost.

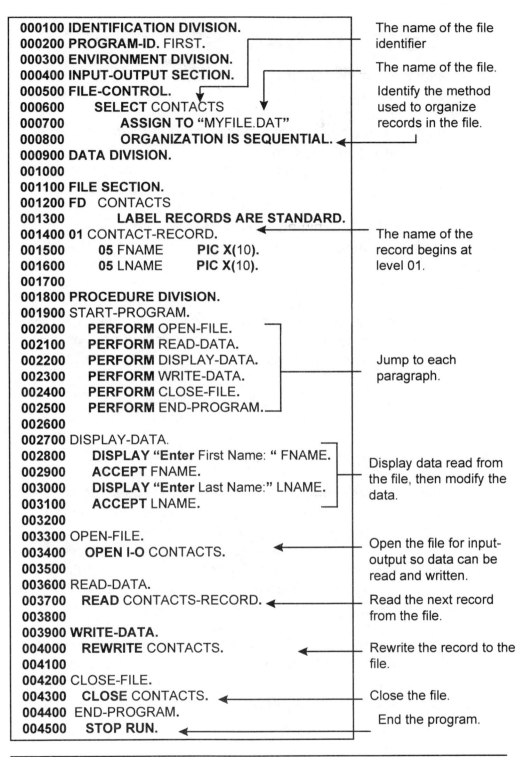

```
000100 IDENTIFICATION DIVISION.
000200 PROGRAM-ID. FIRST.
000300 ENVIRONMENT DIVISION.
000400 INPUT-OUTPUT SECTION.
000500 FILE-CONTROL.
000600     SELECT CONTACTS
000700         ASSIGN TO "MYFILE.DAT"
000800         ORGANIZATION IS SEQUENTIAL.
000900 DATA DIVISION.
001000
001100 FILE SECTION.
001200 FD   CONTACTS
001300         LABEL RECORDS ARE STANDARD.
001400 01 CONTACT-RECORD.
001500     05 FNAME     PIC X(10).
001600     05 LNAME     PIC X(10).
001700
001800 PROCEDURE DIVISION.
001900 START-PROGRAM.
002000     PERFORM OPEN-FILE.
002100     PERFORM READ-DATA.
002200     PERFORM DISPLAY-DATA.
002300     PERFORM WRITE-DATA.
002400     PERFORM CLOSE-FILE.
002500     PERFORM END-PROGRAM.
002600
002700 DISPLAY-DATA.
002800     DISPLAY "Enter First Name: " FNAME.
002900     ACCEPT FNAME.
003000     DISPLAY "Enter Last Name:" LNAME.
003100     ACCEPT LNAME.
003200
003300 OPEN-FILE.
003400     OPEN I-O CONTACTS.
003500
003600 READ-DATA.
003700     READ CONTACTS-RECORD.
003800
003900 WRITE-DATA.
004000     REWRITE CONTACTS.
004100
004200 CLOSE-FILE.
004300     CLOSE CONTACTS.
004400 END-PROGRAM.
004500     STOP RUN.
```

The name of the file identifier

The name of the file.

Identify the method used to organize records in the file.

The name of the record begins at level 01.

Jump to each paragraph.

Display data read from the file, then modify the data.

Open the file for input-output so data can be read and written.

Read the next record from the file.

Rewrite the record to the file.

Close the file.

End the program.

Looping through a File

Some application are designed to do the same thing to every record in a file such as printing payroll checks for all employees.

This requires the program to begin with the first record in the file, do something to the information, then move on to the next record. The program repeats the process until the program reaches the end of the file. This process is called *looping* through a file.

The example on the next page displays every record in the file by executing the **READ** command from within a loop. The loop is created when the **PERFORM** command calls the SHW-DAT paragraph.

The program defines the E-O-F variable in the Working-Storage section. This variable is used as a flag to indicate when the program reaches the end of the file.

The SHW-DAT paragraph is continually called by the **PERFORM** command until the value of the E-O-F variable is "EOF". The E-O-F variable is initialized with spaces that guarantee that the SHW-DAT paragraph will be called at least once.

The SHW-DAT contains a **READ** command that reads a record from the file. After reading the record, the program determines if the end of the file is encountered by using the **AT END** phrase.

The **AT END** phrase is followed by the command to execute if the program detects the end of the file. In this example, the string "EOF" is assigned to the E-O-F variable.

Control returns to the **PERFORM** SHW-DAT sentence that evaluates the value of the E-O-F variable. If the value is "EOF", then the program executes the next sentence that in the example on the next page closes the file, then ends the program.

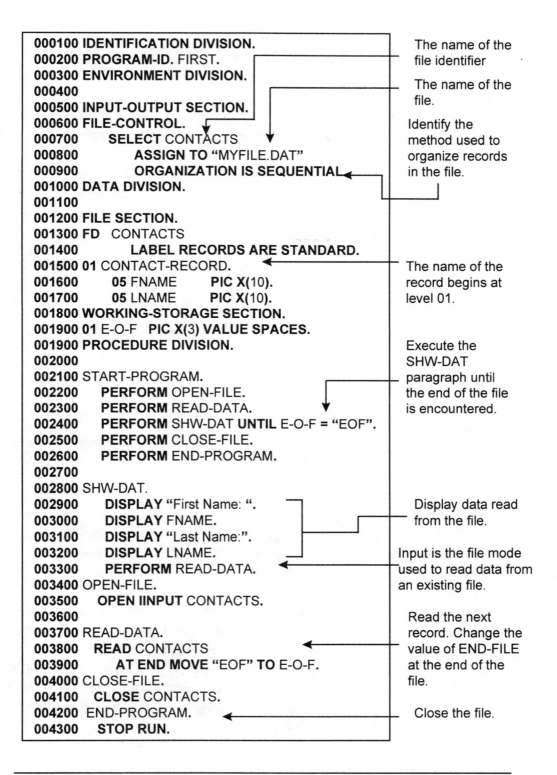

```
000100 IDENTIFICATION DIVISION.
000200 PROGRAM-ID. FIRST.
000300 ENVIRONMENT DIVISION.
000400
000500 INPUT-OUTPUT SECTION.
000600 FILE-CONTROL.
000700     SELECT CONTACTS
000800         ASSIGN TO "MYFILE.DAT"
000900         ORGANIZATION IS SEQUENTIAL
001000 DATA DIVISION.
001100
001200 FILE SECTION.
001300 FD   CONTACTS
001400         LABEL RECORDS ARE STANDARD.
001500 01 CONTACT-RECORD.
001600     05 FNAME     PIC X(10).
001700     05 LNAME     PIC X(10).
001800 WORKING-STORAGE SECTION.
001900 01 E-O-F   PIC X(3) VALUE SPACES.
001900 PROCEDURE DIVISION.
002000
002100 START-PROGRAM.
002200     PERFORM OPEN-FILE.
002300     PERFORM READ-DATA.
002400     PERFORM SHW-DAT UNTIL E-O-F = "EOF".
002500     PERFORM CLOSE-FILE.
002600     PERFORM END-PROGRAM.
002700
002800 SHW-DAT.
002900     DISPLAY "First Name: ".
003000     DISPLAY FNAME.
003100     DISPLAY "Last Name:".
003200     DISPLAY LNAME.
003300     PERFORM READ-DATA.
003400 OPEN-FILE.
003500     OPEN IINPUT CONTACTS.
003600
003700 READ-DATA.
003800   READ CONTACTS
003900       AT END MOVE "EOF" TO E-O-F.
004000 CLOSE-FILE.
004100   CLOSE CONTACTS.
004200 END-PROGRAM.
004300     STOP RUN.
```

The name of the file identifier

The name of the file.

Identify the method used to organize records in the file.

The name of the record begins at level 01.

Execute the SHW-DAT paragraph until the end of the file is encountered.

Display data read from the file.

Input is the file mode used to read data from an existing file.

Read the next record. Change the value of END-FILE at the end of the file.

Close the file.

Creating a Relative File

Information is stored in a file sequentially-that is the second record written to the file is placed behind the first record in the file. This is called a sequential file that is illustrated earlier in this chapter.

Records in a sequential file must be accessed sequentially. For example, if you want to find a record in the middle of the file, the program must read all the records prior to the middle before reading the record you need.

A *relative file* is one where each record is assigned a number called a record number. A *record number* identifies the position of the record within the file, so the first record in the file is assigned record number 1, the second record number 2, and so on.

The record number is used by the program to specify the record needed to be read into memory. This technique is illustrated later in this chapter.

A relative file is created by defining the physical file as relative, shown on the next page. The **SELECT** phrase is used to assign the file identifier variable the name of the physical file.

The **ORGANIZATION** phrase that tells the program how information is arranged in the file is defined as **RELATIVE**. The **ACCESS MODE** phrase describes how the program will access information stored in the file.

The **SEQUENTIAL** access mode is used in this example that enables the program to read and write records sequentially. The dynamic access mode is used to read and write records relatively. The file is opened as **EXTEND** that will create a new file when the **WRITE** command is used. Opening the file as **OUTPUT** also has the same effect. You'll see how to use the **DYNAMIC** access mode and write to the file later in this chapter.

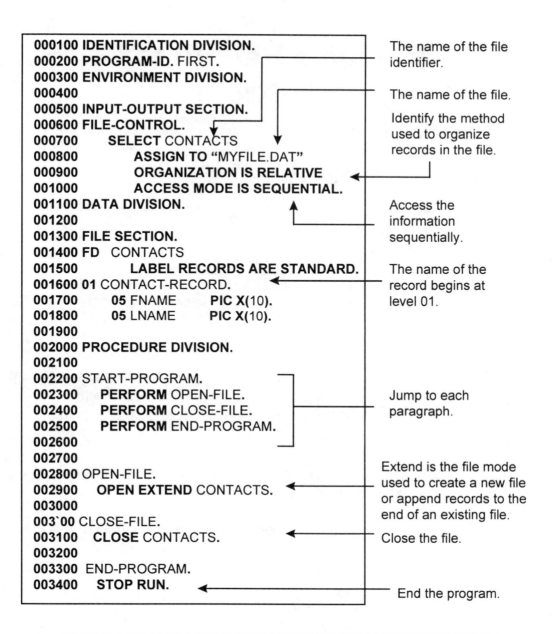

```
000100 IDENTIFICATION DIVISION.          The name of the file
000200 PROGRAM-ID. FIRST.                identifier.
000300 ENVIRONMENT DIVISION.
000400                                    The name of the file.
000500 INPUT-OUTPUT SECTION.
000600 FILE-CONTROL.                      Identify the method
000700     SELECT CONTACTS               used to organize
000800        ASSIGN TO "MYFILE.DAT"     records in the file.
000900        ORGANIZATION IS RELATIVE
001000        ACCESS MODE IS SEQUENTIAL.
001100 DATA DIVISION.                     Access the
001200                                    information
001300 FILE SECTION.                      sequentially.
001400 FD   CONTACTS
001500        LABEL RECORDS ARE STANDARD. The name of the
001600 01 CONTACT-RECORD.                 record begins at
001700     05 FNAME     PIC X(10).       level 01.
001800     05 LNAME     PIC X(10).
001900
002000 PROCEDURE DIVISION.
002100
002200 START-PROGRAM.
002300    PERFORM OPEN-FILE.
002400    PERFORM CLOSE-FILE.
002500    PERFORM END-PROGRAM.            Jump to each
002600                                    paragraph.
002700
002800 OPEN-FILE.                         Extend is the file mode
002900    OPEN EXTEND CONTACTS.           used to create a new file
003000                                    or append records to the
003`00 CLOSE-FILE.                        end of an existing file.
003100    CLOSE CONTACTS.                 Close the file.
003200
003300 END-PROGRAM.
003400    STOP RUN.                       End the program.
```

Facts You Should Know...

A relative file can be created using either the
SEQUENTIAL or the **DYNAMIC** access mode because all
records are written to the file sequentially.

Writing a Record to a Relative File

Information is written to a relative file by using the Write command as is shown on the next page. However, before executing the **WRITE** command, the program must define the relative file.

The physical file is defined in the Environment Division using the **SELECT** phrase. The **SELECT** phrase links the physical file name to the file identifier variable using the **ASSIGN** phrase.

The file must be identified as **RELATIVE** using the **ORGANIZATION** phrase. The **ACCESS MODE** is set to either **SEQUENTIAL** or **DYNAMIC** because records are always written sequentially to the file although the **ACCESS MODE** value is **DYNAMIC**.

The record layout of the file must be defined in the Data Division using the file identifier variable at the **FD** level to identify the file. The name of the record follows at the 01 level and field definitions are described at the 05 level.

The file is opened in the **EXTEND** mode. This will create a new file if one doesn't exist or append the record at the end of the file.

Be cautious if you chose to open the file in the **OUTPUT** mode because the new record will overwrite the existing file that is something you will probably want to avoid.

After assigning values to fields, the record is stored in the file by using the **WRITE** command. The **WRITE** command uses the name of the record to copy all the fields to the file.

Records written to the file are automatically assigned a record number that can be used to locate the record using the **READ** command.

The program closes before terminating.

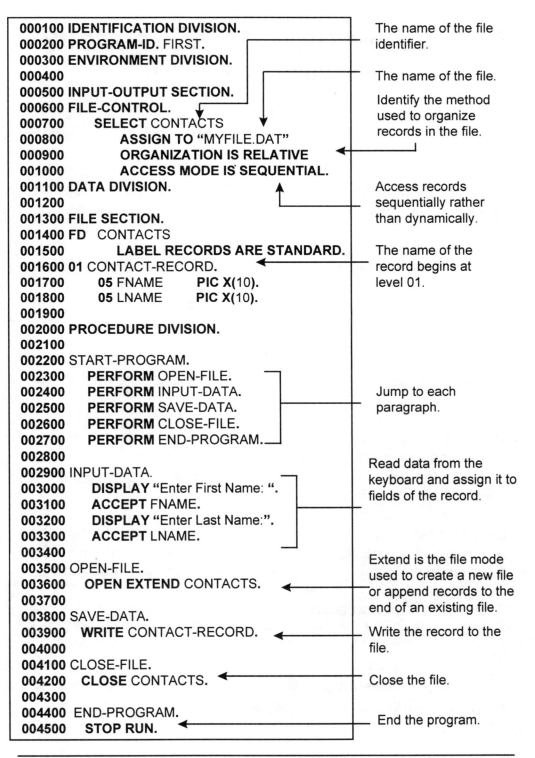

```
000100 IDENTIFICATION DIVISION.
000200 PROGRAM-ID. FIRST.
000300 ENVIRONMENT DIVISION.
000400
000500 INPUT-OUTPUT SECTION.
000600 FILE-CONTROL.
000700      SELECT CONTACTS
000800        ASSIGN TO "MYFILE.DAT"
000900        ORGANIZATION IS RELATIVE
001000        ACCESS MODE IS SEQUENTIAL.
001100 DATA DIVISION.
001200
001300 FILE SECTION.
001400 FD   CONTACTS
001500        LABEL RECORDS ARE STANDARD.
001600 01 CONTACT-RECORD.
001700      05 FNAME     PIC X(10).
001800      05 LNAME     PIC X(10).
001900
002000 PROCEDURE DIVISION.
002100
002200 START-PROGRAM.
002300    PERFORM OPEN-FILE.
002400    PERFORM INPUT-DATA.
002500    PERFORM SAVE-DATA.
002600    PERFORM CLOSE-FILE.
002700    PERFORM END-PROGRAM.
002800
002900 INPUT-DATA.
003000    DISPLAY "Enter First Name: ".
003100    ACCEPT FNAME.
003200    DISPLAY "Enter Last Name:".
003300    ACCEPT LNAME.
003400
003500 OPEN-FILE.
003600    OPEN EXTEND CONTACTS.
003700
003800 SAVE-DATA.
003900    WRITE CONTACT-RECORD.
004000
004100 CLOSE-FILE.
004200    CLOSE CONTACTS.
004300
004400 END-PROGRAM.
004500    STOP RUN.
```

The name of the file identifier.

The name of the file.

Identify the method used to organize records in the file.

Access records sequentially rather than dynamically.

The name of the record begins at level 01.

Jump to each paragraph.

Read data from the keyboard and assign it to fields of the record.

Extend is the file mode used to create a new file or append records to the end of an existing file.

Write the record to the file.

Close the file.

End the program.

Reading a Record Sequentially from a Relative File

Information stored in a relative file can be accessed either sequentially or relatively by specifying the number of the desired record.

You can read information sequentially from a relative file by defining the access mode as **SEQUENTIAL** using the **ACCESS MODE** phrase in the physical definition of the file.

Specifying the access mode as **SEQUENTIAL** prohibits the program from using record numbers to read records stored in the file. Instead, records must be read one after the other beginning with the first record in the file.

The record layout must be defined in the Data Division and list a description of fields in the file as shown in the example on the next page.

The file must be opened in either Input mode or the **I-O** mode. The **INPUT** mode enables information to be read from the file, but not written to the file. In contrast, the **I-O** mode enables the program to read and write data from and to the file.

Once the file is opened, the **READ** command is used to copy the next record from the file into memory. The **READ** command must be followed by the name of the record as defined in the file definition.

Each time the **READ** command is executed, the next record in the field is assigned to field names overwriting the current values of the fields.

The program automatically moves to the next record in the file following a **READ** command and stops when the end of the file is encountered.

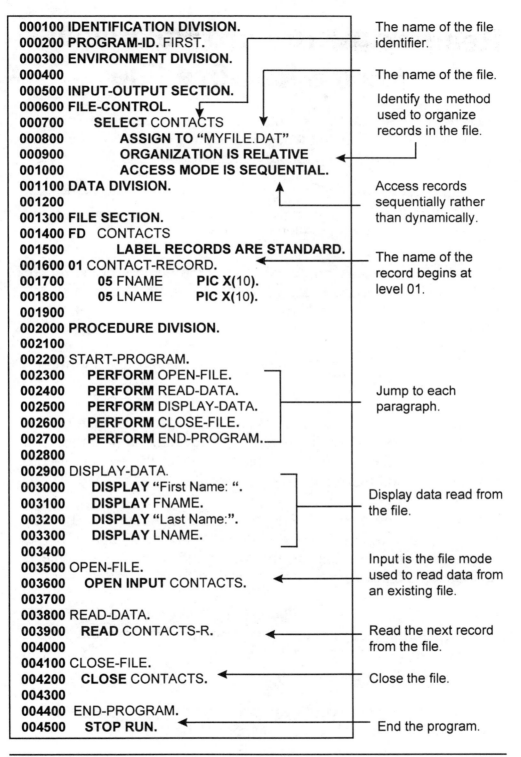

```
000100 IDENTIFICATION DIVISION.
000200 PROGRAM-ID. FIRST.
000300 ENVIRONMENT DIVISION.
000400
000500 INPUT-OUTPUT SECTION.
000600 FILE-CONTROL.
000700      SELECT CONTACTS
000800          ASSIGN TO "MYFILE.DAT"
000900          ORGANIZATION IS RELATIVE
001000          ACCESS MODE IS SEQUENTIAL.
001100 DATA DIVISION.
001200
001300 FILE SECTION.
001400 FD   CONTACTS
001500          LABEL RECORDS ARE STANDARD.
001600 01 CONTACT-RECORD.
001700      05 FNAME      PIC X(10).
001800      05 LNAME      PIC X(10).
001900
002000 PROCEDURE DIVISION.
002100
002200 START-PROGRAM.
002300      PERFORM OPEN-FILE.
002400      PERFORM READ-DATA.
002500      PERFORM DISPLAY-DATA.
002600      PERFORM CLOSE-FILE.
002700      PERFORM END-PROGRAM.
002800
002900 DISPLAY-DATA.
003000      DISPLAY "First Name: ".
003100      DISPLAY FNAME.
003200      DISPLAY "Last Name:".
003300      DISPLAY LNAME.
003400
003500 OPEN-FILE.
003600    OPEN INPUT CONTACTS.
003700
003800 READ-DATA.
003900    READ CONTACTS-R.
004000
004100 CLOSE-FILE.
004200    CLOSE CONTACTS.
004300
004400 END-PROGRAM.
004500    STOP RUN.
```

The name of the file identifier.

The name of the file.

Identify the method used to organize records in the file.

Access records sequentially rather than dynamically.

The name of the record begins at level 01.

Jump to each paragraph.

Display data read from the file.

Input is the file mode used to read data from an existing file.

Read the next record from the file.

Close the file.

End the program.

Reading a Record Relatively from a Relative File

Records in a relative file are numbered based upon the record's position in the file. The first record is assigned record number 1, the second record is assigned record number 2, and so forth.

Previously in this chapter, you learned how to read records from a relative file by accessing the file in the SEQUENTIAL mode without regards to the record number.

Records can be accessed by referring to the number of the record by defining the access mode as DYNAMIC in the definition of the physical file.

The DYNAMIC access mode enables the program to move the file pointer within the file. A *file pointer* is like a finger pointing to one record in the file.

The READ command copies the record pointed to by the file pointer into memory, then moves the file pointer down to the next record in the file. For example, the file pointer moves to the second record when the second READ command is executed.

The program can move the file pointer to any record in the file by specifying the record number in the READ command. This is illustrated in the example on the next page. Notice a variable is defined to hold the desired record number.

Once the file pointer is repositioned in the file, the READ command is executed that copies the data from the file into the record specified in the READ command. The file pointer is moved automatically to the next record.

A drawback in using record numbers to locate data in the file is that the programmer must know the number of the desired record.

```
000100 IDENTIFICATION DIVISION.
000200 PROGRAM-ID. FIRST.
000300 ENVIRONMENT DIVISION.
000400 INPUT-OUTPUT SECTION.
000500 FILE-CONTROL.
000600      SELECT CONTACTS
000700         ASSIGN TO "MYFILE.DAT"
000800         ORGANIZATION IS RELATIVE
000900         ACCESS MODE IS DYNAMIC
001000             RELATIVE KEY IS REC-NUM.
001100 DATA DIVISION.
001200 FILE SECTION.
001300 FD   CONTACTS
001400        LABEL RECORDS ARE STANDARD.
00150001 C-R.
001600      05 FNAME      PIC X(10).
001700      05 LNAME      PIC X(10).
001800 WORKING-STORAGE SECTION.
001900 01 E-O-F  PIC X(3) VALUE SPACES.
002000 77 REC-NUM PIC 9(4) VALUE IS 5.
002100 PROCEDURE DIVISION.
002200 START-PROGRAM.
002300      PERFORM OPEN-FILE.
002400      PERFORM READ-DATA.
002500      PERFORM DISPLAY-DATA.
002600      PERFORM CLOSE-FILE.
002700      PERFORM END-PROGRAM.
002800
002900 OPEN-FILE.
003000    OPEN INPUT CONTACTS.
003100
003200 READ-DATA.
003300    PERFORM UNTIL UNTIL E-O-F = "EOF"
003400       READ CONTACTS
003500       INVALID KEY MOVE "EOF" TO E-O-F.
003600       NOT INVALID KEY PERFORM  DISPLAY C-R.
003700       END-READ
003800    END-PERFORM.
003900
004000 CLOSE-FILE.
004100    CLOSE CONTACTS.
004200 END-PROGRAM.
004300    STOP RUN.
```

The name of the file identifier.

The name of the file.

The method used to organize records.

Access records dynamically.

Identify the key field.

The name of the record begins at level 01.

Define a variable to hold the record number.

Jump to each paragraph.

Continue to execute commands within the PERFORM loop until the end of the file is reached.

Find and read the fifth record.

Signal the end of the file if record is not found.

Display the record if the record is found.

Close the file.

End the program.

Rewriting a Record to a Relative File

An application can overwrite any record in a file by using the **REWRITE** command. The **REWRITE** command copies the value of the fields in memory to the file overwriting the current -record.

Typically, the application will read a record from a file, then modify the record in memory before rewriting the record to the file as is illustrated in the example on the next page.

The access mode for the file can be defined as either **SEQUENTIAL** or **DYNAMIC** since the file pointer will not move between the time the record is copied into memory and the time the record is rewritten to the file.

However, if the program moves the pointer using the **MOVE** command, then be sure the program repositions the file pointer to the appropriate record before rewriting the record to the file. Data could be lost if the file pointer isn't pointed to the correct record in the file.

The **REWRITE** command requires the name of the record as shown on the next page. After the **REWRITE** command is executed, the revised information remains in memory until the next **READ** command is executed.

It is critical that the logical definition of the file corresponds to the record layout of the file, otherwise values in the file could be split and assigned to more than one field.

For example, if the record reserves 5 characters for the first name and the program defines the first name as 10 characters, then the field in the program will contain the value of the first name plus the first five characters of the next field.

COBOL Programmer's Notebook

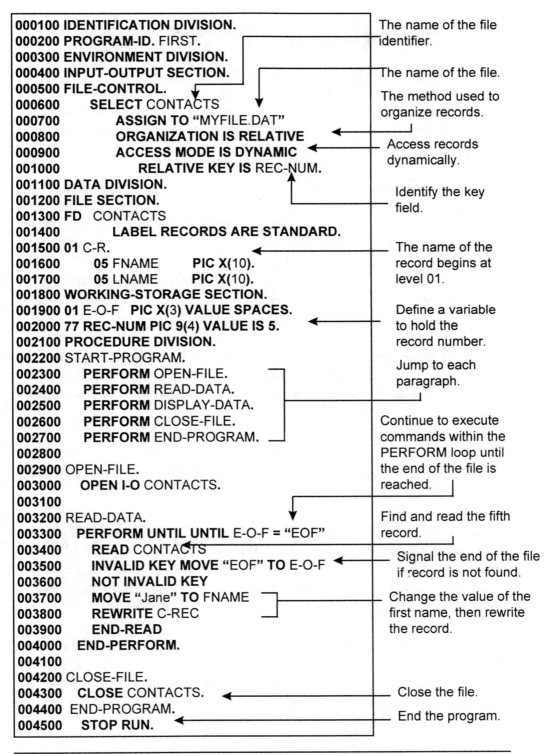

```
000100 IDENTIFICATION DIVISION.
000200 PROGRAM-ID. FIRST.
000300 ENVIRONMENT DIVISION.
000400 INPUT-OUTPUT SECTION.
000500 FILE-CONTROL.
000600     SELECT CONTACTS
000700         ASSIGN TO "MYFILE.DAT"
000800         ORGANIZATION IS RELATIVE
000900         ACCESS MODE IS DYNAMIC
001000             RELATIVE KEY IS REC-NUM.
001100 DATA DIVISION.
001200 FILE SECTION.
001300 FD   CONTACTS
001400         LABEL RECORDS ARE STANDARD.
001500 01 C-R.
001600     05 FNAME      PIC X(10).
001700     05 LNAME      PIC X(10).
001800 WORKING-STORAGE SECTION.
001900 01 E-O-F   PIC X(3) VALUE SPACES.
002000 77 REC-NUM PIC 9(4) VALUE IS 5.
002100 PROCEDURE DIVISION.
002200 START-PROGRAM.
002300     PERFORM OPEN-FILE.
002400     PERFORM READ-DATA.
002500     PERFORM DISPLAY-DATA.
002600     PERFORM CLOSE-FILE.
002700     PERFORM END-PROGRAM.
002800
002900 OPEN-FILE.
003000     OPEN I-O CONTACTS.
003100
003200 READ-DATA.
003300     PERFORM UNTIL UNTIL E-O-F = "EOF"
003400         READ CONTACTS
003500         INVALID KEY MOVE "EOF" TO E-O-F
003600         NOT INVALID KEY
003700         MOVE "Jane" TO FNAME
003800         REWRITE C-REC
003900         END-READ
004000     END-PERFORM.
004100
004200 CLOSE-FILE.
004300     CLOSE CONTACTS.
004400 END-PROGRAM.
004500     STOP RUN.
```

Annotations (right column):

- The name of the file identifier.
- The name of the file.
- The method used to organize records.
- Access records dynamically.
- Identify the key field.
- The name of the record begins at level 01.
- Define a variable to hold the record number.
- Jump to each paragraph.
- Continue to execute commands within the PERFORM loop until the end of the file is reached.
- Find and read the fifth record.
- Signal the end of the file if record is not found.
- Change the value of the first name, then rewrite the record.
- Close the file.
- End the program.

Deleting a Record from a Relative File

Records stored in a relative file can be deleted from the file by using the **DELETE** command as is illustrated in the example on the next page.

An application should locate the record to be deleted by using the record number, then display all or some of the information contained in the record and prompt the user to confirm that the record should be deleted.

The **DELETE** command must specify the name of the record to be deleted. Only the current record is removed from the relative file. The remaining records in the file remain unchanged.

Notice in the example on the next page that the **DELETE** command is executed after the program determines if the record number was found by using the **NOT INVALID KEY** phrase as part of the **READ** command.

Avoid using the **DELETE** command outside of a condition statement. A condition statement determines if a condition is true before executing one or more sentences.

In this example, the key must not be invalid. In other words, the requested record number was found in the file. You could also delete a record based on a value of a field. In this case, the **DELETE** command would be entered within an IF statement block that is executed after the record number is found in the file.

Once a record is deleted, the information is lost. The data is purged from the file and cannot be recovered. It is always wise to make regular backups of files so information can be recovered if data is accidentally deleted from a file.

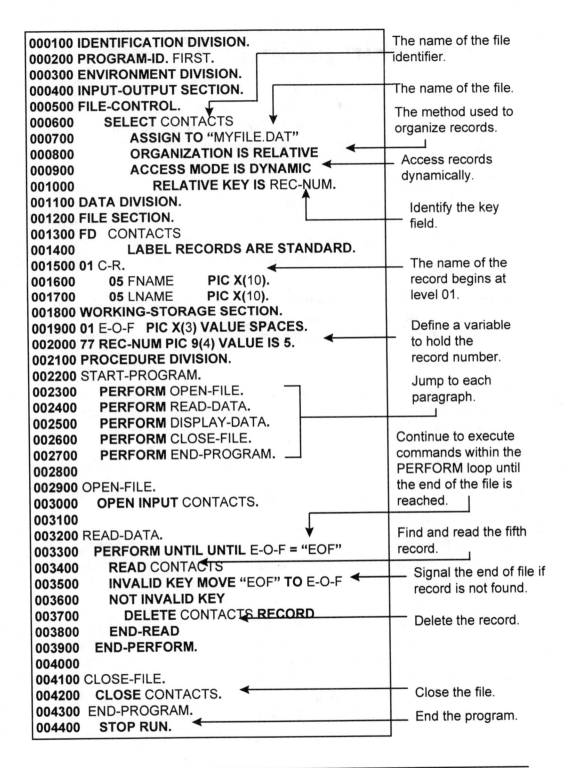

```
000100 IDENTIFICATION DIVISION.
000200 PROGRAM-ID. FIRST.
000300 ENVIRONMENT DIVISION.
000400 INPUT-OUTPUT SECTION.
000500 FILE-CONTROL.
000600     SELECT CONTACTS
000700         ASSIGN TO "MYFILE.DAT"
000800         ORGANIZATION IS RELATIVE
000900         ACCESS MODE IS DYNAMIC
001000             RELATIVE KEY IS REC-NUM.
001100 DATA DIVISION.
001200 FILE SECTION.
001300 FD   CONTACTS
001400         LABEL RECORDS ARE STANDARD.
001500 01 C-R.
001600     05 FNAME      PIC X(10).
001700     05 LNAME      PIC X(10).
001800 WORKING-STORAGE SECTION.
001900 01 E-O-F   PIC X(3) VALUE SPACES.
002000 77 REC-NUM PIC 9(4) VALUE IS 5.
002100 PROCEDURE DIVISION.
002200 START-PROGRAM.
002300     PERFORM OPEN-FILE.
002400     PERFORM READ-DATA.
002500     PERFORM DISPLAY-DATA.
002600     PERFORM CLOSE-FILE.
002700     PERFORM END-PROGRAM.
002800
002900 OPEN-FILE.
003000     OPEN INPUT CONTACTS.
003100
003200 READ-DATA.
003300     PERFORM UNTIL UNTIL E-O-F = "EOF"
003400     READ CONTACTS
003500     INVALID KEY MOVE "EOF" TO E-O-F
003600     NOT INVALID KEY
003700         DELETE CONTACTS RECORD
003800     END-READ
003900     END-PERFORM.
004000
004100 CLOSE-FILE.
004200     CLOSE CONTACTS.
004300 END-PROGRAM.
004400     STOP RUN.
```

The name of the file identifier.

The name of the file.

The method used to organize records.

Access records dynamically.

Identify the key field.

The name of the record begins at level 01.

Define a variable to hold the record number.

Jump to each paragraph.

Continue to execute commands within the PERFORM loop until the end of the file is reached.

Find and read the fifth record.

Signal the end of file if record is not found.

Delete the record.

Close the file.

End the program.

Creating an Indexed File

An *indexed file* is similar to a sequential file except an index is used to locate records in the file. An *index* is similar to an index of a book where key words in the form of a key field are stored in the index along with the position of the corresponding record in the file.

The *key field* is the field within the record used to identify the record. This is typically a unique identifier such as an employee number. A key field is required for every indexed file. This field is also called the *primary key* field. There can be other key fields to the file called *alternate keys* that are discussed later in this chapter.

A file is defined as an indexed file as part of the definition of the physical file that is illustrated on the next page. The definition is contained in the File Control paragraph of the Input-Output section in the Environment Division.

The **SELECT** command identifies the variable assigned the file name of the physical file with the **ASSIGN** phrase. The organization of the file is set as **INDEXED**.

The key field of the file is identified by using the field name in the **RECORD KEY** phrase. This is the field whose value will be searched each time you want to locate a record within the file.

The last line of the physical file definition identifies the manner in which the program will access data in the file. This is called the *access mode* and is set by using the **ACCESS MODE** phrase.

There are three types of access modes. These are **SEQUENTIAL**, **RANDOM**, and **DYNAMIC**. The **SEQUENTIAL** access mode enables the program to access data sequentially in the file although the file is an indexed file. Records will be read one after the other without regards to the index. The **RANDOM** access mode uses the key to locate data. The **DYNAMIC** access mode enables the program to use either method when reading records in the file.

Associate the actual file with the file identifier.

Identify how to access the file.

```
000100 IDENTIFICATION DIVISION.
000200 PROGRAM-ID. FIRST.
000300 ENVIRONMENT DIVISION.
000400
000500 INPUT-OUTPUT SECTION.
000600 FILE-CONTROL.
000700      SELECT CONTACTS
000800          ASSIGN TO "MYFILE.DAT"
000900          ORGANIZATION IS INDEXED
001000          RECORD KEY IS ID-NUM
001100          ACCESS MODE IS DYNAMIC.
001200 DATA DIVISION.
001300
001400 FILE SECTION.
001500 FD   CONTACTS
001600          LABEL RECORDS ARE STANDARD.
001700 01 CONTACT-RECORD.
001800      05 FNAME      PIC X(10).
001900      05 LNAME      PIC X(10).
002000      05 STREET     PIC X(30).
002100      05 CITY       PIC X(30).
002200      05 STATE      PIC X(2).
002300      05 ZIP        PIC X(10).
002400      05 ID-NUM     PIC X(10).
002500
002600 WORKING-STORAGE SECTION.
002700
002800 PROCEDURE DIVISION.
002900
003000  STOP RUN.
```

The name of the file identifier.

The name of the file.

Identify the method used to organize records in the file.

The file descriptor must appear in Area A.

Fields within the record are defined similar to the way variables are defined.

Identify the primary key field used to look up records.

The name of the record begins at level 01.

Facts You Should Know...

The **ACCESS MODE** phrase is used to define how the program is going to access data in the file. There are three access modes: **SEQUENTIAL**, **RANDOM**, and **DYNAMIC**. **SEQUENTIAL** is the default and specified records will be read one after the other. **RANDOM** specified records will be accessed by using a key. **DYNAMIC** allows access both ways and is therefore the choice of many programmers.

Adding Records
to an Indexed File

A file is designed as an indexed file within the physical definition of the file as shown on the next page. The **ORGANIZATION** phrase is set to Indexed and the **RECORD KEY** phrase identifies the key field.

The logical layout of the file must be defined in the File Section of the Data Division. This is where the variable assigned the physical file name is associated with a record layout.

The record layout is defined using the same method as a data structure is defined (Chapter 3). The record is assigned a name at level 01 followed by field definitions on level 05. The field definition must also include the definition of the key field.

It is typical that an application is organized into paragraphs with each paragraph performing a specific function.

Each paragraph is called at the appropriate time in the program by using the **PERFORM** command. This enables the application reuse the same block of code any number of times without having to duplicate code.

Before a record can be added to an indexed file, the file must be opened and data stored into the fields. In this example, the program receives data from the keyboard, but values could also be assigned to fields using the **MOVE** command.

Notice that the file is opened in the **EXTEND** mode that appends the new record at the end of the file. If the file doesn't exist, the program creates a new file.

The **WRITE** command is used with the name of the record to copy values from the fields to the file. The index is automatically updated.

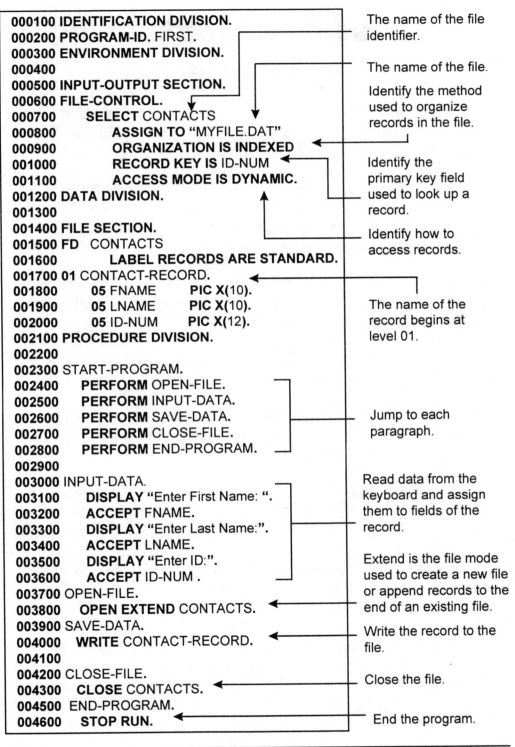

```
000100 IDENTIFICATION DIVISION.
000200 PROGRAM-ID. FIRST.
000300 ENVIRONMENT DIVISION.
000400
000500 INPUT-OUTPUT SECTION.
000600 FILE-CONTROL.
000700     SELECT CONTACTS
000800         ASSIGN TO "MYFILE.DAT"
000900         ORGANIZATION IS INDEXED
001000         RECORD KEY IS ID-NUM
001100         ACCESS MODE IS DYNAMIC.
001200 DATA DIVISION.
001300
001400 FILE SECTION.
001500 FD   CONTACTS
001600         LABEL RECORDS ARE STANDARD.
001700 01 CONTACT-RECORD.
001800     05 FNAME      PIC X(10).
001900     05 LNAME      PIC X(10).
002000     05 ID-NUM     PIC X(12).
002100 PROCEDURE DIVISION.
002200
002300 START-PROGRAM.
002400     PERFORM OPEN-FILE.
002500     PERFORM INPUT-DATA.
002600     PERFORM SAVE-DATA.
002700     PERFORM CLOSE-FILE.
002800     PERFORM END-PROGRAM.
002900
003000 INPUT-DATA.
003100     DISPLAY "Enter First Name: ".
003200     ACCEPT FNAME.
003300     DISPLAY "Enter Last Name:".
003400     ACCEPT LNAME.
003500     DISPLAY "Enter ID:".
003600     ACCEPT ID-NUM .
003700 OPEN-FILE.
003800     OPEN EXTEND CONTACTS.
003900 SAVE-DATA.
004000     WRITE CONTACT-RECORD.
004100
004200 CLOSE-FILE.
004300     CLOSE CONTACTS.
004500 END-PROGRAM.
004600     STOP RUN.
```

Callouts (right column):

- The name of the file identifier.
- The name of the file.
- Identify the method used to organize records in the file.
- Identify the primary key field used to look up a record.
- Identify how to access records.
- The name of the record begins at level 01.
- Jump to each paragraph.
- Read data from the keyboard and assign them to fields of the record.
- Extend is the file mode used to create a new file or append records to the end of an existing file.
- Write the record to the file.
- Close the file.
- End the program.

Reading Records Using an Indexed File

The program must create a physical and logical definition of an indexed file before attempting to access records in the file. This is illustrated in the example on the next page.

Records are located in an indexed file by having the program match a search criteria with values in the key field. For example, the program on the next page reads an ID-NUM from the keyboard and assigns the value to the key field.

Notice the file is opened in the **INPUT** mode. The **INPUT** mode gives the program read-access to the file. The program cannot write to the file, unless the file is opened using the **EXTEND** mode, **OUTPUT** mode, or the **I-O** mode. The **EXTEND** mode and the **OUTPUT** mode prevent the program from reading information in the file. The **I-O** mode enables the program to write or read data.

The **READ** command is used to copy a record from the file into memory. Values are copied into the record that is identified by a name in the **READ** command.

The **KEY IS** phrase identifies the name of the key field and the association of the field within the record. In this example, the ID-NUM field is designed as the key field containing the search criteria.

The program begins searching the index for the search criteria. The **INVALID KEY** phrase is used to determine if the search criteria is found in the index.

The application must determine what to do if the record is found and if the record is not found. The **INVALID KEY** phrase is executed if there isn't a match and the **NOT INVALID KEY** phrase is executed if there is a match. Code beneath these phrases will be executed if the corresponding condition is met.

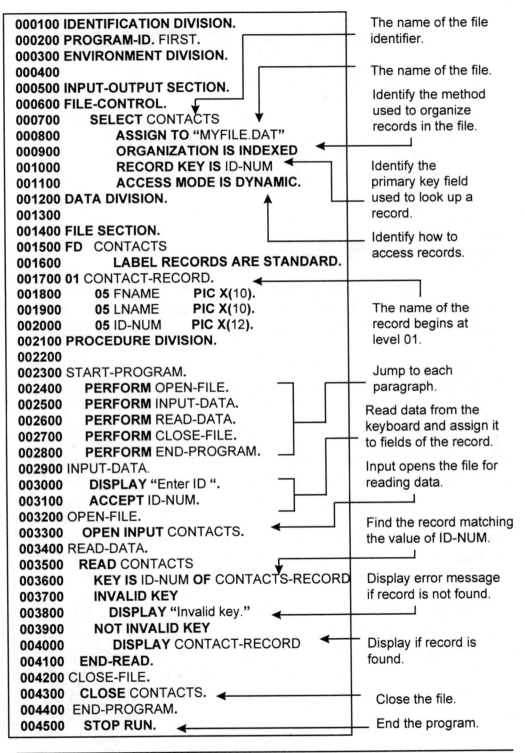

```
000100 IDENTIFICATION DIVISION.
000200 PROGRAM-ID. FIRST.
000300 ENVIRONMENT DIVISION.
000400
000500 INPUT-OUTPUT SECTION.
000600 FILE-CONTROL.
000700     SELECT CONTACTS
000800         ASSIGN TO "MYFILE.DAT"
000900         ORGANIZATION IS INDEXED
001000         RECORD KEY IS ID-NUM
001100         ACCESS MODE IS DYNAMIC.
001200 DATA DIVISION.
001300
001400 FILE SECTION.
001500 FD   CONTACTS
001600         LABEL RECORDS ARE STANDARD.
001700 01 CONTACT-RECORD.
001800     05 FNAME      PIC X(10).
001900     05 LNAME      PIC X(10).
002000     05 ID-NUM     PIC X(12).
002100 PROCEDURE DIVISION.
002200
002300 START-PROGRAM.
002400     PERFORM OPEN-FILE.
002500     PERFORM INPUT-DATA.
002600     PERFORM READ-DATA.
002700     PERFORM CLOSE-FILE.
002800     PERFORM END-PROGRAM.
002900 INPUT-DATA.
003000     DISPLAY "Enter ID ".
003100     ACCEPT ID-NUM.
003200 OPEN-FILE.
003300     OPEN INPUT CONTACTS.
003400 READ-DATA.
003500     READ CONTACTS
003600         KEY IS ID-NUM OF CONTACTS-RECORD
003700     INVALID KEY
003800         DISPLAY "Invalid key."
003900     NOT INVALID KEY
004000         DISPLAY CONTACT-RECORD
004100     END-READ.
004200 CLOSE-FILE.
004300     CLOSE CONTACTS.
004400 END-PROGRAM.
004500     STOP RUN.
```

The name of the file identifier.

The name of the file.

Identify the method used to organize records in the file.

Identify the primary key field used to look up a record.

Identify how to access records.

The name of the record begins at level 01.

Jump to each paragraph.

Read data from the keyboard and assign it to fields of the record.

Input opens the file for reading data.

Find the record matching the value of ID-NUM.

Display error message if record is not found.

Display if record is found.

Close the file.

End the program.

Rewriting Records
in an Indexed File

A record can be read from the file into memory, modified, then rewritten to an indexed file by using the **REWRITE** command. The **REWRITE** command must specify the name of the modified record as shown in the example on the next page.

The physical definition of the file must identify the name of the key used to locate information in the file. The ID-NUM variable is used for this purpose in this sample program.

The file must be opened in the I-O mode that enables the program to read and write data from and to the file. Opening the file in any other mode prevents rewriting data efficiently.

Before executing the **READ** command, the search value must be assigned to the key variable. In this example, the search value is entered into the keyboard and assigned to the ID-NUM value.

The **READ** command begins the search by specifying the name of the record. The program determines if the record is found or not by using the **INVALID KEY** phrase and the **NOT INVALID KEY** phrase.

The **INVALID KEY** phrase identifies sentences that are to be executed if the search criteria isn't found. In contracts, the **NOT INVALID KEY** phrase identifies sentences to be executed if the record is found.

Typically, a message is displayed telling the user the information isn't on file. Once the record is found, new values can be assigned to fields, then the **REWRITE** command is executed copying the copy of the record in memory to the file in the same position in the file as the old record.

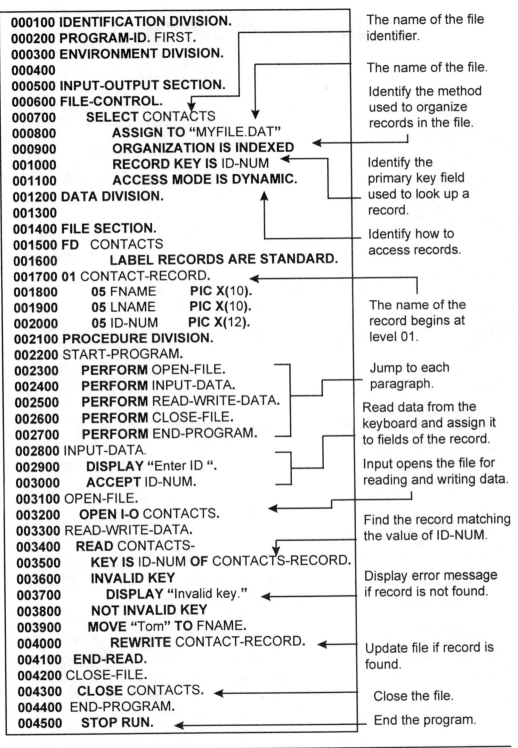

```
000100 IDENTIFICATION DIVISION.
000200 PROGRAM-ID. FIRST.
000300 ENVIRONMENT DIVISION.
000400
000500 INPUT-OUTPUT SECTION.
000600 FILE-CONTROL.
000700     SELECT CONTACTS
000800         ASSIGN TO "MYFILE.DAT"
000900         ORGANIZATION IS INDEXED
001000         RECORD KEY IS ID-NUM
001100         ACCESS MODE IS DYNAMIC.
001200 DATA DIVISION.
001300
001400 FILE SECTION.
001500 FD   CONTACTS
001600         LABEL RECORDS ARE STANDARD.
001700 01 CONTACT-RECORD.
001800     05 FNAME      PIC X(10).
001900     05 LNAME      PIC X(10).
002000     05 ID-NUM     PIC X(12).
002100 PROCEDURE DIVISION.
002200 START-PROGRAM.
002300     PERFORM OPEN-FILE.
002400     PERFORM INPUT-DATA.
002500     PERFORM READ-WRITE-DATA.
002600     PERFORM CLOSE-FILE.
002700     PERFORM END-PROGRAM.
002800 INPUT-DATA.
002900     DISPLAY "Enter ID ".
003000     ACCEPT ID-NUM.
003100 OPEN-FILE.
003200     OPEN I-O CONTACTS.
003300 READ-WRITE-DATA.
003400     READ CONTACTS-
003500     KEY IS ID-NUM OF CONTACTS-RECORD.
003600     INVALID KEY
003700         DISPLAY "Invalid key."
003800     NOT INVALID KEY
003900     MOVE "Tom" TO FNAME.
004000         REWRITE CONTACT-RECORD.
004100   END-READ.
004200 CLOSE-FILE.
004300     CLOSE CONTACTS.
004400 END-PROGRAM.
004500     STOP RUN.
```

The name of the file identifier.

The name of the file.

Identify the method used to organize records in the file.

Identify the primary key field used to look up a record.

Identify how to access records.

The name of the record begins at level 01.

Jump to each paragraph.

Read data from the keyboard and assign it to fields of the record.

Input opens the file for reading and writing data.

Find the record matching the value of ID-NUM.

Display error message if record is not found.

Update file if record is found.

Close the file.

End the program.

Deleting Records in an Indexed File

Records are deleted from an indexed file by using the **DELETE** command followed by the name of the record as shown in the example on the next page.

Before executing the **DELETE** command, the program should first locate the record to be deleted by using the key value and the **READ** command.

The user is prompted to enter a search criteria at the keyboard. The **READ** command attempts to locate the record in the file. An error message is displayed if the record cannot be found.

If the record is found, the application should display all or part of the record on the screen and require that the user confirm this is the record that should be deleted. This isn't shown in the example on the next page due to space limitations.

The **DELETE** command should only be executed after the user confirms that the record should be deleted. Data is lost once the **DELETE** command is executed and can only be recovered if the file was backed up prior to executing the **DELETE** command.

An application can delete records without prompting the user to enter a search criteria or to confirm deleting the record. However, the search criteria must be identified within the program by using either a list of search criteria written into the program or read from another file.

Let's say the employee status file contains employee IDs and employment status and the application is required to delete records in the payroll file of all those employees who have "terminated" as their employment status. The application read the employee status file to identify employee IDs for deletion from the payroll file.

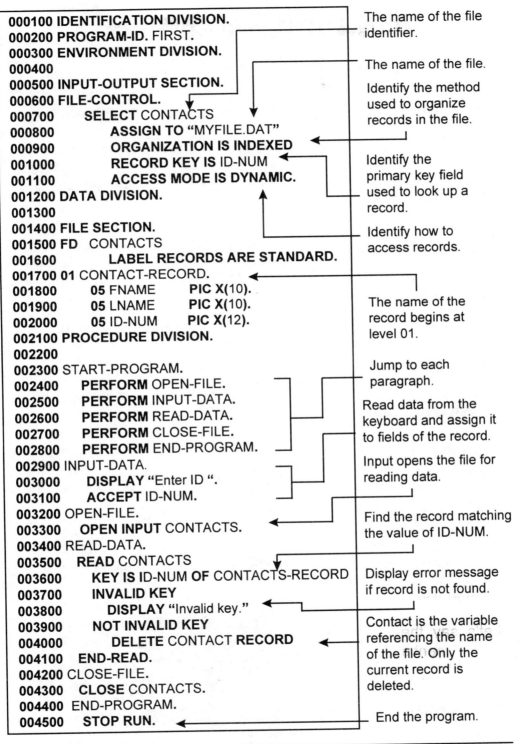

```
000100 IDENTIFICATION DIVISION.
000200 PROGRAM-ID. FIRST.
000300 ENVIRONMENT DIVISION.
000400
000500 INPUT-OUTPUT SECTION.
000600 FILE-CONTROL.
000700     SELECT CONTACTS
000800         ASSIGN TO "MYFILE.DAT"
000900         ORGANIZATION IS INDEXED
001000         RECORD KEY IS ID-NUM
001100         ACCESS MODE IS DYNAMIC.
001200 DATA DIVISION.
001300
001400 FILE SECTION.
001500 FD   CONTACTS
001600         LABEL RECORDS ARE STANDARD.
001700 01 CONTACT-RECORD.
001800     05 FNAME      PIC X(10).
001900     05 LNAME      PIC X(10).
002000     05 ID-NUM     PIC X(12).
002100 PROCEDURE DIVISION.
002200
002300 START-PROGRAM.
002400     PERFORM OPEN-FILE.
002500     PERFORM INPUT-DATA.
002600     PERFORM READ-DATA.
002700     PERFORM CLOSE-FILE.
002800     PERFORM END-PROGRAM.
002900 INPUT-DATA.
003000     DISPLAY "Enter ID ".
003100     ACCEPT ID-NUM.
003200 OPEN-FILE.
003300     OPEN INPUT CONTACTS.
003400 READ-DATA.
003500   READ CONTACTS
003600     KEY IS ID-NUM OF CONTACTS-RECORD
003700     INVALID KEY
003800       DISPLAY "Invalid key."
003900     NOT INVALID KEY
004000         DELETE CONTACT RECORD
004100   END-READ.
004200 CLOSE-FILE.
004300   CLOSE CONTACTS.
004400 END-PROGRAM.
004500     STOP RUN.
```

The name of the file identifier.

The name of the file.

Identify the method used to organize records in the file.

Identify the primary key field used to look up a record.

Identify how to access records.

The name of the record begins at level 01.

Jump to each paragraph.

Read data from the keyboard and assign it to fields of the record.

Input opens the file for reading data.

Find the record matching the value of ID-NUM.

Display error message if record is not found.

Contact is the variable referencing the name of the file. Only the current record is deleted.

End the program.

Using Alternate Keys

Information in a file can be accessed by reading each record sequentially, by selecting records by record number as in a relative file, or matching the value of the primary key as in an indexed file.

The primary key is a value of a field in an indexed file that uniquely identifies the record such as an employee identification number. However, an indexed file can have more than one key that is called an alternate key.

An alternate key is identified in the physical definition of the file by using the **ALTERNATE KEY** phrase as shown in the example on the next page. The **ALTERNATE KEY** phrase is followed by the field used to create the alternate key.

A variable is defined to contain the search value that is used by the **READ** command to locate the record in the file. If the key is not found, then the sentence following the **INVALID KEY** phrase is executed, otherwise the sentence following the **NOT INVALID KEY** phrase is executed.

Once the record is found, the application can display information in the record using the **DISPLAY** command, change information in the record using the **MOVE** or **ACCEPT** commands, and rewrite the modified record to the file using the **REWRITE** command.

An application can search for a record using either the primary key or an alternate key by specifying the key when executing the **READ** command.

An alternate key can have duplicate values by using the **WITH DUPLICATES** following the name of the alternate key in the Select statement. However, only the first record containing duplicate keys is accessed when using the **READ** command.

ALTERNATE KEY IS ZIP **WITH DUPLICATES**.

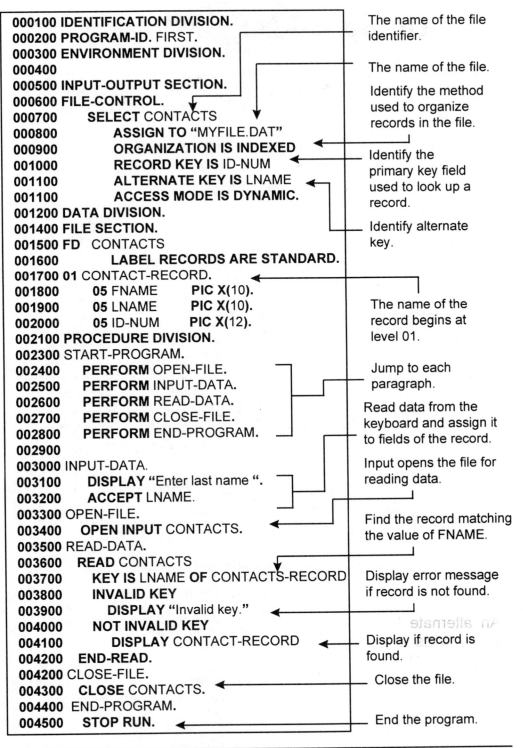

```
000100 IDENTIFICATION DIVISION.
000200 PROGRAM-ID. FIRST.
000300 ENVIRONMENT DIVISION.
000400
000500 INPUT-OUTPUT SECTION.
000600 FILE-CONTROL.
000700     SELECT CONTACTS
000800        ASSIGN TO "MYFILE.DAT"
000900        ORGANIZATION IS INDEXED
001000        RECORD KEY IS ID-NUM
001100        ALTERNATE KEY IS LNAME
001100        ACCESS MODE IS DYNAMIC.
001200 DATA DIVISION.
001400 FILE SECTION.
001500 FD   CONTACTS
001600        LABEL RECORDS ARE STANDARD.
001700 01 CONTACT-RECORD.
001800     05 FNAME     PIC X(10).
001900     05 LNAME     PIC X(10).
002000     05 ID-NUM    PIC X(12).
002100 PROCEDURE DIVISION.
002300 START-PROGRAM.
002400     PERFORM OPEN-FILE.
002500     PERFORM INPUT-DATA.
002600     PERFORM READ-DATA.
002700     PERFORM CLOSE-FILE.
002800     PERFORM END-PROGRAM.
002900
003000 INPUT-DATA.
003100     DISPLAY "Enter last name ".
003200     ACCEPT LNAME.
003300 OPEN-FILE.
003400     OPEN INPUT CONTACTS.
003500 READ-DATA.
003600     READ CONTACTS
003700        KEY IS LNAME OF CONTACTS-RECORD
003800        INVALID KEY
003900          DISPLAY "Invalid key."
004000        NOT INVALID KEY
004100          DISPLAY CONTACT-RECORD
004200     END-READ.
004200 CLOSE-FILE.
004300     CLOSE CONTACTS.
004400 END-PROGRAM.
004500     STOP RUN.
```

The name of the file identifier.

The name of the file.

Identify the method used to organize records in the file.

Identify the primary key field used to look up a record.

Identify alternate key.

The name of the record begins at level 01.

Jump to each paragraph.

Read data from the keyboard and assign it to fields of the record.

Input opens the file for reading data.

Find the record matching the value of FNAME.

Display error message if record is not found.

Display if record is found.

Close the file.

End the program.

Working with
File Errors

- SELECT OPTIONAL
- Sequential I-O File Status
- Relative I-O File Status
- Indexed I-O File Status
- Trapping the File Status

SELECT OPTIONAL

In the example applications shown in Chapter 8, an assumption was made that the file existed whenever an attempt was made to open a file using the **OPEN** command.

This assumption may not be valid and could lead to an application to stop running whenever it cannot find a file. Unfortunately, such an error happens when the application is running rather than when the application is compiled.

Errors occurring when a program is running are called run-time errors and can happen at any time including when the programmer is not available to fix the problem.

Errors occurring when a program is compiled are called compiler errors that always happen when the programmer is available to correct the error.

The availability of a file to an application might be critical to the success of the application such as a program that writes payroll checks.

However, rarely would a programmer want the application to stop running. Instead, the programmer is likely to have the application detect the error, then prompt the user to rectify the problem.

For example, the application could display a message telling the user to load the file on the disk, then press a character on the keyboard when the file is loaded.

The application must be told not to stop the application if a file can't be found by using the **OPTIONAL** phrase following the **SELECT** command when the physical file is defined. This technique is illustrated in the example on the next page. Instead of stopping the application, the **OPEN** command returns an end-of-file status if the file is unavailable.

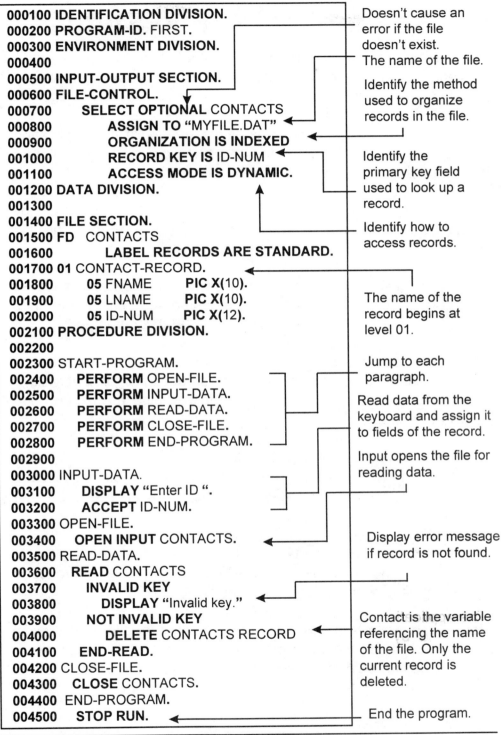

```
000100 IDENTIFICATION DIVISION.
000200 PROGRAM-ID. FIRST.
000300 ENVIRONMENT DIVISION.
000400
000500 INPUT-OUTPUT SECTION.
000600 FILE-CONTROL.
000700      SELECT OPTIONAL CONTACTS
000800          ASSIGN TO "MYFILE.DAT"
000900          ORGANIZATION IS INDEXED
001000          RECORD KEY IS ID-NUM
001100          ACCESS MODE IS DYNAMIC.
001200 DATA DIVISION.
001300
001400 FILE SECTION.
001500 FD   CONTACTS
001600          LABEL RECORDS ARE STANDARD.
001700 01 CONTACT-RECORD.
001800      05 FNAME       PIC X(10).
001900      05 LNAME       PIC X(10).
002000      05 ID-NUM      PIC X(12).
002100 PROCEDURE DIVISION.
002200
002300 START-PROGRAM.
002400      PERFORM OPEN-FILE.
002500      PERFORM INPUT-DATA.
002600      PERFORM READ-DATA.
002700      PERFORM CLOSE-FILE.
002800      PERFORM END-PROGRAM.
002900
003000 INPUT-DATA.
003100      DISPLAY "Enter ID ".
003200      ACCEPT ID-NUM.
003300 OPEN-FILE.
003400      OPEN INPUT CONTACTS.
003500 READ-DATA.
003600      READ CONTACTS
003700      INVALID KEY
003800          DISPLAY "Invalid key."
003900      NOT INVALID KEY
004000          DELETE CONTACTS RECORD
004100      END-READ.
004200 CLOSE-FILE.
004300      CLOSE CONTACTS.
004400 END-PROGRAM.
004500      STOP RUN.
```

Doesn't cause an error if the file doesn't exist.

The name of the file.

Identify the method used to organize records in the file.

Identify the primary key field used to look up a record.

Identify how to access records.

The name of the record begins at level 01.

Jump to each paragraph.

Read data from the keyboard and assign it to fields of the record.

Input opens the file for reading data.

Display error message if record is not found.

Contact is the variable referencing the name of the file. Only the current record is deleted.

End the program.

Sequential I-O File Status

We assumed in examples in Chapter 8 that all the files existed and all file commands functioned flawlessly. As you've seen previously in this chapter, both assumptions can be wrong.

You can tell the application to continue running if the application cannot locate a file by using the **OPTIONAL** phrase in the **SELECT** command as shown previously in this chapter.

You can also determine if a file command executed successfully by having the application examine the return code from the file command.

A return code is a two-digit value that corresponds to the success or failure of the execution of a file command. File commands include **OPEN**, **CLOSE**, **READ**, **WRITE**, and **REWRITE** commands.

The return code is assigned to a variable that can be evaluated by the application to determine if an error occurred or if it was a successful operation. You'll see how to examine the return code later in this chapter.

A successful execution returns a 00 value for the return code. Any other value indicates the operation failed for some reason. A return code value greater than 00 means that trouble was detected by the file command.

There can be many kinds of problems encountered by a file command using a sequential file. The value of the return code corresponds to a particular error.

For example, a return code value of 10 means the file doesn't exist or the end of the file was encountered. A complete list of return code values for sequential files is shown on the next page.

Error	Error Description
00	Operation was successful.
04	Incorrect record size was copied from the file by **READ**.
05	File doesn't exist.
07	Tape drive option was specified, but file was on a disk. Just a warning. The operation was successful.
10	Could not read from the file because the file didn't exist or the end of the file was encountered.
30	Unknown file error. File could not be accessed probably because of a problem with the operating system.
34	An attempt was made to write beyond the end of the file.
35	An attempt was made to open a file that doesn't exist.
37	The file can't be opened in **EXTEND**, **OUTPUT**, or **I-O** mode probably because of security restriction on the file.
38	The file couldn't be opened because the file is locked.
39	The file doesn't match the attributes defined in the program.
41	An attempt was made to open a file that is already opened.
42	An attempt was made to close a file that wasn't opened.
43	An attempt was made to rewrite a record that wasn't first read from the file.
44	An attempt was made to rewrite a record that is larger or smaller than the record on the file.
46	An attempt was made to read a record after a read failure.
47	An attempt was made to read from a file that was opened as **OUTPUT** or **EXTEND**.
48	An attempt was made to write to a file that was opened for reading.
49	An attempt was made to rewrite a record to a file that was not opened in **I-O** mode.

Relative I-O File Status

A relative file is one where records are stored sequentially in the file; however, each record is identified by a record number. The record number corresponds to the position of the record in the file.

An application can locate a record in a relative file by reading each record sequentially or by searching for a specific record number. These techniques were illustrated in Chapter 8.

Each time an attempt is made to access a record in a relative file, the attempt could fail. This could happen for many reasons such as when the application tries to locate a record that doesn't exist in the file.

The only way an application knows if an error has occurred is by examining the value of the return code of the file command. A return code is a two-digit value assigned by the file command to a variable designated by the programmer.

The value of the return code corresponds to the success or failure of the file command. A return code value of 00 means the operation was successful. A value greater than 00 indicates trouble. The file command detected an error.

There are many errors that can be uncovered by a file command. Each error is assigned a specific error code. A complete list of these codes for a relative file is shown on the next page.

Your application should evaluate the value of the return code after each execution of a file command to determine if the command executed properly. You'll see how to examine the value of the return code later in this chapter.

Typically, an application that encounters a file error will attempt to take corrective action if possible rather than stopping it altogether. However, some errors cannot be corrected by the application as you'll see when reviewing the errors on the next page.

Error	Error Description
00	Operation was successful.
04	Incorrect record size was copied from the file by READ.
05	File doesn't exist.
10	Could not read from the file because the file didn't exist or the end of the file was encountered.
14	An attempt was made to sequentially read a file, but the key defined in the program iwas too small. Try adding an additional digit to the definition.
22	An attempt was made to write a record that would have duplicated a key value.
23	An attempt was made to read a record that doesn't exist.
24	An attempt was made to write a record beyond the size of the file.
30	Unknown file error. File could not be accessed probably because of a problem with the operating system.
34	An attempt was made to write beyond the end of the file.
35	An attempt was made to open a file that doesn't exist.
37	The file can't be opened in EXTEND, OUTPUT, or I-O mode probably because of security restriction on the file.
38	The file couldn't be opened because the file was locked.
39	The file doesn't match the attributes defined in the program.
41	An attempt was made to open a file that was opened.
42	An attempt was made to close a file that wasn't opened.
43	An attempt was made to rewrite a record that wasn't first read from the file.
44	An attempt was made to write a record that is larger or smaller than the record on the file.
46	An attempt was made to read a record after a read failure.
47	An attempt was made to read from a file that was opened as OUTPUT or EXTEND.
48	An attempt was made to write to a file that was opened for reading.
49	An attempt was made to rewrite a record to a file that was not opened in I-O mode.

Indexed I-O File Status

An indexed file uses an index to locate records in the file quickly. As you'll recall from Chapter 8, an index is like an index to a book and contains key words of each record along with the number of the record.

Records are located in an indexed file by the application specifying a key value that is similar to the words in an index of a book. An employee identification number is a typical key value of records in an employee file.

Each time an application accesses an indexed file, the application should examine the value of the return code supplied by a file command. File commands are **OPEN**, **CLOSE**, **READ**, **WRITE**, and **REWRITE** commands.

The two-digit value of the return code determines the success or failure of the file command. The value is assigned by the file command to a variable defined by the programmer. You'll see how this is done later in this chapter.

Each value returned by the file command corresponds to a successful execution that has the value 00 or one of several errors. Each error is assigned its own error code.

The next page contains the possible return values for an indexed file. Your application should be able to react to all these errors. Some errors can be rectified by requesting assistance from the user such as when the file can't be found.

Other errors such as an unknown file error requires the application to display a message informing the user of a problem, then stopping the application. It is the responsibility of the user to track down and fix the error.

You can intuitively distinguish between errors your application can fix and those left to the user to resolve.

Error	Error Description
00	Operation was successful.
02	A duplicate key value was added to an alternate key.
04	Incorrect record size was copied from the file by READ.
05	File doesn't exist.
10	Could not read from the file because the file didn't exist or the end of the file was encountered.
21	An attempt was made to change the value of a primary key.
22	An attempt was made to write a record that would have duplicated a key value.
23	An attempt was made to read a record that doesn't exist.
24	An attempt was made to write a record beyond the size of the file.
30	Unknown file error. File could not be accessed probably because of a problem with the operating system.
35	An attempt was made to open a file that doesn't exist.
37	The file can't be opened in EXTEND, OUTPUT, or I-O mode probably because of security restriction on the file.
38	The file couldn't be opened because the file is locked.
39	The file doesn't match the attributes defined in the program.
41	An attempt was made to open a file that is already opened.
42	An attempt was made to close a file that wasn't opened.
43	An attempt was made to rewrite a record that wasn't first read from the file.
44	An attempt was made to write a record that is larger or smaller than the record on the file.
46	An attempt was made to read a record after a read failure.
47	An attempt was made to read from a file that was opened as OUTPUT or EXTEND.
48	An attempt was made to write to a file that was opened for reading.
49	An attempt was made to rewrite a record to a file that was not opened in I-O mode.

Trapping the File Status

There are three steps required for an application to trap and evaluate the value of return codes from a file command. The first step is to identify the variable to use to store the return code value.

The variable is identified in the physical definition of the file by using the **FILE STATUS IS** phrase as shown on the next page. The **FILE STATUS IS** phrase is followed by the name of the variable used to store the return code.

The next step is for the application to define the variable. Typically, the variable is defined in the Working-Storage **Section** at level 77. The variable must be a two-digit numeric variable.

The final step is to create a routine that evaluates the value of the variable each time a file command is executed.

The example on the next page examines the value of the FSTAT variable after an attempt is made to open the CONTACTS file. The IF statement determines if the value of the variable is not 00 that means the **OPEN** command had problems executing.

Sentences within the IF statement block display the value of the **FSTAT** variable then end the application. The user is expected to compare the error code against the list of errors.

Typically, an application will call another paragraph when an error is detected rather than displaying the error code on the screen. The paragraph should contain sentences to appropriately handle all possible errors that could be encountered by the application.

It is important for an application to immediately evaluate the value of the return code following the execution of a file command. The program should not continue on the normal flow if any error is detected.

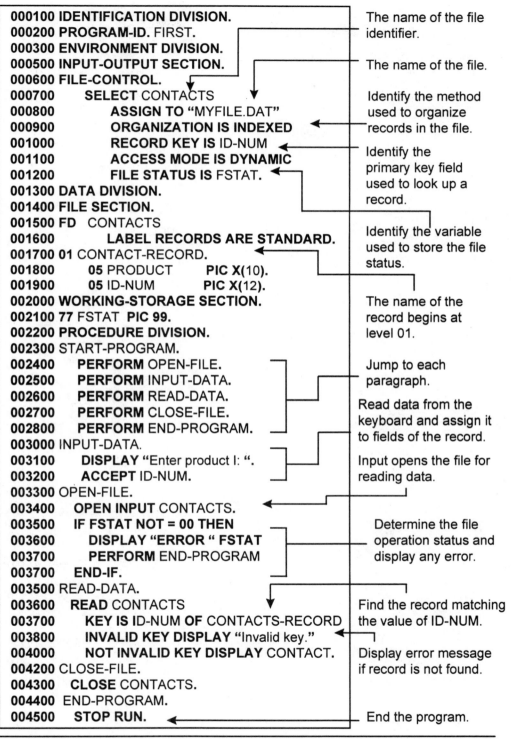

```
000100 IDENTIFICATION DIVISION.                    The name of the file
000200 PROGRAM-ID. FIRST.                          identifier.
000300 ENVIRONMENT DIVISION.
000500 INPUT-OUTPUT SECTION.                        The name of the file.
000600 FILE-CONTROL.
000700      SELECT CONTACTS                         Identify the method
000800          ASSIGN TO "MYFILE.DAT"              used to organize
000900          ORGANIZATION IS INDEXED             records in the file.
001000          RECORD KEY IS ID-NUM
001100          ACCESS MODE IS DYNAMIC              Identify the
001200          FILE STATUS IS FSTAT.               primary key field
001300 DATA DIVISION.                               used to look up a
001400 FILE SECTION.                                record.
001500 FD  CONTACTS
001600          LABEL RECORDS ARE STANDARD.         Identify the variable
001700 01 CONTACT-RECORD.                           used to store the file
001800     05 PRODUCT     PIC X(10).                status.
001900     05 ID-NUM      PIC X(12).
002000 WORKING-STORAGE SECTION.                     The name of the
002100 77 FSTAT  PIC 99.                            record begins at
002200 PROCEDURE DIVISION.                          level 01.
002300 START-PROGRAM.
002400     PERFORM OPEN-FILE.                       Jump to each
002500     PERFORM INPUT-DATA.                      paragraph.
002600     PERFORM READ-DATA.
002700     PERFORM CLOSE-FILE.                      Read data from the
002800     PERFORM END-PROGRAM.                     keyboard and assign it
003000 INPUT-DATA.                                  to fields of the record.
003100     DISPLAY "Enter product I: ".
003200     ACCEPT ID-NUM.                           Input opens the file for
003300 OPEN-FILE.                                   reading data.
003400     OPEN INPUT CONTACTS.
003500     IF FSTAT NOT = 00 THEN                   Determine the file
003600       DISPLAY "ERROR " FSTAT                 operation status and
003700       PERFORM END-PROGRAM                    display any error.
003700     END-IF.
003500 READ-DATA.
003600     READ CONTACTS                            Find the record matching
003700       KEY IS ID-NUM OF CONTACTS-RECORD       the value of ID-NUM.
003800       INVALID KEY DISPLAY "Invalid key."
004000       NOT INVALID KEY DISPLAY CONTACT.       Display error message
004200 CLOSE-FILE.                                  if record is not found.
004300     CLOSE CONTACTS.
004400 END-PROGRAM.
004500     STOP RUN.                                End the program.
```

Working with
Sorting and Merging

- Creating a Sort Definition
- Sort into Another File
- Changing the Order of the Sort
- Upper- and Lowercase Sorts
- Sorting Duplicates
- Sorting a File to a Procedure
- Sorting a Procedure to a File
- Sorting a Procedure to a Procedure
- Merging Files
- Changing the Order of the Merge
- Upper- and Lowercase Merge
- Merging Duplicates
- Merge a File to a Procedure

Creating a Sort Definition

Data is grouped together into records in a file. A *record* is a group of related data such as a person's name and address. Records are stored sequentially in a file where the first record entered into the file is followed by the second record, and so on.

An application typically requires records to be placed in a different order called a sort order. Records can be sorted by using the SORT command.

The SORT command rearranges records in a file based on fields identified in the SORT command. For example, records can be sorted by the last name field in a record.

There are five components of the SORT command. These are the name of the work file, the source file, the destination file, the field used to sort the record, and the direction of the sort.

The *work file* is an intermediate file used by the SORT command to temporarily store records during the sort operation. The source file is the file containing the unsorted records. The destination file is the file that will contain the sorted records.

The field used for the sort is called the *key to the sort*. Don't confuse the sort key with the key to the file. They can be different or the same field.

The direction of the sort determines whether the first record in the sorted file starts with A or Z or in the case of a numeric field, the lowest or highest number.

As you'll see later in this chapter, data can be sorted to and from a file or a procedure. Data in a procedure is stored in memory.

```
000100 IDENTIFICATION DIVISION.
000200 PROGRAM-ID. FIRST.
000300 ENVIRONMENT DIVISION.
000400
000500 INPUT-OUTPUT SECTION.
000600 FILE-CONTROL.
000700     SELECT WORK-FILE
000800         ASSIGN TO "TMP.DAT".
000900     SELECT EMP
001000         ASSIGN TO "MYFILE.DAT".
001100     SELECT SORT-EMP
001200         ASSIGN TO "SORTFILE.DAT".
001300 DATA DIVISION.
001400
001500 FILE SECTION.
001600 SD WORK-FILE
001700     LABEL RECORDS ARE STANDARD.
001800 01 EMP-WK.
001900     05 FNAME      PIC X(10).
002000     05 LNAME      PIC X(10).
002100     05 ID-NUM     PIC X(2).
002200 FD EMP
002300     LABEL RECORDS ARE STANDARD.
002400 01 EMP-INPUT.
002500     05 FNAME      PIC X(10).
002600     05 LNAME      PIC X(10).
002700     05 ID-NUM     PIC X(2).
002800 FD SORT-EMP
002900     LABEL RECORDS ARE STANDARD.
003000 01 EMP-OUTPUT.
003100     05 FNAME      PIC X(10).
003200     05 LNAME      PIC X(10).
003300     05 ID-NUM     PIC X(2).
003400 PROCEDURE DIVISION.
003500
003600 START-PROGRAM.
003700     SORT WORK-FILE
003800     ON ASCENDING KEY ID-NUM OF EMP-WK
003900     USING EMP
004000     GIVING SORT-EMP.
004100 END-PROGRAM.
004200     STOP RUN.
```

Identify the work file used to sort records.

Identify the file containing the unsorted data.

Identify the file where the sorted data will be written.

Define the sort work file using the special SD level.

Sort records in the workfile.

Sort by the value of the ID-NUM field.

Sort into Another File

The contents of a file can be sorted with the results stored in another field by defining the files in the File-Control paragraph of the Input-Output Section of the Environment Division.

Three files must be defined. The first is the work file that is the temporary file used to store records. The second file is the source file which contains the unsorted record. The third file is the destination file which will contain the sorted records.

All three files are linked to a file identifier variable using the **SELECT** command as is illustrated in the example on the next page. The file identifier variable is used in the **SORT** command whenever it is necessary to reference the file.

Reference to the work file is made following the **SORT** command. The sort key is specified using the **ON** phrase. In the example on the opposite page, the ID-NUM file of the EMP-WK file that is a reference to the work file that is used to sort records.

The **USING** phrase identifies the source file to use in the sort and the **GIVING** phrase references the destination file.

The records used in all three files are defined in the Data Division. Notice that the **SD** special level is used to define the work file. This is called the sort descriptor. The source and destination files are defined at the **FD** special level called the file descriptor.

The layout of all files must be the same. There can be more than one key used in the sort. Enter the keys in the **ON** phrase separating each with a space.

The left-most key is the primary sort. Let's say last name and first name are two keys used for the sort. Records will be sorted by last name, then within last name sorted by first name.

```
000100 IDENTIFICATION DIVISION.
000200 PROGRAM-ID. FIRST.
000300 ENVIRONMENT DIVISION.
000400
000500 INPUT-OUTPUT SECTION.
000600 FILE-CONTROL.
000700      SELECT WORK-FILE
000800          ASSIGN TO "TMP.DAT".
000900      SELECT EMP
001000          ASSIGN TO "MYFILE.DAT".
001100      SELECT SORT-EMP
001200          ASSIGN TO "SORTFILE.DAT".
001300 DATA DIVISION.
001400
001500 FILE SECTION.
001600 SD WORK-FILE
001700      LABEL RECORDS ARE STANDARD.
001800 01 EMP-WK.
001900      05 FNAME      PIC X(10).
002000      05 LNAME      PIC X(10).
002100      05 ID-NUM     PIC X(2).
002200 FD EMP
002300      LABEL RECORDS ARE STANDARD.
002400 01 EMP-INPUT.
002500      05 FNAME      PIC X(10).
002600      05 LNAME      PIC X(10).
002700      05 ID-NUM     PIC X(2).
002800 FD SORT-EMP
002900      LABEL RECORDS ARE STANDARD.
003000 01 EMP-OUTPUT.
003100      05 FNAME      PIC X(10).
003200      05 LNAME      PIC X(10).
003300      05 ID-NUM     PIC X(2).
003400 PROCEDURE DIVISION.
003500
003600 START-PROGRAM.
003700      SORT WORK-FILE
003800      ON ASCENDING KEY ID-NUM OF EMP-WK
003900      USING EMP
004000      GIVING SORT-EMP.
004100 END-PROGRAM.
004200      STOP RUN.
```

Identify the work file used to sort records.

Identify the file containing the unsorted data.

Identify the file where the sorted data will be written.

Define the sort work file using the special SD level.

Define the file containing the data to be sorted.

Define the file used to store the sorted data.

Sort records in the workfile.

Sort by the value of the ID-NUM field.

The file containing the records to be sorted.

The file where the sorted records will be stored.

Changing the Order of the Sort

Records are stored sequentially in a file regardless of whether a file is a relative file or an indexed file. The first record entered into the file is the first record stored and the pattern continues throughout the file.

In a relative file, records are accessed by record number that is the position number assigned to the record based upon the record's location in the file.

An application can access and display records in numerical order based on the value of the record number that is the same as if the application read records sequentially in the file. This is not sorting the file.

In an indexed file, records are accessed by a key field. There needs to be at least one key field called the primary key, but an indexed file can have several alternate keys. Keys are stored in sorted order.

However, the **SORT** command is the only way to display records in numeric or alphabetical order. You've seen previously in this chapter how to use the **SORT** command to change the order of the file.

By default all records are sorted in ascending order. You can reverse the sort by specifying **DESCENDING** in the **ON** phrase of the **SORT** command. This is illustrated in the example on the opposite page.

The direction of the sort only affects the records in the destination file. Records in the source file remain unchanged. Records in the work file are also in sorted order; however, the application won't directly access the work file, so the direction of the sort in the work file is irrelevant to the application.

```
000100 IDENTIFICATION DIVISION.
000200 PROGRAM-ID. FIRST.
000300 ENVIRONMENT DIVISION.
000400
000500 INPUT-OUTPUT SECTION.
000600 FILE-CONTROL.
000700     SELECT WORK-FILE
000800         ASSIGN TO "TMP.DAT".
000900     SELECT EMP
001000         ASSIGN TO "MYFILE.DAT".
001100     SELECT SORT-EMP
001200         ASSIGN TO "SORTFILE.DAT".
001300 DATA DIVISION.
001400
001500 FILE SECTION.
001600 SD WORK-FILE
001700     LABEL RECORDS ARE STANDARD.
001800 01 EMP-WK.
001900     05 FNAME      PIC X(10).
002000     05 LNAME      PIC X(10).
002100     05 ID-NUM     PIC X(2).
002200 FD EMP
002300     LABEL RECORDS ARE STANDARD.
002400 01 EMP-INPUT.
002500     05 FNAME      PIC X(10).
002600     05 LNAME      PIC X(10).
002700     05 ID-NUM     PIC X(2).
002800 FD SORT-EMP
002900     LABEL RECORDS ARE STANDARD.
003000 01 EMP-OUTPUT.
003100     05 FNAME      PIC X(10).
003200     05 LNAME      PIC X(10).
003300     05 ID-NUM     PIC X(2).
003400 PROCEDURE DIVISION.
003500
003600 START-PROGRAM.
003700     SORT WORK-FILE
003800     ON DESCENDING KEY ID-NUM OF EMP-WK
003900     USING EMP
004000     GIVING SORT-EMP.
004100 END-PROGRAM.
004200     STOP RUN.
```

Identify the work file used to sort records.

Identify the file containing the unsorted data.

Identify the file where the sorted data will be written.

Define the sort work file using the special SD level.

Define the file containing the data to be sorted.

Define the file used to store the sorted data.

Sort records in the workfile.

Sort by the value of the ID-NUM field in descending order.

The file containing the records to be sorted.

The file where the sorted records will be stored.

Upper- and Lowercase Sorts

Programmers are occasionally disappointed by the results of sorting records with keys containing uppercase and lowercase letters because the uppercase letters are above the lowercase letter in the destination file as illustrated below.

Bob
Jones
bob

At first glance it appears the SORT command failed to work properly, but that's not the case. The information was sorted properly, although the order is not what most of us would expect.

The problem rest with the way computers recognize characters. A character is represented by a numeric value based on either the ASCII code or the EBCDIC code.

Uppercase characters are assigned values from 65 through 90. For example, value 65 is the character A and the value 90 is the character Z.

Lowercase characters are assigned values greater than 90 such as the value 97 is the character a and the value 122 is the character z. The SORT command sorts records based on the numeric value. Therefore, uppercase Z comes before lowercase A.

You can fix this problem by defining a new alphabet in the Special-Names paragraph of the Configuration Section in the Environment Division as shown on the next page.

Define the alphabet using the **ALPHABET** phrase by placing lowercase letters alongside their corresponding uppercase letters. The **SORT** command then uses the new alphabet that properly sorts records.

```
000100 IDENTIFICATION DIVISION.
000200 PROGRAM-ID. FIRST.
000300 ENVIRONMENT DIVISION.
000400 CONFIGURATION SECTION.
000500 SPECIAL-NAMES.
000600 ALPHABET myOwn IS
000700 "AaBbCcDcEeFfGgHhIiJjKkLlMmNnOoPpQq
000800 RrSsTtUuVvWwXxYyZz".
000900 INPUT-OUTPUT SECTION.
001000 FILE-CONTROL.
001100     SELECT WORK-FILE
001200         ASSIGN TO "TMP.DAT".
001300     SELECT EMP
001400         ASSIGN TO "MYFILE.DAT".
001500     SELECT SORT-EMP
001600         ASSIGN TO "SORTFILE.DAT".
001700 DATA DIVISION.
001900 FILE SECTION.
002000 SD WORK-FILE
002100     LABEL RECORDS ARE STANDARD.
002200 01 EMP-WK.
002300     05 FNAME      PIC X(10).
002400     05 LNAME      PIC X(10).
002500     05 ID-NUM     PIC X(2).
002600 FD EMP
002700     LABEL RECORDS ARE STANDARD.
002800 01 EMP-INPUT.
002900     05 FNAME      PIC X(10).
003000     05 LNAME      PIC X(10).
003100     05 ID-NUM     PIC X(2).
003200 FD SORT-EMP
003300     LABEL RECORDS ARE STANDARD.
003400 01 EMP-OUTPUT.
003500     05 FNAME      PIC X(10).
003600     05 LNAME      PIC X(10).
003700     05 ID-NUM     PIC X(2).
003800 PROCEDURE DIVISION.
003900     SORT WORK-FILE
004000     ON DESCENDING KEY LNAME OF EMP-WK
004100     USING EMP
004200     GIVING SORT-EMP.
004300     STOP RUN.
```

Identify the alphabetic to be used for the sort.

Identify the file containing the unsorted data.

Identify the file where the sorted data will be written.

Define the sort work file using the special SD level.

Define the file containing the data to be sorted.

Define the file used to store the sorted data.

Sort records in the workfile.

Sort by the value of the ID-NUM field in descending order.

The file containing the records to be sorted.

The file where the sorted records will be stored.

Sorting Duplicates

Records are uniquely identified in a file by the value of the primary key such as an employee identification number. No two records can have the same primary key value although more than one record can have the same alternate key value as shown in **Chapter 8**.

The **SORT** command uses the sort key value specified by the application to sort records in the source file. The sort key can be different than the primary key of the file. Therefore, it is likely multiple records can have the same sort key value.

Duplicate sort key values can be included in the sort by specifying the **WITH DUPLICATES IN ORDER** phrase when executing the **SORT** command.

The example on the opposite page shows how to use the **WITH DUPLICATES IN ORDER** phrase in an application. Notice the phrase is typically placed below the **ON** phrase although the phrase can be placed in any order as long as they are fall between the **SORT** command and the period following the last sentence in the **SORT** command.

All duplicate sort key values will appear grouped together in the proper sort sequence as specified by the sort direction in the **ON** phrase.

The example on the next page places records in the EMP-WK file in last name order. Since it is likely for the file to contain records of people with same last name, the **WITH DUPLICATES IN ORDER** phrase is used to assure no duplicate record is left out of the sorted destination file.

```
000100 IDENTIFICATION DIVISION.
000200 PROGRAM-ID. FIRST.
000300 ENVIRONMENT DIVISION.
000400
000500 INPUT-OUTPUT SECTION.
000600 FILE-CONTROL.
000700     SELECT WORK-FILE
000800         ASSIGN TO "TMP.DAT".
000900     SELECT EMP
001000         ASSIGN TO "MYFILE.DAT".
001100     SELECT SORT-EMP
001200         ASSIGN TO "SORTFILE.DAT".
001300 DATA DIVISION.
001400
001500 FILE SECTION.
001600 SD WORK-FILE
001700     LABEL RECORDS ARE STANDARD.
001800 01 EMP-WK.
001900     05 FNAME      PIC X(10).
002000     05 LNAME      PIC X(10).
002100     05 ID-NUM     PIC X(2).
002200 FD EMP
002300     LABEL RECORDS ARE STANDARD.
002400 01 EMP-INPUT.
002500     05 FNAME      PIC X(10).
002600     05 LNAME      PIC X(10).
002700     05 ID-NUM     PIC X(2).
002800 FD SORT-EMP
002900     LABEL RECORDS ARE STANDARD.
003000 01 EMP-OUTPUT.
003100     05 FNAME      PIC X(10).
003200     05 LNAME      PIC X(10).
003300     05 ID-NUM     PIC X(2).
003400 PROCEDURE DIVISION.
003500
003600 START-PROGRAM.
003700     SORT WORK-FILE
003800     ON ASCENDING KEY LNAME OF EMP-WK
003900     WITH DUPLICATES IN ORDER
003900     USING EMP
004000     GIVING SORT-EMP.
004100 END-PROGRAM.
004200     STOP RUN.
```

Identify the work file used to sort records.

Identify the file containing the unsorted data.

Identify the file where the sorted data will be written.

Define the sort work file using the special SD level.

Define the file containing the data to be sorted.

Define the file used to store the sorted data.

Sort records in the workfile.

Sort by the value of the ID-NUM field in ascending order.

Including duplicate values in sort.

Sorting a File to a Procedure

Previously in this chapter you have seen how records in a file can be sorted and written to a new file. You can also copy the sorted records to a procedure.

A procedure is a paragraph that contains sentences that can be used with records stored in the work file. This is illustrated in the example on the next page.

The **SORT** command is told to reference a procedure rather than a destination file by using the **OUTPUT PROCEDURE IS** phrase in the **SORT** command.

The **OUTPUT PROCEDURE IS** phrase must specify the paragraph name containing the sentences to be executed once the source file is sorted.

The example on the next page jumps to the **DISPLAY-DATA** paragraph when the **SORT** command is finished sorting records. The **DISPLAY-DATA** paragraph executes a series of sentences one of which displays the record from the work file on the screen.

The paragraph loops through the work file displaying each record until the end of file is encountered. The **AT END** phrase causes the value "1" to be assigned to the **EOF-VAR** variable that breaks the **PERFORM** loop and returns to the sentence at the end of the last sentence in the **SORT** command that ends the program.

Although records are displayed on the screen, the same routine can be used to assign sorted records to the elements of an array. The array can then be used to further process records.

Make sure the variable used to signal the end of the file is defined and initialized before it is used in the **PERFORM** command loop, otherwise a compiler error will occur.

```
000100 IDENTIFICATION DIVISION.
000200 PROGRAM-ID. FIRST.
000300 ENVIRONMENT DIVISION.
000400
000500 INPUT-OUTPUT SECTION.
000600 FILE-CONTROL.
000700     SELECT WORK-FILE
000800         ASSIGN TO "TMP.DAT".
000900     SELECT EMP
001000         ASSIGN TO "MYFILE.DAT".
001100 DATA DIVISION.
001200
001300 FILE SECTION.
001400 SD WORK-FILE
001500     LABEL RECORDS ARE STANDARD.
001600 01 EMP-WK.
001700     05 FNAME      PIC X(10).
001800     05 LNAME      PIC X(10).
002000     05 ID-NUM     PIC X(2).
002100 FD EMP
002200     LABEL RECORDS ARE STANDARD.
002300 01 EMP-INPUT.
002400     05 FNAME      PIC X(10).
002500     05 LNAME      PIC X(10).
002600     05 ID-NUM     PIC X(2).
002700 WORKING-STORAGE SECTION
002800 77 EOF-VAR PIX X VALUE "0".
002900     88 EOF-VAL VALUE "1".
003000 PROCEDURE DIVISION.
003100
003200 START-PROGRAM.
003300     SORT WORK-FILE
003400     ON ASCENDING KEY ID-NUM OF EMP-WK
003500     USING EMP
003600     OUTPUT PROCEDURE IS DISPLAY-DATA.
003700     STOP RUN.
003800 DISPLAY-DATA.
003900     PERFORM UNTIL EOF-VAL
004000         RETURN WORK-FILE
004100         AT END
004200             MOVE "1" TO EOF-VAR
004300         NOT AT END
004500             DISPLAY EMP-WK
004600         END-RETURN
004700     END-PERFORM.
```

Identify the work file used to sort records.

Identify the file containing the unsorted data.

Define the sort workfile using the special SD level.

Define the file containing the data to be sorted.

Sort records in the workfile.

The results of the sort is sent to a procedure.

Signal the end of the file.

Display the sorted records.

Sorting a Procedure to a File

A procedure is a paragraph in an application that can contain data. Data in a procedure can be sorted by using the **SORT** command and the results of which can be written to a file.

Two files must be physically defined in the File-Control paragraph of the Input-Output Section of the Environment Division. One file is the work file that is used as temporary storage while the information is being sorted. The other file is the destination file where the sorted information will ultimately be stored.

Likewise, the same two files must be logically defined in the File Section of the Data Division as illustrated in the example on the opposite page.

Both files must have the same definition and the definitions must correspond to the data in the procedure that will be sorted using the **SORT** command. A mismatch of file definitions could lead to unreliable results.

The information to be sorted must be assembled into a record as illustrated in the GET-DATA paragraph in the example. Data for each field must be positioned within the record according to the file definition, then enclosed within double quotations.

A word of caution. Make sure each field begins in the proper position. Space can be used as a filler if necessary between the last character of the previous field and the first character of the next field. The **MOVE** command is used to assign the complete record to the work file.

Notice the **INPUT** phrase is used with the **SORT** command to specify the paragraph name that contains the unsorted data. The **SORT** command automatically calls the paragraph to gather the information before sorting begins.

```
000100 IDENTIFICATION DIVISION.
000200 PROGRAM-ID. FIRST.
000300 ENVIRONMENT DIVISION.
000400
000500 INPUT-OUTPUT SECTION.
000600 FILE-CONTROL
000700     SELECT WORK-FILE
000800         ASSIGN TO "TMP.DAT".
000900     SELECT OUT-EMP
001000         ASSIGN TO "MYFILE.DAT".
001100 DATA DIVISION.
001200
001300 FILE SECTION.
001400 SD WORK-FILE
001500     RECORD CONTAINS 10 CHARACTERS.
001600 01 EMP-WK.
001700     05 FNAME      PIC X(3).
001800     05 LNAME      PIC X(5).
001900     05 ID-NUM     PIC X(2).
002000 FD OUT-EMP
002100     LABEL RECORDS ARE STANDARD.
002200 01 EMP-OUTPUT.
002300     05 FNAME      PIC X(3).
002400     05 LNAME      PIC X(5).
002500     05 ID-NUM     PIC X(2).
002600 PROCEDURE DIVISION.
002700
002800 START-PROGRAM.
002900     SORT WORK-FILE
003000     ON ASCENDING KEY ID-NUM OF EMP-WK
003100     INPUT PROCEDURE GET-DATA
003200     GIVING OUT-EMP.
003300     STOP RUN.
003400 GET-DATA.
003500     MOVE "JoeSmith01" TO EMP-WK.
003600     RELEASE EMP-WK.
003700     MOVE "MaeAdams04" TO EMP-WK.
003800     RELEASE EMP-WK.
003900     MOVE "BobJones02" TO EMP-WK.
004000     RELEASE EMP-WK.
004100     MOVE "SueMarks04" TO EMP-WK.
004200     RELEASE EMP-WK.
004300     MOVE "SanCarrs03" TO EMP-WK.
004400     RELEASE EMP-WK.
```

Identify the work file used to sort records.

Identify the file that will contain the sorted data.

Define the sort work file using the special SD level.

Define the file that will contain the sorted data.

The procedure that will supply the data to be sorted.

The file containing the sorted records.

Records to be sorted.

Sorting a Procedure
to a Procedure

Records stored in memory can also be sorted in memory without having to create a source or destination file. This process is called sorting a procedure to a procedure.

A procedure is a paragraph that can contain information as illustrated on the next page. There are two procedures used in this example. These are GET-DATA and DISPLAY-DATA.

The GET-DATA procedure assembles information in the form of a record making sure the record layout corresponds to the logical definition of the work file.

Each field in the record begins in the exact character position as is specified in the work file definition. Unexpected results can occur if the record layout isn't strictly followed.

The value of the fields are enclosed within double quotations and is assigned to the work file using the **MOVE** command. The **RELEASE** phrase causes the record to be written to the work file.

Notice the work file is a physical file that must be defined although the source and destination of the sort is in memory. This is because the **SORT** command uses a file to reorder records.

The **SORT** command uses the **INPUT** and **OUTPUT** phrases to identify the source and destination procedures. Each phrase is followed by the name of the paragraph.

In this example, the DISPLAY-DATA paragraph steps through the work file displaying each record on the screen. The process continues until the **AT END** phrase detects the end of the work file at which time a signal is given to end the procedure.

```
000100 IDENTIFICATION DIVISION.
000200 PROGRAM-ID. FIRST.
000300 ENVIRONMENT DIVISION.
000400 INPUT-OUTPUT SECTION.
000500 FILE-CONTROL.
000600      SELECT WORK-FILE
000700          ASSIGN TO "TMP.DAT".
000800 DATA DIVISION.
000900 FILE SECTION.
001000 SD WORK-FILE
001100      RECORD CONTAINS 22 CHARACTERS.
001200 01 EMP-WK.
001300      05 FNAME      PIC X(3).
001400      05 LNAME      PIC X(5).
001500      05 ID-NUM     PIC X(2).
001600 WORKING-STORAGE SECTION
001700 77 EOF-VAR PIX X VALUE "0".
001800      88 EOF-VAL VALUE "1".
001900 PROCEDURE DIVISION.
002000 START-PROGRAM.
002100      SORT WORK-FILE
002200      ON ASCENDING KEY ID-NUM.
002300      INPUT PROCEDURE GET-DATA.
002400      OUTPUT PROCEDURE DISPLAY-DATA.
002500      STOP RUN.
002600 GET-DATA.
002700      MOVE "JoeSmith01" TO EMP-WK.
002800      RELEASE EMP-WK.
002900      MOVE "MaeAdams04" TO EMP-WK.
003000      RELEASE EMP-WK.
003100      MOVE "BobJones02" TO EMP-WK.
003200      RELEASE EMP-WK.
003300      MOVE "SueMarks04" TO EMP-WK.
003400      RELEASE EMP-WK.
003500 DISPLAY-DATA.
003600      PERFORM UNTIL EOF-VAL
003700          RETURN WORK-FILE
003800          AT END
003900              MOVE "1" TO EOF-VAR
004000          NOT AT END
004100              DISPLAY EMP-WK
004200          END-RETURN
004300      END-PERFORM.
```

Identify the work file used to sort records.

Define the sort workfile using the special SD level.

The variable to signal the end of file.

The procedure that will supply the data to be sorted.

The procedure that will display the sorted data.

Define the records to be sorted.

Display the sorted records.

Merging Files

Two sorted files can be merged to form one file by using the **MERGE** command. The **MERGE** command is very similar to the **SORT** command in that information is reordered based upon the value of a sort key.

A *sort key* is one or more fields within the field the value of which is placed in alphabetical or numerical order depending on the data type of the field.

The example on the next page illustrates how to merge together two files. Three files are physically defined in the **File-Control** paragraph of the Input-Output section in the Environment Division.

The first is the work file that is used by the **MERGE** command to assemble both files into one. The second file is a file that contains presorted information that will be merged with the third file. The results of the merge is written to the third file.

The physical files can be defined in any order since the name of each file is used in the **MERGE** command to identify the role of the file in the merge.

Although files are being merged, the logical definition of the work file must occur at the special **SD** level that is the sort descriptor. The sort file and the files to be merged must be defined in the File Section of the Data Division.

The **MERGE** command specifies the name of the work file and defines the first file for the merge with the **USING** phrase. The other merge file that will contain sort records from both files is identified using the **GIVING** phrase.

A word of caution. The **USING** phrase must identify the name of a file containing records that will be merged with the second file. You can't merge records in a procedure with a file.

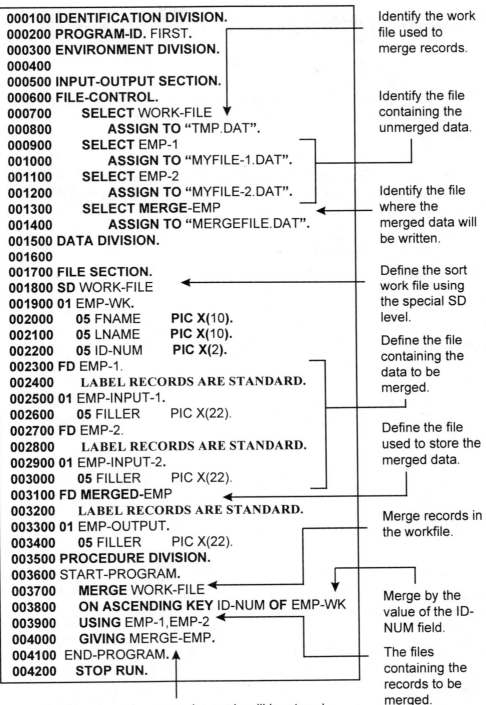

```
000100 IDENTIFICATION DIVISION.
000200 PROGRAM-ID. FIRST.
000300 ENVIRONMENT DIVISION.
000400
000500 INPUT-OUTPUT SECTION.
000600 FILE-CONTROL.
000700     SELECT WORK-FILE
000800         ASSIGN TO "TMP.DAT".
000900     SELECT EMP-1
001000         ASSIGN TO "MYFILE-1.DAT".
001100     SELECT EMP-2
001200         ASSIGN TO "MYFILE-2.DAT".
001300     SELECT MERGE-EMP
001400         ASSIGN TO "MERGEFILE.DAT".
001500 DATA DIVISION.
001600
001700 FILE SECTION.
001800 SD WORK-FILE
001900 01 EMP-WK.
002000     05 FNAME     PIC X(10).
002100     05 LNAME     PIC X(10).
002200     05 ID-NUM    PIC X(2).
002300 FD EMP-1.
002400     LABEL RECORDS ARE STANDARD.
002500 01 EMP-INPUT-1.
002600     05 FILLER    PIC X(22).
002700 FD EMP-2.
002800     LABEL RECORDS ARE STANDARD.
002900 01 EMP-INPUT-2.
003000     05 FILLER    PIC X(22).
003100 FD MERGED-EMP
003200     LABEL RECORDS ARE STANDARD.
003300 01 EMP-OUTPUT.
003400     05 FILLER    PIC X(22).
003500 PROCEDURE DIVISION.
003600 START-PROGRAM.
003700     MERGE WORK-FILE
003800     ON ASCENDING KEY ID-NUM OF EMP-WK
003900     USING EMP-1,EMP-2
004000     GIVING MERGE-EMP.
004100 END-PROGRAM.
004200     STOP RUN.
```

Identify the work file used to merge records.

Identify the file containing the unmerged data.

Identify the file where the merged data will be written.

Define the sort work file using the special SD level.

Define the file containing the data to be merged.

Define the file used to store the merged data.

Merge records in the workfile.

Merge by the value of the ID-NUM field.

The files containing the records to be merged.

The file where the merged records will be stored.

Changing the Order of the Merge

Files that are merged together are presorted by using the **SORT** command that is illustrated previously in this chapter. The **SORT** command rearranges the natural order in which records are sorted in a file.

Records are stored sequentially in a file regardless if a file is a relative file or an indexed file. The first record entered into the file is the first record stored and the pattern continues throughout the file.

By default, all records are placed in ascending order by the **SORT** command. You learned how to reverse the sort by specifying **DESCENDING** in the **ON** phrase of the **SORT** command.

Files that are to be merged must have the same record layout, however each can be sorted in a different direction. The first file might be in ascending order while the other file is in descending order.

You can reorder records in the same direction in both files by specifying the sort direction in the **ON** phrase as is illustrated in the example on the next page.

The **ON** phase can be set to **ASCENDING** or **DESCENDING**. All the records in the merged file will be reordered. However, only the final merged file reflects the new order. The first file identified by the **USING** phrase remains unaffected by the sort.

In this example, all the records in the merge file is sorted in descending order based on the value of the LNAME field which contains a person's last name.

Notice that the actual sort occurs in the work file rather than in either of the merging files. The merging files remain untouched until the merge and the sort are completed and the merged records are written to the file identified in the **GIVING** phrase.

```
000100 IDENTIFICATION DIVISION.
000200 PROGRAM-ID. FIRST.
000300 ENVIRONMENT DIVISION.
000400
000500 INPUT-OUTPUT SECTION.
000600 FILE-CONTROL.
000700     SELECT WORK-FILE
000800         ASSIGN TO "TMP.DAT".
000900     SELECT EMP
001000         ASSIGN TO "MYFILE.DAT".
001100     SELECT MERGED-EMP
001200         ASSIGN TO "MERGEFILE.DAT".
001300 DATA DIVISION.
001400
001500 FILE SECTION.
001600 SD WORK-FILE
001700     LABEL RECORDS ARE STANDARD.
001800 01 EMP-WK.
001900     05 FNAME      PIC X(10).
002000     05 LNAME      PIC X(10).
002100     05 ID-NUM     PIC X(2).
002200 FD EMP
002300     LABEL RECORDS ARE STANDARD.
002400 01 EMP-INPUT.
002500     05 FNAME      PIC X(10).
002600     05 LNAME      PIC X(10).
002700     05 ID-NUM     PIC X(2).
002800 FD MERGED-EMP
002900     LABEL RECORDS ARE STANDARD.
003000 01 EMP-OUTPUT.
003100     05 FNAME      PIC X(10).
003200     05 LNAME      PIC X(10).
003300     05 ID-NUM     PIC X(2).
003400 PROCEDURE DIVISION.
003500
003600 START-PROGRAM.
003700     MERGE WORK-FILE
003800     ON DESCENDING KEY LNAME OF EMP-WK
003900     USING EMP
004000     GIVING MERGED-EMP.
004100 END-PROGRAM.
004200     STOP RUN.
```

Identify the work file used to merge records.

Identify the file containing the unmerged data.

Identify the file where the merged data will be written.

Define the sort work file using the special SD level.

Define the file containing the data to be sorted.

Define the file used to store the merged data.

Merge records in the workfile.

Merge by the value of the LNAME field in descending order.

The file containing the records to be merged.

The file where the merged records will be stored.

Upper- and Lowercase Merge

The results of a merger between two sorted files is frequently disappointing because uppercase and lowercase letters are sorted improperly. Uppercase letters are above the lowercase letter in the merged file as illustrated below.

It seems that the **MERGE** command failed to properly reorganize the file; however, information was sorted properly. The problem lies with the way computers recognize characters.

A character is represented by a numeric value based on either the ASCII code or the EBCDIC code. Uppercase characters are assigned values from 65 through 90. For example value 65 is the character A and the value 90 is the character z.

Lowercase characters are assigned values greater than 90 such as the value 97 is the character a and the value 122 is the character z. The MERGE command sorts records based on the numeric value not the alphabetical value. Therefore, uppercase Z comes before lowercase A.

By defining a new alphabet in the Special-Names paragraph of the Configuration Section in the Environment Division the problem can be fixed. This is illustrated on the opposite page.

The **ALPHABET** phrase places lowercase letters alongside their corresponding uppercase letter within double quotations that becomes the standard alphabet for the application.

The **MERGE** command then uses the new alphabet to sort records once two files are merged into the work file. For example, the new alphabet now has character value 97 coming after character value 65. Character 97 is lowercase a and character 65 is uppercase a.

```
000100 IDENTIFICATION DIVISION.
000200 PROGRAM-ID. FIRST.
000300 ENVIRONMENT DIVISION.
000400 CONFIGURATION SECTION.
000500 SPECIAL-NAMES.
000600 ALPHABET myOwn IS
000700 "AaBbCcDcEeFfGgHhIiJjKkLlMmNnOoPpQq
000800 RrSsTtUuVvWwXxYyZz".
000900 INPUT-OUTPUT SECTION.
001000 FILE-CONTROL.
001100     SELECT WORK-FILE
001200         ASSIGN TO "TMP.DAT".
001300     SELECT EMP
001400         ASSIGN TO "MYFILE.DAT".
001500     SELECT MERGED-EMP
001600         ASSIGN TO "MERGEFILE.DAT".
001700 DATA DIVISION.
001900 FILE SECTION.
002000 SD WORK-FILE
002100     LABEL RECORDS ARE STANDARD.
002200 01 EMP-WK.
002300     05 FNAME      PIC X(10).
002400     05 LNAME      PIC X(10).
002500     05 ID-NUM     PIC X(2).
002600 FD EMP
002700     LABEL RECORDS ARE STANDARD.
002800 01 EMP-INPUT.
002900     05 FNAME      PIC X(10).
003000     05 LNAME      PIC X(10).
003100     05 ID-NUM     PIC X(2).
003200 FD MERGED-EMP
003300     LABEL RECORDS ARE STANDARD.
003400 01 EMP-OUTPUT.
003500     05 FNAME      PIC X(10).
003600     05 LNAME      PIC X(10).
003700     05 ID-NUM     PIC X(2).
003800 PROCEDURE DIVISION.
003900     MERGE WORK-FILE
004000     ON DESCENDING KEY LNAME OF EMP-WK
004100     USING EMP
004200     GIVING MERGED-EMP.
004300     STOP RUN.
```

Identify alphabetic to be used for the merge.

Identify file containing the unmerged data.

Identify the file where the merged data will be written.

Define the merge work file using the special SD level.

Define the file containing the data to be merged.

Define the file used to store the merged data.

Merge records in the workfile.

Mergeby the value of the ID-NUM field in descending order.

The file containing the records to be merged.

The file where the merged records will be stored.

Merging Duplicates

The **MERGE** command uses the sort key value specified by the application to sort merged records in the work file. The sort key can be different than the primary key of the file. Therefore, it is likely multiple records can have the same sort key value.

As illustrated in Chapter 8, records are uniquely identified in a file by the value of the primary key such as an employee identification number. No two records can have the same primary key value although more than one record can have the same alternate key value.

Duplicate sort key values can be included in the sort by specifying the **WITH DUPLICATES IN ORDER** phrase when executing the **SORT** command as shown on the next page.

Notice the **WITH DUPLICATES IN ORDER** phrase is typically placed below the **ON** phrase although the phrase can be placed in any order as long as they fall between the **MERGE** command and the period following the last sentence in the **MERGE** command.

The **MERGE** command groups together all duplicate sort key values in the proper sort sequence as specified by the sort direction in the **ON** phrase.

Records in the EMP-WK file in last name order are found in the example on the opposite page. Since it is likely for the file to contain records of people with the same last name, the **WITH DUPLICATES IN ORDER** phrase is used to assure no duplicate record is left out of the sorted merged file.

A word of caution. Make sure you create a new alphabet as shown previously in this chapter so uppercase and lowercase duplication sort keys appear correctly in the merged file.

```
000100 IDENTIFICATION DIVISION.
000200 PROGRAM-ID. FIRST.
000300 ENVIRONMENT DIVISION.
000400
000500 INPUT-OUTPUT SECTION.
000600 FILE-CONTROL.
000700     SELECT WORK-FILE
000800          ASSIGN TO "TMP.DAT".
000900     SELECT EMP
001000          ASSIGN TO "MYFILE.DAT".
001100     SELECT MERGE-EMP
001200          ASSIGN TO "MERGEFILE.DAT".
001300 DATA DIVISION.
001400
001500 FILE SECTION.
001600 SD WORK-FILE
001700     LABEL RECORDS ARE STANDARD.
001800 01 EMP-WK.
001900     05 FNAME      PIC X(10).
002000     05 LNAME      PIC X(10).
002100     05 ID-NUM     PIC X(2).
002200 FD EMP
002300     LABEL RECORDS ARE STANDARD.
002400 01 EMP-INPUT.
002500     05 FNAME      PIC X(10).
002600     05 LNAME      PIC X(10).
002700     05 ID-NUM     PIC X(2).
002800 FD MERGED-EMP
002900     LABEL RECORDS ARE STANDARD.
003000 01 EMP-OUTPUT.
003100     05 FNAME      PIC X(10).
003200     05 LNAME      PIC X(10).
003300     05 ID-NUM     PIC X(2).
003400 PROCEDURE DIVISION.
003500
003600 START-PROGRAM.
003700     MERGE WORK-FILE
003800     ON ASCENDING KEY LNAME OF EMP-WK
003900     WITH DUPLICATES IN ORDER
004000     USING EMP
004100     GIVING MERGED-EMP.
004200 END-PROGRAM.
004300     STOP RUN.
```

Identify the work file used to merge records.

Identify the file containing the un- merged data.

Identify file where the merged data will be written.

Define the merge work file using the special SD level.

Define the file containing the data to be merged.

Define the file used to store the merged data.

Merge records in the workfile.

Merge by the value of the ID-NUM field in ascending order.

Include duplicate values in the merge.

Merge a File to a Procedure

Records from a presorted file can be merged with a procedure by specifying the name of the procedure in the **MERGE** command.

The **MERGE** command references a procedure rather than a destination file by using the **OUTPUT PROCEDURE IS** phrase in the **SORT** command.

A *procedure* is a paragraph that contains sentences that do something with records stored in the work file.

The **OUTPUT PROCEDURE IS** phrase must specify the name of the paragraph containing the sentences to be executed once the source file is merged.

The example on the next page jumps to the **DISPLAY-DATA** paragraph when the **MERGE** command is finished merging records. The **DISPLAY-DATA** paragraph execute a series of sentences one of which displays the record from the work file on the screen.

The paragraph loops through the work file displaying each record until the end of file is encountered. The **AT END** phrase causes the value "1" to be assigned to the **EOF-VAR** variable that breaks the **PERFORM** loop and returns to the sentence at the end of the last sentence in the **MERGE** command that ends the program.

Although records are displayed on the screen, the same routine can be used to assign merged records to the elements of an array. The array can then be used to further process records.

Make sure the variable used to signal the end of the file is defined and initialized before it is used in the **PERFORM** command loop, otherwise a compiler error will occur.

```
000100 IDENTIFICATION DIVISION.
000200 PROGRAM-ID. FIRST.
000300 ENVIRONMENT DIVISION.
000400
000500 INPUT-OUTPUT SECTION.
000600 FILE-CONTROL.
000700     SELECT WORK-FILE
000800         ASSIGN TO "TMP.DAT".
000900     SELECT EMP
001000         ASSIGN TO "MYFILE.DAT".
001100 DATA DIVISION.
001200
001300 FILE SECTION.
001400 SD WORK-FILE
001500     LABEL RECORDS ARE STANDARD.
001600 01 EMP-WK.
001700     05 FNAME     PIC X(10).
001800     05 LNAME     PIC X(10).
002000     05 ID-NUM    PIC X(2).
002100 FD EMP
002200     LABEL RECORDS ARE STANDARD.
002300 01 EMP-INPUT.
002400     05 FNAME     PIC X(10).
002500     05 LNAME     PIC X(10).
002600     05 ID-NUM    PIC X(2).
002700 WORKING-STORAGE SECTION
002800 77 EOF-VAR PIC X VALUE "0".
002900     88 EOF-VAL VALUE "1".
003000 PROCEDURE DIVISION.
003100
003200 START-PROGRAM.
003300     MERGE WORK-FILE
003400     ON ASCENDING KEY ID-NUM OF EMP-WK
003500     USING EMP
003600     OUTPUT PROCEDURE IS DISPLAY-DATA.
003700     STOP RUN.
003800 DISPLAY-DATA.
003900     PERFORM UNTIL EOF-VAL
004000         RETURN WORK-FILE
004100         AT END
004200             MOVE "1" TO EOF-VAR
004300         NOT AT END
004400             DISPLAY EMP-WK
004500         END-RETURN
004600     END-PERFORM.
```

Identify the work file used to merge records.

Identify the file containing the unmerged data.

Define the merge workfile using the special SD level.

Define the file containing the data to be merged.

Merge records in the workfile.

The results of the merge is sent to a procedure.

Signal the end of the file.

Display the merged records.

Chapter Eleven

Working with
the Printer

- Defining a Physical Printer
- Preparing to Print a Record
- Printing a Record
- Print a Record from a Sequential File
- Printing All Records in a File
- Printing Records from an Indexed File
- Printing Text With Fields
- Creating a Report Layout
- Printing Fields in Columns
- Printing Report Title
- Printing Column Headings
- Printing Report Trailer
- Determining the End of the Page
- Printing Page Numbers at Top Left of Page
- Printing Page Numbers at Top Right of Page
- Printing Page Numbers at Bottom Left of Page
- Printing Page Numbers at Bottom Right of Page
- Create Multiline Text

Defining a Physical Printer

We tend to think of a printer as a device that spits out documents generated by an application. However, to a COBOL application a printer is a file similar to other files used by the application.

As is presented in Chapter 8, a file is defined in two ways within a COBOL application. These are as a logical file and as a physical file.

A logical file is the conceptual organization of data that is to be written to the file. The logical definition describes how information is prepared in memory to be written to the file by the application.

Before this can happen, the application must have information about the physical file. The *physical file* is the name of the file located on a device such as a disk or tape drive. When an application is printing, the file name is specified as the printer.

The physical file is defined in the File Control paragraph of the Input-Output section within the Environment Division as shown in the example on the next page.

The file definition begins with the **SELECT** command that is followed by the name of the variable used throughout the program to refer to the file name. In this case, PTR-FILE is associated with the printer. Every time the application needs to print, reference is made to the PTR-FILE.

The **ASSIGN** command is used to assign the name of the file to the variable. You cannot use the **MOVE** command to store a value to this variable. The name of the file is the reserved word **PRINTER**.

The physical file definition must also identify how records are organized in the file. Records sent to a printer can be organized one way the **ORGANIZATION IS LINE** is as shown on the next page. This tells the application the printer is a line printer.

```
000100 IDENTIFICATION DIVISION.
000200 PROGRAM-ID. FIRST.
000300 ENVIRONMENT DIVISION.
000400
000500 INPUT-OUTPUT SECTION.
000600 FILE-CONTROL.
000700     SELECT CONTACTS
000800         ASSIGN TO "MYFILE.DAT"
000900         ORGANIZATION IS SEQUENTIAL.
001000     SELECT PTR-FILE
001100         ASSIGN TO PRINTER
001200         ORGANIZATION IS LINE SEQUENTIAL.
001300 DATA DIVISION.
001400
001500 FILE SECTION.
001600 FD   CONTACTS
001700         LABEL RECORDS ARE STANDARD.
001800 01 CONTACT-RECORD.
001900     05 FILLER     PIC X(1).
002000     05 FNAME      PIC X(10).
002100     05 LNAME      PIC X(10).
002200
002300 FD PTR-FILE
002400    LABEL RECORDS ARE OMITTED.
002500 01 PTR-RECORD    PIC X(21).
002600
002700 WORKING-STORAGE SECTION.
002800
002900 PROCEDURE DIVISION.
003000
003100  STOP RUN.
```

Associate the printer with the printer identifier.

Defines the physical printer.

The size of the record is the sum of the size of fields and labels to be printed.

The file containing records that will be printed.

Identifies how records are to be sent to the printer.

Define the logical layout of the printer.

Facts You Should Know...

An application writes records to a printer similar to how records are written to a file. A printer is considered a file opened in the **OUTPUT** mode.

A printer must be assigned an identifier that is used throughout the application whenever information is to be written to the printer.

Preparing to Print a Record

A printer is treated as a file by a COBOL application by associating the reserved word **PRINTER** with a variable used throughout the program any time the program needs to reference the printer.

This association takes place when the file, in this case the printer, is physically defined in the program. You saw how this is done previously in the chapter.

As shown in Chapter 8, all files used by the program must have a physical and logical definition. The *physical definition* tells the application where the physical file is located. (Remember the printer is considered a file by the program.)

The *logical definition* of the file tells how information is organized in the file. In Chapter 8, you learned how information is logically grouped together. The group is called a record. Each record contains one or more pieces of information called fields. The order and size of the fields within the record are called the record layout.

The logical definition of a file describes the record layout of the file. In the case of a printer, the logical definition describes the data that will be sent to the printer for printing.

Typically, information that is to be printed is stored in structured variables within the application as shown in the example on the opposite page. A structured variable is a data structured defined in the **Working-Storage Section** of the application.

The local definition of a printer is defined in the **File Section** and must exactly match the data structure of the variables that are to be printed.

Notice both the printer and the data structure have the same record layout.

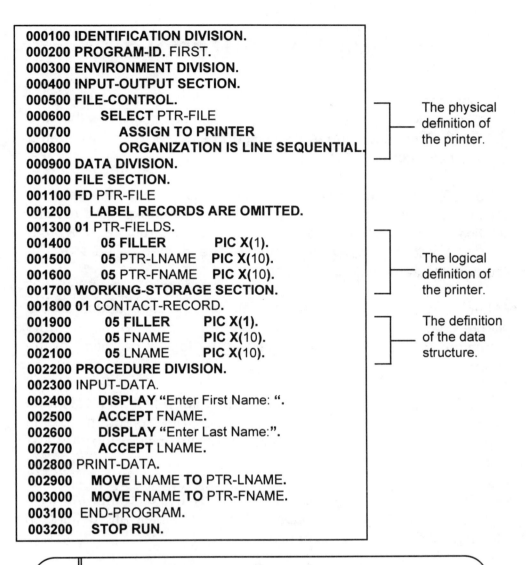

```
000100 IDENTIFICATION DIVISION.
000200 PROGRAM-ID. FIRST.
000300 ENVIRONMENT DIVISION.
000400 INPUT-OUTPUT SECTION.
000500 FILE-CONTROL.
000600     SELECT PTR-FILE
000700         ASSIGN TO PRINTER
000800         ORGANIZATION IS LINE SEQUENTIAL.
000900 DATA DIVISION.
001000 FILE SECTION.
001100 FD PTR-FILE
001200     LABEL RECORDS ARE OMITTED.
001300 01 PTR-FIELDS.
001400     05 FILLER       PIC X(1).
001500     05 PTR-LNAME   PIC X(10).
001600     05 PTR-FNAME   PIC X(10).
001700 WORKING-STORAGE SECTION.
001800 01 CONTACT-RECORD.
001900     05 FILLER       PIC X(1).
002000     05 FNAME       PIC X(10).
002100     05 LNAME       PIC X(10).
002200 PROCEDURE DIVISION.
002300 INPUT-DATA.
002400     DISPLAY "Enter First Name: ".
002500     ACCEPT FNAME.
002600     DISPLAY "Enter Last Name:".
002700     ACCEPT LNAME.
002800 PRINT-DATA.
002900   MOVE LNAME TO PTR-LNAME.
003000   MOVE FNAME TO PTR-FNAME.
003100 END-PROGRAM.
003200     STOP RUN.
```

The physical definition of the printer.

The logical definition of the printer.

The definition of the data structure.

Facts You Should Know...

A printer must be defined physically and logically by the application before any information can be printed.

The logical definition of the printer must exactly match the logical definition of the data structure containing the information that is to be printed.

Printing a Record

An application collects information from a file or from the keyboard and assigns the data to variables previously defined within the program. This technique is discussed in Chapter 8 and illustrated on the next page.

The logical definition of the printer must exactly match the definition of the data structure, otherwise you'll receive unexpected results. Notice on the opposite page, both the data structure CONTACT-RECORD and the logical definition of the printer called PTR-FILE contain the same field descriptions.

After the program stores information into the data structure, the **MOVE** command is used to copy the data from a field in the data structure to the corresponding field in the logical definition of the printer.

In this example, the user is prompted to enter a first and last name into the keyboard that is assigned by the program to the appropriate element of the data structure using the **ACCEPT** command.

The **MOVE** command is then used to copy the data into the PTR-FNAME and PTR-LNAME variables. These variables are defined in the logical definition of the printer.

Printing occurs when the **WRITE** command is called. The **WRITE** command requires the name of the variable that contains the information that is to be printed.

In this example, the name of the record is used in place of the name of the variable. The record name PTR-REC is defined at the 01 level in the logical definition of the printer. The contents of each variable associated with the record is sent to the printer for printing even if no value is assigned to the variable.

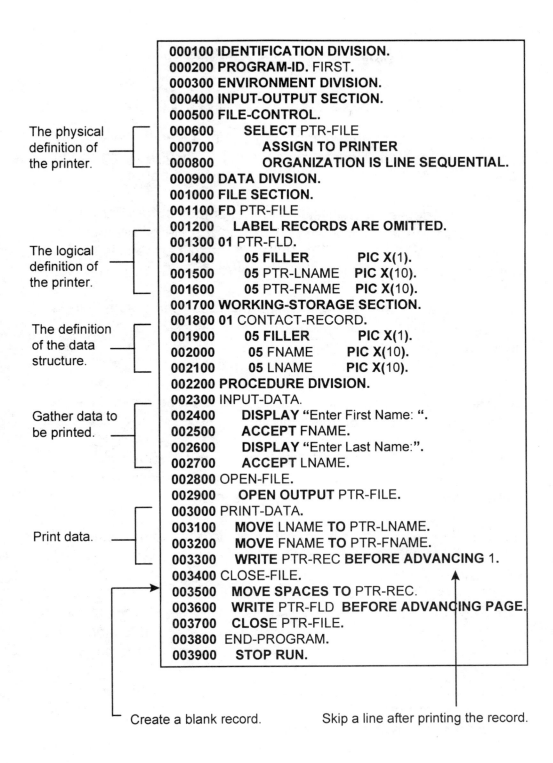

The physical definition of the printer.

The logical definition of the printer.

The definition of the data structure.

Gather data to be printed.

Print data.

```
000100 IDENTIFICATION DIVISION.
000200 PROGRAM-ID. FIRST.
000300 ENVIRONMENT DIVISION.
000400 INPUT-OUTPUT SECTION.
000500 FILE-CONTROL.
000600     SELECT PTR-FILE
000700         ASSIGN TO PRINTER
000800             ORGANIZATION IS LINE SEQUENTIAL.
000900 DATA DIVISION.
001000 FILE SECTION.
001100 FD PTR-FILE
001200     LABEL RECORDS ARE OMITTED.
001300 01 PTR-FLD.
001400     05 FILLER        PIC X(1).
001500     05 PTR-LNAME  PIC X(10).
001600     05 PTR-FNAME  PIC X(10).
001700 WORKING-STORAGE SECTION.
001800 01 CONTACT-RECORD.
001900     05 FILLER        PIC X(1).
002000     05 FNAME        PIC X(10).
002100     05 LNAME        PIC X(10).
002200 PROCEDURE DIVISION.
002300 INPUT-DATA.
002400     DISPLAY "Enter First Name: ".
002500     ACCEPT FNAME.
002600     DISPLAY "Enter Last Name:".
002700     ACCEPT LNAME.
002800 OPEN-FILE.
002900     OPEN OUTPUT PTR-FILE.
003000 PRINT-DATA.
003100     MOVE LNAME TO PTR-LNAME.
003200     MOVE FNAME TO PTR-FNAME.
003300     WRITE PTR-REC BEFORE ADVANCING 1.
003400 CLOSE-FILE.
003500     MOVE SPACES TO PTR-REC.
003600     WRITE PTR-FLD BEFORE ADVANCING PAGE.
003700     CLOSE PTR-FILE.
003800 END-PROGRAM.
003900     STOP RUN.
```

Create a blank record.   Skip a line after printing the record.

Print a Record
from a Sequential File

A program can print information stored in a sequential file by reading data from the file into memory then writing the data to the printer that is illustrated in the example on the next page.

The program defines the physical file that contains the information to be printed in the Environment Division and the file name must be associated with a variable. The file must also be identified as a sequential file using the **ORGANIZATION** phrase.

The description of the file must define the record and each field in the Data Division of the program. The type and size of each field must correspond to the layout of records stored in the file, otherwise information will be misread from the file.

Likewise, the logical definition of the printer must be defined with a similar layout as shown on the opposite page.

After the file is opened, information can be read from the file using the **READ** command. The **READ** command must be followed by the name of the file as defined in the file descriptor.

The next record in the file is assigned to the appropriate field name, then field names can be referenced by the program any time the program needs to access the value of the field.

Data is only copied into memory whenever the **READ** command is executed by the program. The information remains unchanged in the file even if the program changes values of fields in memory.

Information stored in the fields are then copied using the **MOVE** command to the record layout described in the logical definition of the printer after which the information is printed.

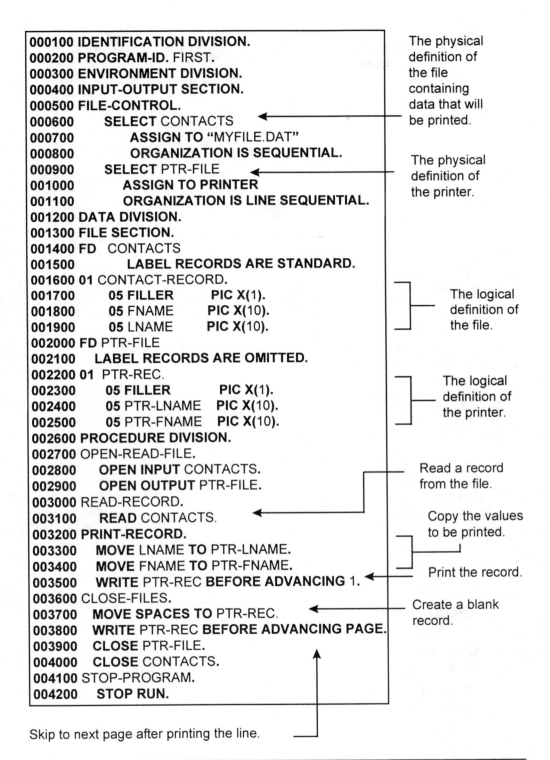

```
000100 IDENTIFICATION DIVISION.
000200 PROGRAM-ID. FIRST.
000300 ENVIRONMENT DIVISION.
000400 INPUT-OUTPUT SECTION.
000500 FILE-CONTROL.
000600     SELECT CONTACTS
000700         ASSIGN TO "MYFILE.DAT"
000800         ORGANIZATION IS SEQUENTIAL.
000900     SELECT PTR-FILE
001000         ASSIGN TO PRINTER
001100         ORGANIZATION IS LINE SEQUENTIAL.
001200 DATA DIVISION.
001300 FILE SECTION.
001400 FD   CONTACTS
001500         LABEL RECORDS ARE STANDARD.
001600 01 CONTACT-RECORD.
001700     05 FILLER     PIC X(1).
001800     05 FNAME      PIC X(10).
001900     05 LNAME      PIC X(10).
002000 FD PTR-FILE
002100     LABEL RECORDS ARE OMITTED.
002200 01  PTR-REC.
002300     05 FILLER     PIC X(1).
002400     05 PTR-LNAME  PIC X(10).
002500     05 PTR-FNAME  PIC X(10).
002600 PROCEDURE DIVISION.
002700 OPEN-READ-FILE.
002800     OPEN INPUT CONTACTS.
002900     OPEN OUTPUT PTR-FILE.
003000 READ-RECORD.
003100     READ CONTACTS.
003200 PRINT-RECORD.
003300     MOVE LNAME TO PTR-LNAME.
003400     MOVE FNAME TO PTR-FNAME.
003500     WRITE PTR-REC BEFORE ADVANCING 1.
003600 CLOSE-FILES.
003700     MOVE SPACES TO PTR-REC.
003800     WRITE PTR-REC BEFORE ADVANCING PAGE.
003900     CLOSE PTR-FILE.
004000     CLOSE CONTACTS.
004100 STOP-PROGRAM.
004200     STOP RUN.
```

The physical definition of the file containing data that will be printed.

The physical definition of the printer.

The logical definition of the file.

The logical definition of the printer.

Read a record from the file.

Copy the values to be printed.

Print the record.

Create a blank record.

Skip to next page after printing the line.

Printing All Records in a File

Typically a COBOL application is required to print all the records in a file. This requires the program to read and print records constantly until there are no more records in a file.

The program must begin with the first record in the file, print the information, then move on to the next record. The program repeats the process until the program reaches the end of the file. This process is called *looping* through a file.

The example on the next page prints every record in the file by executing the **READ** command from within a loop. The loop is created when the **PERFORM** command calls the PRT-DAT paragraph.

The program defines the EOF-VAL variable in the Working-Storage section. This variable is used as a flag to indicate when the program reaches the end of the file.

The PRT-DAT paragraph is continually called by the **PERFORM** command until the value of the EOF-VAL variable is "EOF". The EOF-VAL variable is initialized with spaces that guarantee that the PRT-DAT paragraph will be called at least once.

The PRT-DAT contains a **READ** command that reads a record from the file. After reading the record, the program determines if the end of the file is encountered by using the **AT END** phrase.

The **AT END** phrase is followed by the command to execute if the program detects the end of the file. In this example, the string "EOF" is assigned to the EOF-VAL variable.

Control returns to the **PERFORM** PRT-DAT sentence that evaluates the value of the EOF-VAL variable. If the value is "EOF", then the program executes the next sentence, which in the example on the next page closes the file, then ends the program.

```
000100 IDENTIFICATION DIVISION.
000200 PROGRAM-ID. FIRST.
000300 ENVIRONMENT DIVISION.
000400 INPUT-OUTPUT SECTION.
000500 FILE-CONTROL.
000600     SELECT CONTACTS          ◄────
000700         ASSIGN TO "MYFILE.DAT"
000800         ORGANIZATION IS SEQUENTIAL.
000900     SELECT PTR-FILE    ◄────
001000         ASSIGN TO PRINTER
001100         ORGANIZATION IS LINE SEQUENTIAL.
001200 DATA DIVISION.
001300 FILE SECTION.
001400 FD   CONTACTS
001500         LABEL RECORDS ARE STANDARD.
001600 01 CONTACT-RECORD.
001700     05 FILLER      PIC X(1).
001800     05 FNAME       PIC X(10).
001900     05 LNAME       PIC X(10).
002000 FD PTR-FILE
002100   LABEL RECORDS ARE OMITTED.
002200 01  PTR-REC.
002300     05 FILLER      PIC X(1).
002400     05 PTR-LNAME   PIC X(10).
002500     05 PTR-FNAME   PIC X(10).
002600 WORKING-STORAGE SECTION.
002700 01 EOF-VAL   PIC X(3) VALUE SPACES.
002800 PROCEDURE DIVISION.
002900     PERFORM OPEN-FILE.
003000     PERFORM PTR-DAT UNTIL EOF-VAL = "EOF".
003100     MOVE SPACES TO PTR-REC.
003200     WRITE PTR-REC BEFORE ADVANCING PAGE.
003300     CLOSE PTR-FILE CONTACTS.
003400     STOP RUN.
003500 PTR-DAT.
003600     READ CONTACTS
003700         AT END MOVE "EOF" TO E0F-VAL.
003800     IF E0F-VAL NOT = "EOF"
003900         MOVE LNAME TO PTR-LNAME
004000         MOVE FNAME TO PTR-FNAME
004100         WRITE PTR-REC BEFORE ADVANCING 1
004200     END-IF.
004300 OPEN-FILE.
004400     OPEN INPUT CONTACTS.
004500     OPEN OUTPUT PTR-FILE.
```

The physical definition of the file containing data that will be printed.

The physical definition of the printer.

The logical definition of the file.

The logical definition of the printer.

Keep calling until the value is "EOF".

Read a record from the file.

Copy the values to be printed.

Print the record.

Printing Records from an Indexed File

Records are located in an indexed file by having the program match a search criteria with values in the key field. For example, the program on the next page reads an ID-NUM from the keyboard and assigns the value to the key field.

Notice the file is opened in the INPUT mode. The INPUT mode gives the program read-access to the file. The program cannot write to the file, unless the file is opened using the EXTEND mode, OUTPUT mode, or the I-O mode. The EXTEND mode and the OUTPUT mode prevent the program from reading information in the file. The I-O mode enables the program to write or read data.

The READ command is used to copy a record from the file into memory. Values are copied into the record that is identified by name in the READ command.

The KEY IS phrase identifies the name of the key field and the association of the field within the record. In this example, the ID-NUM field is designed as the key field containing the search criteria.

The program begins searching the index for the search criteria. The INVALID KEY phrase is used to determine if the search criteria is found in the index.

The INVALID KEY phrase is executed if there isn't a match and the NOT INVALID KEY phrase is executed if there is a match. Code beneath these phrases will be executed if the corresponding condition is met.

If the record in the file matches the search criteria, the data is copied from the file into memory, then copied to the printer record layout, and finally printed using the WRITE command.

```
000100 IDENTIFICATION DIVISION.
000200 PROGRAM-ID. FIRST.
000300 ENVIRONMENT DIVISION.
000500 INPUT-OUTPUT SECTION.
000600 FILE-CONTROL.
000700     SELECT CONTACTS              ◄──────────
000800         ASSIGN TO "MYFILE.DAT"
000900         ORGANIZATION IS INDEXED
001000         RECORD KEY IS ID-NUM
001100         ACCESS MODE IS DYNAMIC.
001200     SELECT PTR-FILE             ◄──────────
001300         ASSIGN TO PRINTER
001400         ORGANIZATION IS LINE SEQUENTIAL.
001500 DATA DIVISION.
001600 FILE SECTION.
001700
001800 FD   CONTACTS
001900 01 CONTACT-RECORD.
002000     05 FILLER       PIC X(1).
002100     05 LNAME        PIC X(10).
002200     05 ID-NUM       PIC X(2).
002300 FD PTR-FILE
002400     LABEL RECORDS ARE OMITTED.
002500 01  PTR-REC.
002600     05 FILLER        PIC X(1).
002700     05 PTR-LNAME     PIC X(10).
002800     05 PTR-ID-NUM    PIC X(2).
002900 WORKING-STORAGE SECTION.
003000 01 WS-ID-NUM       PIC X(2) VALUE "42".  ◄──────
003100 PROCEDURE DIVISION.
003200     OPEN INPUT CONTACTS.
003300     OPEN OUTPUT PTR-FILE.
003400     MOVE WS-ID-NUM TO ID-NUM.
003500     READ CONTACTS                ◄──────────
003600      KEY IS ID-NUM OF CONTACTS-RECORD
003700      INVALID KEY DISPLAY "Invalid key."
003780      NOT INVALID KEY
003900        MOVE LNAME TO PTR-LNAME
004000        MOVE FNAME TO PTR-FNAME
004100        WRITE PTR-REC BEFORE ADVANCING 1
004200     END-READ.
004300     MOVE SPACES TO PTR-REC.
004400     WRITE PTR-REC BEFORE ADVANCING PAGE..
004500     CLOSE PTR-FILE CONTACTS .
004600     STOP RUN.
```

The physical definition of the file containing data that will be printed.

The physical definition of the printer.

The logical definition of the file.

The logical definition of the printer.

Define the search value.

Read a record from the file.

Copy the values to be printed.

Print the record.

Printing Text with Fields

Throughout this chapter you learned how to write information from the keyboard or from a file into memory, then how to write the information to the printer.

You've noticed that only the data itself is printed. Nothing on the printed document describes the data. In previous examples, a person's first and last name is printed.

Although we can easily identify the data as a person's name, printed documents should identify the data with text sometimes called a *label* such as:

First : Bob Last: Smith

A program can print a label identifying data by incorporating the text in the logical definition of the printer. The opposite page logically defines a printer as havinng two fields and two labels.

The position of the labels and fields in the detail record definition must be in the order in which they are to be printed on the page. In this case, label "First:" is printed first followed by the person's first name, then the label "Last" followed by the person's last name.

Notice each label is identified with a unique name (LABEL-1) and uses the **PIC** phrase to define the number of characters in the label. The text of the label is assigned a text of the label by using the **VALUE** phrase.

The program changes the value of the fields within the logical definition of the printer after new data is read into memory using the **MOVE** command. The **WRITE** command writes the complete record including the labels to the printer.

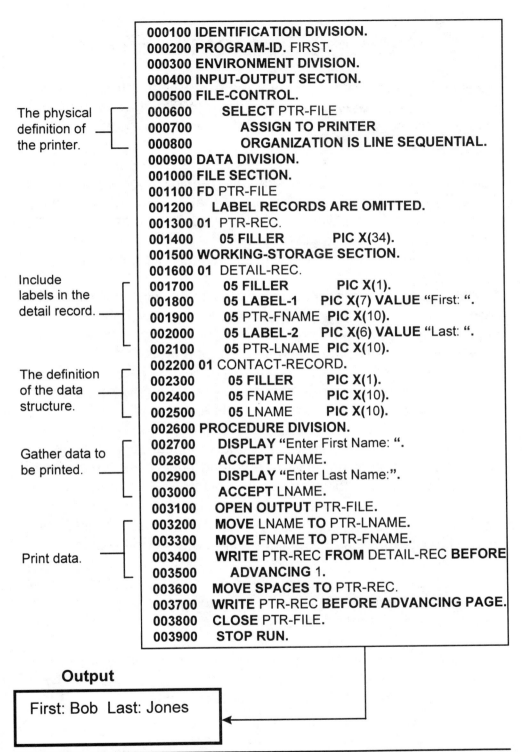

The physical definition of the printer.

Include labels in the detail record.

The definition of the data structure.

Gather data to be printed.

Print data.

```
000100 IDENTIFICATION DIVISION.
000200 PROGRAM-ID. FIRST.
000300 ENVIRONMENT DIVISION.
000400 INPUT-OUTPUT SECTION.
000500 FILE-CONTROL.
000600        SELECT PTR-FILE
000700          ASSIGN TO PRINTER
000800            ORGANIZATION IS LINE SEQUENTIAL.
000900 DATA DIVISION.
001000 FILE SECTION.
001100 FD PTR-FILE
001200    LABEL RECORDS ARE OMITTED.
001300 01  PTR-REC.
001400      05 FILLER         PIC X(34).
001500 WORKING-STORAGE SECTION.
001600 01  DETAIL-REC.
001700      05 FILLER        PIC X(1).
001800      05 LABEL-1     PIC X(7) VALUE "First: ".
001900      05 PTR-FNAME  PIC X(10).
002000      05 LABEL-2     PIC X(6) VALUE "Last: ".
002100      05 PTR-LNAME  PIC X(10).
002200 01 CONTACT-RECORD.
002300      05 FILLER        PIC X(1).
002400      05 FNAME        PIC X(10).
002500      05 LNAME        PIC X(10).
002600 PROCEDURE DIVISION.
002700      DISPLAY "Enter First Name: ".
002800      ACCEPT FNAME.
002900      DISPLAY "Enter Last Name:".
003000      ACCEPT LNAME.
003100      OPEN OUTPUT PTR-FILE.
003200      MOVE LNAME TO PTR-LNAME.
003300      MOVE FNAME TO PTR-FNAME.
003400      WRITE PTR-REC FROM DETAIL-REC BEFORE
003500         ADVANCING 1.
003600      MOVE SPACES TO PTR-REC.
003700      WRITE PTR-REC BEFORE ADVANCING PAGE.
003800      CLOSE PTR-FILE.
003900      STOP RUN.
```

Output

First: Bob Last: Jones

Creating a Report Layout

Previously in this chapter you learned how to place text to the left of each printed data to describe the data to the reader. This technique is adequate for some printing applications where many records are not printed.

However, many COBOL applications require information to be printed in a more pleasing report format where the first page contains a report title, fields are displayed in columns, each row represents a record, each column is identified by text, and additional information is printed on the last page of the report.

The remaining of this chapter is devoted to showing how to print a report using a COBOL application. You'll notice that such a report requires information to be printed in specific locations on the paper. Those locations are determined by the report layout.

A *report layout* is a plan containing the components of the report and where on the paper the components are printed.

There are many report styles. Here is a typical style that begins with a *report header* that is text appearing only on the first page of the report. This is followed by a *column header* that is text describing the contents of each column, A column header is usually printed at the top of every page except for the first page where the column header is printed below the report header.

Following the column header are the *details* of the report that consisting of records. At the end of each page there is a *page trailer* v typically contains the page number.

You can design your own report layout by plotting the components of a report on graph paper as shown on the opposite page. Each square represents a character position on the page.

Each box represents a character position on the report.

The report header prints on the first page of the report.

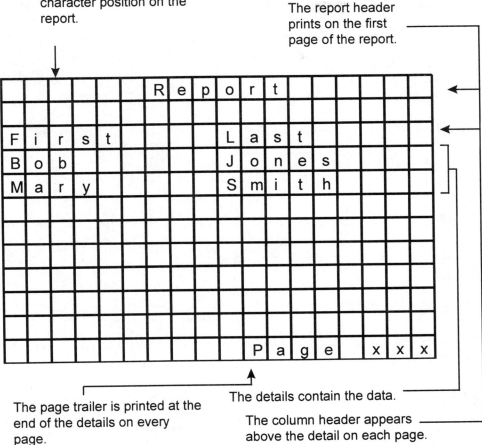

The page trailer is printed at the end of the details on every page.

The details contain the data.

The column header appears above the detail on each page.

Facts You Should Know...

○

The number of character positions on a page depends on the size of the paper. The example above is for illustrative purposes only and is not indented to represent a standard size paper.

○

○

In addition to the components described in the example, a report can be designed to have a *page header* containing text that prints at the top of every page and a *report trailer* for text to be printed only at the end of the report.

Printing Fields in Columns

A common report style is to place each record in a single row with each field starting at the same character position on the page. This gives the impression that fields are divided into columns in the report.

As described in Chapter 8, fields are defined as having a specific number of characters such as the first and last name fields in the example on the opposite page each contain no more than 10 characters.

The fixed size of each field makes it easy to design a report where the value of each field is placed in a column. The first character of each value of the same field always starts at the same position in the report.

Fields are printed in the order in which they are defined in the definition of the detail record as is illustrated in the File Section of the program on the next page.

Spaces can be inserted between fields on the report by defining a filler within the printer description. A *filler* is defined as having a specific number of spaces or literal characters. Typically, spaces are used to separate values contained in two fields when they are printed on the page.

You define a filler as having any number of spaces. However, it is very common that a fixed number of spaces is used to separate all columns in the report. This is to give the report a more balanced presentation.

You can determine the size of the filler by adding together the size of all the fields that are to be printed. Subtract the sum from the total number of characters on a page, then divide the difference by the number of columns to arrive at the size of the filler.

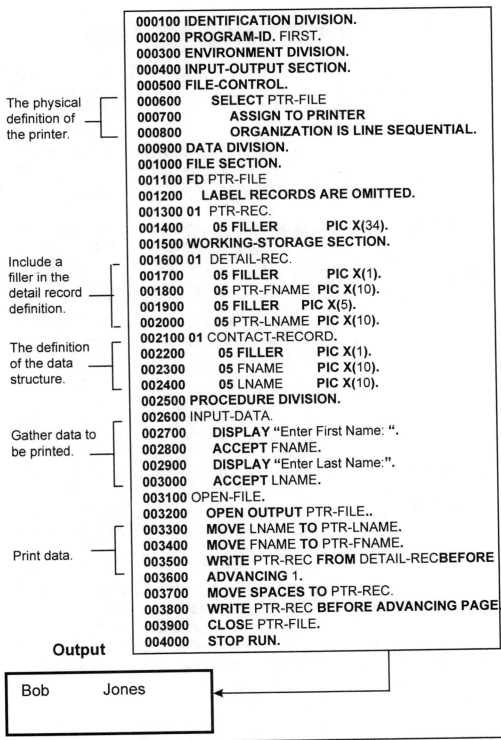

The physical definition of the printer.

```
000100 IDENTIFICATION DIVISION.
000200 PROGRAM-ID. FIRST.
000300 ENVIRONMENT DIVISION.
000400 INPUT-OUTPUT SECTION.
000500 FILE-CONTROL.
000600     SELECT PTR-FILE
000700         ASSIGN TO PRINTER
000800             ORGANIZATION IS LINE SEQUENTIAL.
000900 DATA DIVISION.
001000 FILE SECTION.
001100 FD PTR-FILE
001200     LABEL RECORDS ARE OMITTED.
001300 01  PTR-REC.
001400         05 FILLER        PIC X(34).
001500 WORKING-STORAGE SECTION.
001600 01  DETAIL-REC.
001700         05 FILLER        PIC X(1).
001800         05 PTR-FNAME PIC X(10).
001900         05 FILLER     PIC X(5).
002000         05 PTR-LNAME  PIC X(10).
002100 01 CONTACT-RECORD.
002200         05 FILLER       PIC X(1).
002300         05 FNAME        PIC X(10).
002400         05 LNAME        PIC X(10).
002500 PROCEDURE DIVISION.
002600 INPUT-DATA.
002700     DISPLAY "Enter First Name: ".
002800     ACCEPT FNAME.
002900     DISPLAY "Enter Last Name:".
003000     ACCEPT LNAME.
003100 OPEN-FILE.
003200     OPEN OUTPUT PTR-FILE..
003300     MOVE LNAME TO PTR-LNAME.
003400     MOVE FNAME TO PTR-FNAME.
003500     WRITE PTR-REC FROM DETAIL-RECBEFORE
003600     ADVANCING 1.
003700     MOVE SPACES TO PTR-REC.
003800     WRITE PTR-REC BEFORE ADVANCING PAGE.
003900     CLOSE PTR-FILE.
004000     STOP RUN.
```

Include a filler in the detail record definition.

The definition of the data structure.

Gather data to be printed.

Print data.

Output

Bob	Jones

Printing Report Title

The title of a report typically consists of the name of the report, the date, and other information that helps someone identify the data contained in the report.

The report title is commonly called the *report header* and is printed only on the first page of the report. There is nothing in COBOL that defines a report header from other text printed on the page.

A report header is a data structure that contains characters printed whenever a new report is created. It is the responsibility of the programmer to write the report header data structure to the printer whenever the report runs.

As illustrated on the opposite page, the report header data structure is defined within the Working-Storage Section of the Data Division.

Members of the report header data structure are defined as a filler. A filler contains literal characters or spaces and are printed in the order in which the filler is defined in the data structure.

Typically, information contained in the report header such as the title of the report needs to be centered on the page. There is no automatic function to center the text on a page. Instead, you must align the title by assigning spaces to the filler within the report header data structure.

Plot the title in the center of the graph paper using the technique illustrated previously in this chapter. Count the number of character positions appearing to the left of the first character in the title. This is the value of the number of spaces required to be assigned to the first filler in the data structure. This is shown in the example on the next page.

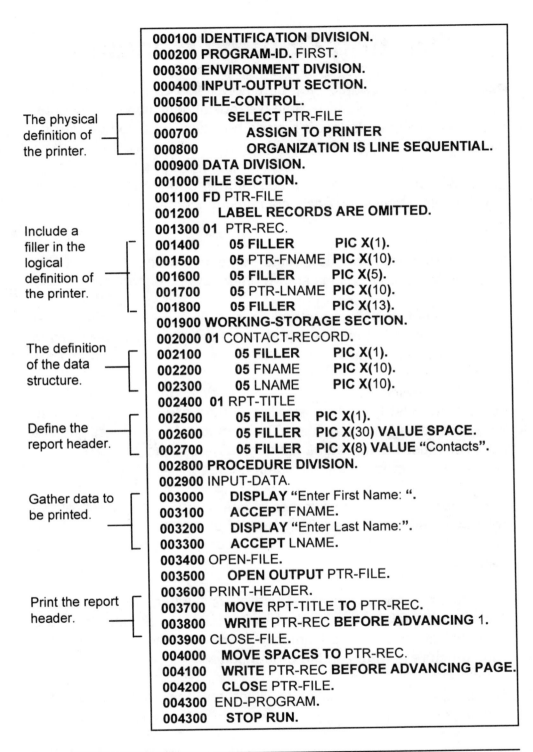

| The physical definition of the printer. | ```
000100 IDENTIFICATION DIVISION.
000200 PROGRAM-ID. FIRST.
000300 ENVIRONMENT DIVISION.
000400 INPUT-OUTPUT SECTION.
000500 FILE-CONTROL.
000600     SELECT PTR-FILE
000700        ASSIGN TO PRINTER
000800           ORGANIZATION IS LINE SEQUENTIAL.
``` |

```
000100 IDENTIFICATION DIVISION.
000200 PROGRAM-ID. FIRST.
000300 ENVIRONMENT DIVISION.
000400 INPUT-OUTPUT SECTION.
000500 FILE-CONTROL.
000600     SELECT PTR-FILE                          | The physical
000700        ASSIGN TO PRINTER                        definition of
000800           ORGANIZATION IS LINE SEQUENTIAL.      the printer.
000900 DATA DIVISION.
001000 FILE SECTION.
001100 FD PTR-FILE
001200     LABEL RECORDS ARE OMITTED.
001300 01  PTR-REC.                                 | Include a
001400        05 FILLER      PIC X(1).                filler in the
001500        05 PTR-FNAME PIC X(10).                 logical
001600        05 FILLER      PIC X(5).                definition of
001700        05 PTR-LNAME PIC X(10).                 the printer.
001800        05 FILLER      PIC X(13).
001900 WORKING-STORAGE SECTION.
002000 01 CONTACT-RECORD.                           | The definition
002100        05 FILLER      PIC X(1).                of the data
002200        05 FNAME       PIC X(10).               structure.
002300        05 LNAME       PIC X(10).
002400 01 RPT-TITLE
002500        05 FILLER    PIC X(1).                 | Define the
002600        05 FILLER    PIC X(30) VALUE SPACE.      report header.
002700        05 FILLER    PIC X(8) VALUE "Contacts".
002800 PROCEDURE DIVISION.
002900 INPUT-DATA.
003000     DISPLAY "Enter First Name: ".            | Gather data to
003100     ACCEPT FNAME.                              be printed.
003200     DISPLAY "Enter Last Name:".
003300     ACCEPT LNAME.
003400 OPEN-FILE.
003500     OPEN OUTPUT PTR-FILE.
003600 PRINT-HEADER.                                | Print the report
003700     MOVE RPT-TITLE TO PTR-REC.                 header.
003800     WRITE PTR-REC BEFORE ADVANCING 1.
003900 CLOSE-FILE.
004000     MOVE SPACES TO PTR-REC.
004100     WRITE PTR-REC BEFORE ADVANCING PAGE.
004200     CLOSE PTR-FILE.
004300 END-PROGRAM.
004300     STOP RUN.
```
```

Printing Column Headings

Previously in this chapter you saw how fields can be printed in a column. Fields are defined within the logical definition of the printer and fillers are used to insert spaces between the columns making the columns evenly distributed throughout the width of the report.

Each column should contain a column name to identify the data in the column. Names of each column are contained in a column header.

A *column header* is a data structured defined in the Working-Storage Section of the Data Division as shown on the opposite page.

Each element of the data structure is a filler that contains either characters used to form the name of the column or spaces used to separate column names.

Typically, the first filler in the column header data structure is the name of the first field. This is followed by a filler that uses spaces to separate the column names. The number of spaces assigned to the filler must be the same number as are used in the filler for printing fields, otherwise the column names will misalign.

A word of caution. The number of characters in the name of the column must not exceed the number of characters in the field, otherwise the column name will appear over more than one column.

The column header data structure is written to the printer immediately before the data is written to the printer. It is the responsibility of the programmer to make sure the column header data structure is written in the proper sequence.

The program on the next page illustrates how to create column headings for a report.

```
000100 IDENTIFICATION DIVISION.
000200 PROGRAM-ID. FIRST.
000300 ENVIRONMENT DIVISION.
000400 INPUT-OUTPUT SECTION.
000500 FILE-CONTROL.
000600     SELECT PTR-FILE
000700       ASSIGN TO PRINTER
000800         ORGANIZATION IS LINE SEQUENTIAL.
000900 DATA DIVISION.
001000 FILE SECTION.
001100 FD PTR-FILE
001200     LABEL RECORDS ARE OMITTED.
001300 01 PTR-REC.
001400     05 FILLER      PIC X(1).
001500     05 PTR-FNAME  PIC X(10).
001600     05 FILLER      PIC X(5).
001700     05 PTR-LNAME  PIC X(10).
001800 WORKING-STORAGE SECTION.
001900 01 CONTACT-RECORD.
002000     05 FILLER      PIC X(1).
002100     05 FNAME       PIC X(10).
002200     05 LNAME       PIC X(10).
002300 01 COL-HEAD.
002400     05 FILLER      PIC X(1).
002500     05 FILLER      PIC X(5) VALUE "First".
002600     05 FILLER      PIC X(5) VALUE SPACES.
002700     05 FILLER      PIC X(4) VALUE "Last".
002800 PROCEDURE DIVISION.
002900 INPUT-DATA.
003000     DISPLAY "Enter First Name: ".
003100     ACCEPT FNAME.
003200     DISPLAY "Enter Last Name:".
003300     ACCEPT LNAME.
003400 OPEN-FILE.
003500     OPEN OUTPUT PTR-FILE.
003600 PRINT-DATA.
003700     MOVE COL-HEAD TO PTR-REC.
003800     WRITE PTR-REC BEFORE ADVANCING 1.
003900 CLOSE-FILE.
004000     MOVE SPACES TO PTR-REC.
004100     WRITE PTR-REC BEFORE ADVANCING PAGE.
004200     CLOSE PTR-FILE.
004300 END-PROGRAM.
004400     STOP RUN.
```

Labels (left margin annotations):

- The physical definition of the printer. → (lines 000600–000800)
- Include a filler in the logical definition of the printer. → (lines 001400–001700)
- The definition of the data structure. → (lines 002000–002200)
- Define the column header. → (lines 002400–002700)
- Gather data to be printed. → (lines 003000–003300)
- Print the column header. → (lines 003700–003800)

Printing Report Trailer

Some reports require information to be printed on the last page of the report. This information is called the *report trailer* and can consist of a variety of data, but typically includes a sentence indicating the report is finished printing.

You don't have to include a report trailer on your report especially if the only information contained on the page is the message telling the user that this is the last page of the report.

The report trailer is created by defining a data structure as in the example on the next page in the Working-Storage Section of the Data Division.

The report trailer data structure defines fillers each of which is assigned text that will appear on the last page or spaces used to properly position the text on the page.

Notice that the number of character positions assigned to the filler does not have to correspond to any data in the report. An exception is if the report trailer contains the sum of one or more columns of data in the report. In this case, the spacing of data must correspond to the proper column position. You'll see how this is done later in this chapter.

Previously in this chapter, you've seen examples where spaces are assigned to the printer record after all the data is printed. The spaces formed a blank record that was then written to the last page of the report.

Instead of assigning a blank record as the last record of the report, you can assign the report trailer record to the printer record. This will cause the report trailer to be written to the printer.

You can see an example of this in the CLOSE-FILE paragraph on the opposite page.

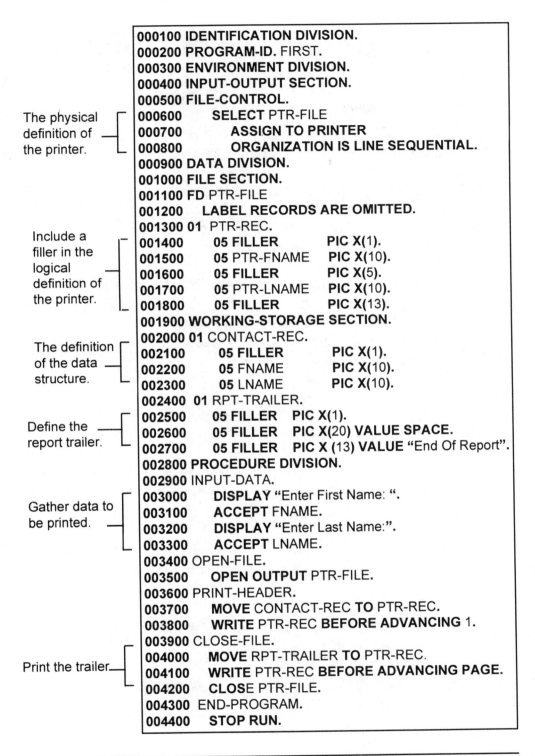

```
000100 IDENTIFICATION DIVISION.
000200 PROGRAM-ID. FIRST.
000300 ENVIRONMENT DIVISION.
000400 INPUT-OUTPUT SECTION.
000500 FILE-CONTROL.
000600     SELECT PTR-FILE
000700         ASSIGN TO PRINTER
000800         ORGANIZATION IS LINE SEQUENTIAL.
000900 DATA DIVISION.
001000 FILE SECTION.
001100 FD PTR-FILE
001200     LABEL RECORDS ARE OMITTED.
001300 01 PTR-REC.
001400     05 FILLER        PIC X(1).
001500     05 PTR-FNAME     PIC X(10).
001600     05 FILLER        PIC X(5).
001700     05 PTR-LNAME     PIC X(10).
001800     05 FILLER        PIC X(13).
001900 WORKING-STORAGE SECTION.
002000 01 CONTACT-REC.
002100     05 FILLER        PIC X(1).
002200     05 FNAME         PIC X(10).
002300     05 LNAME         PIC X(10).
002400 01 RPT-TRAILER.
002500     05 FILLER    PIC X(1).
002600     05 FILLER    PIC X(20) VALUE SPACE.
002700     05 FILLER    PIC X (13) VALUE "End Of Report".
002800 PROCEDURE DIVISION.
002900 INPUT-DATA.
003000     DISPLAY "Enter First Name: ".
003100     ACCEPT FNAME.
003200     DISPLAY "Enter Last Name:".
003300     ACCEPT LNAME.
003400 OPEN-FILE.
003500     OPEN OUTPUT PTR-FILE.
003600 PRINT-HEADER.
003700     MOVE CONTACT-REC TO PTR-REC.
003800     WRITE PTR-REC BEFORE ADVANCING 1.
003900 CLOSE-FILE.
004000     MOVE RPT-TRAILER TO PTR-REC.
004100     WRITE PTR-REC BEFORE ADVANCING PAGE.
004200     CLOSE PTR-FILE.
004300 END-PROGRAM.
004400     STOP RUN.
```

Annotations (left margin):

- The physical definition of the printer. → lines 000600–000800
- Include a filler in the logical definition of the printer. → lines 001400–001800
- The definition of the data structure. → lines 002100–002300
- Define the report trailer. → lines 002500–002700
- Gather data to be printed. → lines 003000–003300
- Print the trailer → lines 004000–004200

Determining the End
of the Page

Throughout this chapter you've learned there isn't an automatic feature of COBOL that positions the printer to the next line nor automatically continues printing to the next page.

Each application that prints data and text must track the lines on the page to determine if there is enough room to print another line. If there isn't, then the application must eject the current page and begin printing at the top of the next page.

The example on the next page illustrates a technique for tracking lines on a page. Notice a variable called LINE-CT is defined in the Working-Storage Section of the Data Division. This variable is initialized with the value 1 using the **VALUE** phrase to indicate printing is taking place on the first line of the page.

Records are read from a file, then written to the printer. After a record is printed, the printer is moved to the next line on the page using the **ADVANCING** 1 phrase.

Also, the value of the LINE-CT variable is incremented by one using the **COMPUTE** command. An **IF** statement is used to determine if the current value of the LINE-CT variable is less than 55.

The value 55 represents the maximum number of printable lines on a page and can vary depending on the length of the paper used for printing.

If the current value of LINE-CT exceeds 54, then the program writes a blank record and begins a new page.

Also, the value of LINE-CT is reset to 1 indicating printing will take place on the first line of the new page.

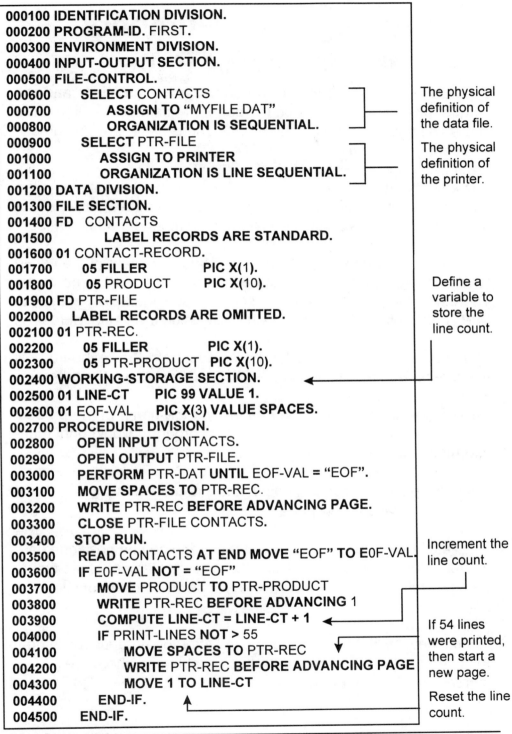

```
000100 IDENTIFICATION DIVISION.
000200 PROGRAM-ID. FIRST.
000300 ENVIRONMENT DIVISION.
000400 INPUT-OUTPUT SECTION.
000500 FILE-CONTROL.
000600     SELECT CONTACTS                              ⎤  The physical
000700         ASSIGN TO "MYFILE.DAT"                   ⎬  definition of
000800         ORGANIZATION IS SEQUENTIAL.             ⎦  the data file.
000900     SELECT PTR-FILE                              ⎤  The physical
001000         ASSIGN TO PRINTER                        ⎬  definition of
001100         ORGANIZATION IS LINE SEQUENTIAL.        ⎦  the printer.
001200 DATA DIVISION.
001300 FILE SECTION.
001400 FD  CONTACTS
001500         LABEL RECORDS ARE STANDARD.
001600 01 CONTACT-RECORD.
001700     05 FILLER          PIC X(1).
001800     05 PRODUCT         PIC X(10).                   Define a
001900 FD PTR-FILE                                         variable to
002000    LABEL RECORDS ARE OMITTED.                       store the
002100 01 PTR-REC.                                         line count.
002200     05 FILLER          PIC X(1).
002300     05 PTR-PRODUCT   PIC X(10).
002400 WORKING-STORAGE SECTION.
002500 01 LINE-CT    PIC 99 VALUE 1.
002600 01 EOF-VAL    PIC X(3) VALUE SPACES.
002700 PROCEDURE DIVISION.
002800     OPEN INPUT CONTACTS.
002900     OPEN OUTPUT PTR-FILE.
003000     PERFORM PTR-DAT UNTIL EOF-VAL = "EOF".
003100     MOVE SPACES TO PTR-REC.
003200     WRITE PTR-REC BEFORE ADVANCING PAGE.
003300     CLOSE PTR-FILE CONTACTS.
003400     STOP RUN.                                    Increment the
003500     READ CONTACTS AT END MOVE "EOF" TO E0F-VAL.  line count.
003600     IF E0F-VAL NOT = "EOF"
003700         MOVE PRODUCT TO PTR-PRODUCT
003800         WRITE PTR-REC BEFORE ADVANCING 1
003900         COMPUTE LINE-CT = LINE-CT + 1            If 54 lines
004000         IF PRINT-LINES NOT > 55                  were printed,
004100             MOVE SPACES TO PTR-REC               then start a
004200             WRITE PTR-REC BEFORE ADVANCING PAGE  new page.
004300             MOVE 1 TO LINE-CT
004400         END-IF.                                  Reset the line
004500     END-IF.                                      count.
```

Printing Page Numbers
at Top Left of Page

Each page of a report should be numbered sequentially and the number placed somewhere on the page. Pages must be numbered and positioned by the application. There isn't any automatic numbering feature available in COBOL.

The key to numbering pages is to write a routine that maintains the page count. This requires the programmer to create a variable that will be used to store a value equal to the number of pages printed.

In the example on the next page, the PG-NUM element of the PG-HD (page header) data structure is defined as containing three digits. Therefore, the report should not contain more than 999 pages. PG-NUM is also initialized with the value 1 by using the **VALUE** phrase.

The program reads a value for the product from the keyboard until the letter Q is entered that signifies the user is quitting the program.

Each page contains the page header and the name of the product in this example. However, a more typical program would print more information on the page.

After the page header is printed, the program prints the product name, then starts a new page.

The value of PG-NUM is the page number and can be positioned at the top left of the page by making the PG-NUM element of the first element in the PG-HEADER structure as shown on the opposite page.

Notice the **COMPUTE** command is used after the product is printed to increment the value of the **PG-NUM** variable and, therefore, increasing the page number of the report.

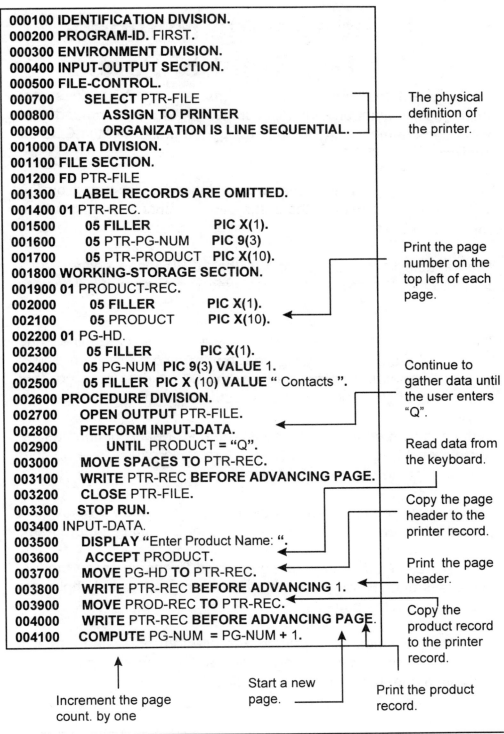

```
000100 IDENTIFICATION DIVISION.
000200 PROGRAM-ID. FIRST.
000300 ENVIRONMENT DIVISION.
000400 INPUT-OUTPUT SECTION.
000500 FILE-CONTROL.
000700     SELECT PTR-FILE
000800        ASSIGN TO PRINTER
000900        ORGANIZATION IS LINE SEQUENTIAL.
001000 DATA DIVISION.
001100 FILE SECTION.
001200 FD PTR-FILE
001300     LABEL RECORDS ARE OMITTED.
001400 01 PTR-REC.
001500     05 FILLER          PIC X(1).
001600     05 PTR-PG-NUM     PIC 9(3)
001700     05 PTR-PRODUCT    PIC X(10).
001800 WORKING-STORAGE SECTION.
001900 01 PRODUCT-REC.
002000     05 FILLER          PIC X(1).
002100     05 PRODUCT         PIC X(10).
002200 01 PG-HD.
002300     05 FILLER          PIC X(1).
002400     05 PG-NUM  PIC 9(3) VALUE 1.
002500     05 FILLER  PIC X (10) VALUE " Contacts ".
002600 PROCEDURE DIVISION.
002700     OPEN OUTPUT PTR-FILE.
002800     PERFORM INPUT-DATA.
002900         UNTIL PRODUCT = "Q".
003000     MOVE SPACES TO PTR-REC.
003100     WRITE PTR-REC BEFORE ADVANCING PAGE.
003200     CLOSE PTR-FILE.
003300     STOP RUN.
003400 INPUT-DATA.
003500     DISPLAY "Enter Product Name: ".
003600     ACCEPT PRODUCT.
003700     MOVE PG-HD TO PTR-REC.
003800     WRITE PTR-REC BEFORE ADVANCING 1.
003900     MOVE PROD-REC TO PTR-REC.
004000     WRITE PTR-REC BEFORE ADVANCING PAGE.
004100     COMPUTE PG-NUM = PG-NUM + 1.
```

The physical definition of the printer.

Print the page number on the top left of each page.

Continue to gather data until the user enters "Q".

Read data from the keyboard.

Copy the page header to the printer record.

Print the page header.

Copy the product record to the printer record.

Increment the page count. by one

Start a new page.

Print the product record.

Printing Page Numbers at Top Right of Page

As is presented earlier in this chapter, COBOL does not automatically number reports. You won't find a command that prints page numbers and increments page numbers in the COBOL language.

However, you can build your own routine as is illustrated on the opposite page. In this example, the page number is printed on the right side of the top of the page.

The variable PG-NUM is defined in the PG-HD (page header) data structure. This is the variable assigned the page number for the report.

The position within the PG-HD data structure determines the location where the page will appear on the report. On the previous page, the PG-NUM is defined first in the PG-HD data structure that causes the page number to appear at the top right of the page.

In the example on the opposite page, the PG-NUM is defined as the last element in the PG-HD data structure. This causes the number to appear at the top right of the page.

The program reads a value for the product from the keyboard until the letter Q is entered that signifies the user is quitting the program.

Each page contains the page header and the name of the product in this example. However, a more typical program would print more information on the page.

After the page header is printed, the program prints the name of the product, then starts a new page, and increments the PG-NUM variable before reading the next product from the keyboard.

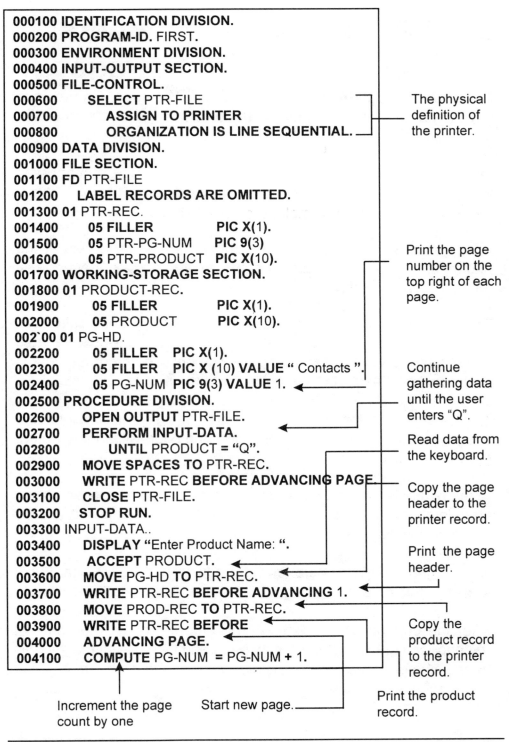

```
000100 IDENTIFICATION DIVISION.
000200 PROGRAM-ID. FIRST.
000300 ENVIRONMENT DIVISION.
000400 INPUT-OUTPUT SECTION.
000500 FILE-CONTROL.
000600     SELECT PTR-FILE
000700        ASSIGN TO PRINTER
000800        ORGANIZATION IS LINE SEQUENTIAL.
000900 DATA DIVISION.
001000 FILE SECTION.
001100 FD PTR-FILE
001200    LABEL RECORDS ARE OMITTED.
001300 01 PTR-REC.
001400     05 FILLER          PIC X(1).
001500     05 PTR-PG-NUM   PIC 9(3)
001600     05 PTR-PRODUCT  PIC X(10).
001700 WORKING-STORAGE SECTION.
001800 01 PRODUCT-REC.
001900     05 FILLER          PIC X(1).
002000     05 PRODUCT        PIC X(10).
002`00 01 PG-HD.
002200     05 FILLER   PIC X(1).
002300     05 FILLER   PIC X (10) VALUE " Contacts ".
002400     05 PG-NUM  PIC 9(3) VALUE 1.
002500 PROCEDURE DIVISION.
002600     OPEN OUTPUT PTR-FILE.
002700     PERFORM INPUT-DATA.
002800        UNTIL PRODUCT = "Q".
002900     MOVE SPACES TO PTR-REC.
003000     WRITE PTR-REC BEFORE ADVANCING PAGE.
003100     CLOSE PTR-FILE.
003200     STOP RUN.
003300 INPUT-DATA..
003400     DISPLAY "Enter Product Name: ".
003500     ACCEPT PRODUCT.
003600     MOVE PG-HD TO PTR-REC.
003700     WRITE PTR-REC BEFORE ADVANCING 1.
003800     MOVE PROD-REC TO PTR-REC.
003900     WRITE PTR-REC BEFORE
004000     ADVANCING PAGE.
004100     COMPUTE PG-NUM  = PG-NUM + 1.
```

The physical definition of the printer.

Print the page number on the top right of each page.

Continue gathering data until the user enters "Q".

Read data from the keyboard.

Copy the page header to the printer record.

Print the page header.

Copy the product record to the printer record.

Increment the page count by one

Start new page.

Print the product record.

Printing Page Numbers at Bottom Left of Page

Page numbers can be printed anywhere on the page. On previous pages you saw how to print a page number in either corner at the beginning of the page.

In those examples, the variable containing the page number was an element of the page header. The page header is the information that is printed at the beginning of every page.

It isn't uncommon to have page numbers printed in reports at the end of the page. Text that appears at the end of the page is contained with the page trailer.

The example on the opposite page defines a page trailer called PG-TR that consists of two elements. The first is the PG-NUM variable that is used to store the current page number. The other element is a filler that fills the rest of the positions in the record.

The position of the PG-NUM element within page trailer data structure determines the location where the page will appear on the report.

In the example on the opposite page, the PG-NUM is defined as the first element in the page trailer. This causes the number to appear at the bottom left of the page.

The program reads a value for the product from the keyboard until the letter Q is entered that signifies the user is quitting the program.

After the product data is printed, the program prints the name of the page trailer, then starts a new page and increments the PG-NUM variable before reading the next product from the keyboard.

```
000100 IDENTIFICATION DIVISION.
000200 PROGRAM-ID. FIRST.
000300 ENVIRONMENT DIVISION.
000400 INPUT-OUTPUT SECTION.
000500 FILE-CONTROL.
000700     SELECT PTR-FILE
000800        ASSIGN TO PRINTER
000900        ORGANIZATION IS LINE SEQUENTIAL.
001000 DATA DIVISION.
001100 FILE SECTION.
001200 FD PTR-FILE
001300     LABEL RECORDS ARE OMITTED.
001400 01 PTR-REC.
001500     05 FILLER        PIC X(1).
001600     01 PTR-PG-NUM PIC 9(3)
001700     05 PTR-PRODUCT  PIC X(10).
001800 WORKING-STORAGE SECTION.
001900 01 PRODUCT-REC.
002000     05 FILLER        PIC X(1).
002100     05 PRODUCT    PIC X(10).
002200 01 PG-TR.
002300     05 FILLER     PIC X(1).
002400     05 PG-NUM    PIC 9(3) VALUE 1.
002500     05 FILLER    PIC X (10).
002600 PROCEDURE DIVISION.
002700     OPEN OUTPUT PTR-FILE.
002800     PERFORM INPUT-DATA.
002900        UNTIL PRODUCT = "Q".
003000     MOVE SPACES TO PTR-REC.
003100     WRITE PTR-REC BEFORE ADVANCING PAGE.
003200     CLOSE PTR-FILE CONTACTS.
003300     STOP RUN.
003400 INPUT-DATA.
003500     DISPLAY "Enter Product Name: ".
003600     ACCEPT PRODUCT.
003600     MOVE PROD-REC TO PTR-REC.
003800     WRITE PTR-REC BEFORE ADVANCING 1.
003900     MOVE PG-TR TO PTR-REC.
004000     WRITE PTR-REC BEFORE
004100     ADVANCING PAGE.
004200     COMPUTE PG-NUM = PG-NUM + 1.
```

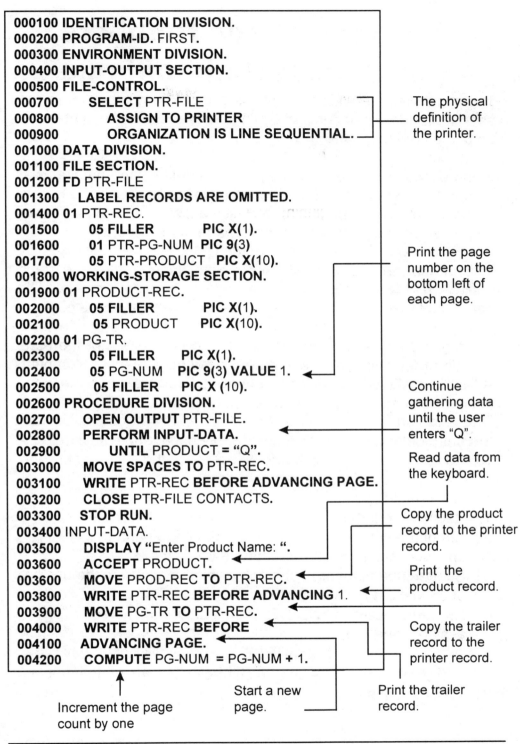

The physical definition of the printer.

Print the page number on the bottom left of each page.

Continue gathering data until the user enters "Q".

Read data from the keyboard.

Copy the product record to the printer record.

Print the product record.

Copy the trailer record to the printer record.

Increment the page count by one

Start a new page.

Print the trailer record.

Printing Page Numbers at Bottom Right of Page

The position of the variable containing the page number within the page trailer data structure determines where the page number will be printed on the page.

In the example on the previous page, PG-NUM is the variable used to hold the current page number and is defined as the first element of the page trailer data structure. This causes the page number to be printed on the bottom left of each page of the report.

In contrast, the example on the opposite page defines the same variable as the last element in the page trailer data structure. The page number is therefore printed at the bottom right on the page.

Page numbers can be centered on the top or bottom of the page by using fillers within the record before the page number is printed. A filler is assigned a specific number of characters that correspond to spaces when the filler is printed on the line.

It is your job to determine the number of characters to assign to the filler to force the page number to be printed in the center of the line. Here's how this is done.

1. Count the number of characters that will fit on the line.
2. Count the number of characters in the page number including any label such as PAGE 52 where PAGE is the label.
3. Subtract the number of characters in the page from the number of characters in the line.
4. Divide the result in half. This is the number of characters to assign to the filler.

EXAMPLE

72 = 80 characters on the line - 8 characters for the page number
31 = 72 remaining characters \ 2.

FILLER   PIC X(31).

```
000100 IDENTIFICATION DIVISION.
000200 PROGRAM-ID. FIRST.
000300 ENVIRONMENT DIVISION.
000400 INPUT-OUTPUT SECTION.
000500 FILE-CONTROL.
000700     SELECT PTR-FILE
000800         ASSIGN TO PRINTER
000900         ORGANIZATION IS LINE SEQUENTIAL.
001000 DATA DIVISION.
001100 FILE SECTION.
001200 FD PTR-FILE
001300     LABEL RECORDS ARE OMITTED.
001400 01 PTR-REC.
001500     05 FILLER        PIC X(1).
001600     01 PTR-PG-NUM  PIC 9(3)
001700     05 PTR-PRODUCT   PIC X(10).
001800 WORKING-STORAGE SECTION.
001900 01 PRODUCT-REC.
002000     05 FILLER        PIC X(1).
002100     05 PRODUCT   PIC X(10).
002200 01 PG-TR.
002300     05 FILLER        PIC X(1).
002400     05 PG-NUM  PIC 9(3) VALUE 1.
002500     05 FILLER  PIC X (10) VALUE " Contacts ".
002600 PROCEDURE DIVISION.
002700     OPEN OUTPUT PTR-FILE.
002800     PERFORM INPUT-DATA.
002900         UNTIL PRODUCT = "Q".
003000     MOVE SPACES TO PTR-REC.
003100     WRITE PTR-REC BEFORE ADVANCING PAGE.
003200     CLOSE PTR-FILE CONTACTS.
003200     STOP RUN.
003300 INPUT-DATA..
003400     DISPLAY "Enter Product Name: ".
003500     ACCEPT PRODUCT.
003600     MOVE PROD-REC TO PTR-REC.
003700     WRITE PTR-REC BEFORE ADVANCING 1.
003800     MOVE PG-TR TO PTR-REC.
003900     WRITE PTR-REC BEFORE
004000     ADVANCING PAGE.
004100     COMPUTE PG-NUM = PG-NUM + 1.
```

The physical definition of the printer.

Print the page number on the bottom right of each page.

Continue gathering data until the user enters "Q".

Read data from the keyboard.

Copy the product record to the printer record.

Print the product record.

Copy the trailer record to the printer record.

Print the trailer record.

Increment the page count by one

Start a new page

Create Multiline Text

Throughout this chapter you learned how to create a report header, column headings, a report trailer, and a page trailer. These are typical components of a report that contains textual information that explains the data printed in the report.

Each of these components printed text on a single line in the example previously shown in this chapter. Typically, programmers will be required to use more than one line such as when there is insufficient column width to print all the text in a column heading.

You can add as many lines as necessary by defining a data structure for each line, then entering the appropriate text to be printed on the line.

This technique is illustrated on the opposite page where the program creates a two-line column heading. You can use this same technique to create additional lines in the other components of a report.

Each data structure defines a line and contains text that will appear on that line. This can become confusing at times because text contained in the data structure does not make sense when you read it in the program.

For example, the first data structure has two column headings that read "First" and "Last". You may ask yourself, first and last of what. It isn't until you read the text in the second structure that you complete the thought with the words "Name" and "Name".

Another area that can become confusing is when the lines are printed on the page. Each line must be printed separately as illustrated at the end of the program on the next page.

The column position of each line must match the column position of the data record, otherwise the columns will misalign.

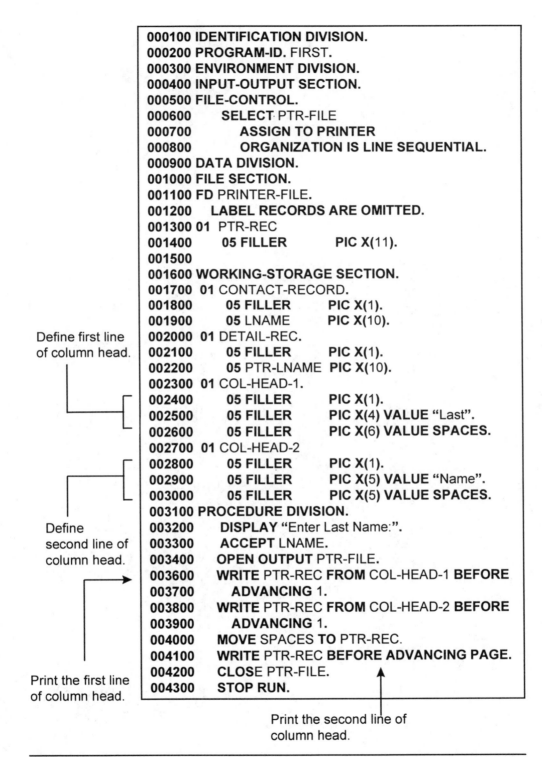

```
000100 IDENTIFICATION DIVISION.
000200 PROGRAM-ID. FIRST.
000300 ENVIRONMENT DIVISION.
000400 INPUT-OUTPUT SECTION.
000500 FILE-CONTROL.
000600     SELECT PTR-FILE
000700        ASSIGN TO PRINTER
000800           ORGANIZATION IS LINE SEQUENTIAL.
000900 DATA DIVISION.
001000 FILE SECTION.
001100 FD PRINTER-FILE.
001200     LABEL RECORDS ARE OMITTED.
001300 01 PTR-REC
001400       05 FILLER         PIC X(11).
001500
001600 WORKING-STORAGE SECTION.
001700 01 CONTACT-RECORD.
001800       05 FILLER      PIC X(1).
001900       05 LNAME       PIC X(10).
002000 01 DETAIL-REC.
002100       05 FILLER      PIC X(1).
002200       05 PTR-LNAME   PIC X(10).
002300 01 COL-HEAD-1.
002400       05 FILLER      PIC X(1).
002500       05 FILLER      PIC X(4) VALUE "Last".
002600       05 FILLER      PIC X(6) VALUE SPACES.
002700 01 COL-HEAD-2
002800       05 FILLER      PIC X(1).
002900       05 FILLER      PIC X(5) VALUE "Name".
003000       05 FILLER      PIC X(5) VALUE SPACES.
003100 PROCEDURE DIVISION.
003200     DISPLAY "Enter Last Name:".
003300     ACCEPT LNAME.
003400     OPEN OUTPUT PTR-FILE.
003600     WRITE PTR-REC FROM COL-HEAD-1 BEFORE
003700        ADVANCING 1.
003800     WRITE PTR-REC FROM COL-HEAD-2 BEFORE
003900        ADVANCING 1.
004000     MOVE SPACES TO PTR-REC.
004100     WRITE PTR-REC BEFORE ADVANCING PAGE.
004200     CLOSE PTR-FILE.
004300     STOP RUN.
```

Define first line of column head.

Define second line of column head.

Print the first line of column head.

Print the second line of column head.

Working to Solve the Year 2000 Problem

What Is the
Year 2000 Problem?

There isn't a day that doesn't go by when you hear about how the year 2000 problem is going to stop all the computers in the world from working on January 1, 2000.

The problem is a serious one. Consider, do you have money in the bank? If you answer yes, then you're wrong. Another question, does your employer have money in the bank to keep the business running and to pay you. Again if you answer yes, you're wrong.

We live in a cashless society. Instead of cash, we use book-entry to keep track of who owes whom cash. For example, the bank records in a computer database cash it owes you. This is called your bank account. The same holds true with your employer.

What would happen if the bank couldn't get at this database? The bank wouldn't process any transactions until the problem was fixed. This means the bank can't give you or your employer cash nor transfer funds electronically to other financial institutions such as what occurs when someone cashes your check.

Why would computers stop working? It is because programs that manipulate dates probably aren't programmed to handle the year 2000.

Dates are typically stored as mmddyy where the century digit is dropped and assumed to be 19. So come the year 2000, the year of the date will be 00 and computer programs will either assume it is 1900 or stop altogether because the program cannot use a year 00. An example is shown on the next page.

The real year 2000 problem is trying to find all the places in all the programs where dates are manipulated, then to fix and test all the programs before January 1, 2000. This chapters shows how to find and fix such routines in COBOL programs.

The following program calculates a person's birth year by subtracting the year from the current date. The current date is obtained by the program by requesting the date from the operating system using the DATE request.

What is the person's age if 80, the birth year of the person in this example, is subtracted from the current year? It all depends if the system's date is two or four digits and if the operating system is year 2000 compliant.

```
000100 IDENTIFICATION DIVISION.
000200 PROGRAM-ID. FIRST.
000300 ENVIRONMENT DIVISION.
000400 INPUT-OUTPUT SECTION.
000500 FILE-CONTROL.
000900 DATA DIVISION.
001700 WORKING-STORAGE SECTION.
001800 01 BIRTH-DATE.
001800    05 BIRTH-YR    PIC 9(2).
001800    05 BIRTH-MO    PIC 9(2).
001800    05 BIRTH-DAY   PIC 9(62).
001800 01 CUR-DATE.
001800    05 CUR -YR     PIC 9(2).
001800    05 CUR -MO     PIC 9(2).
001800    05 CUR -DAY    PIC 9(2).
001800 01 AGE            PIC 9(3).
000900 PROCEDURAL DIVISION.
001800    MOVE 80 TO BIRTH-YR.
001800    ACCEPT  CUR-DATE FROM DATE.
001800    COMPUTE AGE = CUR -YR - BIRTH-YR.
001800    DISPLAY AGE.
004200    STOP RUN.
```

The Year 2000 Problem

99	00
− 80	− 80
19	− 80

DATE

COBOL programs determine the current date by making a request to the operating system by using the reserved word **DATE**. **DATE** polls the operating system for the system's date, then returns the value to the application.

The request is typically made by initially creating a variable that will be used to store the date within the application. The variable is defined as **PIC X**(6).

Next, the **ACCEPT** command is used to issue the request for the date from the operating system, then assign the return value to the date variable. This is illustrated in the example on the opposite page.

Notice the **FROM** phrase is used with within the sentence. The **FROM** phrase identifies where the **ACCEPT** command is to find the data to assign to the date variable.

A word of caution. The **DATE** reserved word returns a two-character year on some operating system. This means the year 2000 is returned as 00. Check with the documentation that came with your COBOL compiler to determine if the compiler adjusts the date to include the century.

Problems can occur with routines that manipulate dates based upon the return value of **DATE** if the century characters aren't returned. The date routine within the program may not manipulate dates properly.

Routines that use the **DATE** reserved word must be examined to determine if it is affected by the year 2000 problem. If so, then the routine must be rewritten to remove the year 2000 bug from the application.

Techniques for fixing this problem are presented throughout this chapter and can be incorporated in routines with **DATE**.

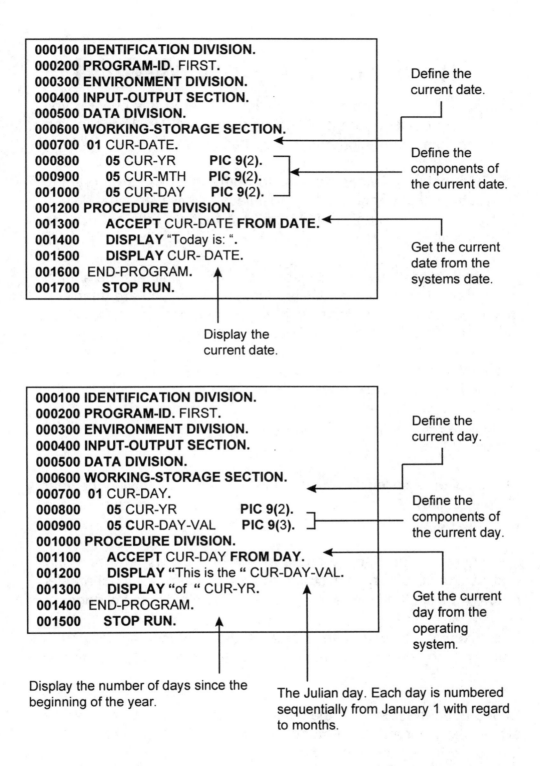

```
000100 IDENTIFICATION DIVISION.
000200 PROGRAM-ID. FIRST.
000300 ENVIRONMENT DIVISION.
000400 INPUT-OUTPUT SECTION.
000500 DATA DIVISION.
000600 WORKING-STORAGE SECTION.
000700 01 CUR-DATE.
000800    05 CUR-YR     PIC 9(2).
000900    05 CUR-MTH    PIC 9(2).
001000    05 CUR-DAY    PIC 9(2).
001200 PROCEDURE DIVISION.
001300    ACCEPT CUR-DATE FROM DATE.
001400    DISPLAY "Today is: ".
001500    DISPLAY CUR- DATE.
001600 END-PROGRAM.
001700    STOP RUN.
```

Define the current date.

Define the components of the current date.

Get the current date from the systems date.

Display the current date.

```
000100 IDENTIFICATION DIVISION.
000200 PROGRAM-ID. FIRST.
000300 ENVIRONMENT DIVISION.
000400 INPUT-OUTPUT SECTION.
000500 DATA DIVISION.
000600 WORKING-STORAGE SECTION.
000700 01 CUR-DAY.
000800    05 CUR-YR         PIC 9(2).
000900    05 CUR-DAY-VAL    PIC 9(3).
001000 PROCEDURE DIVISION.
001100    ACCEPT CUR-DAY FROM DAY.
001200    DISPLAY "This is the " CUR-DAY-VAL.
001300    DISPLAY "of " CUR-YR.
001400 END-PROGRAM.
001500    STOP RUN.
```

Define the current day.

Define the components of the current day.

Get the current day from the operating system.

Display the number of days since the beginning of the year.

The Julian day. Each day is numbered sequentially from January 1 with regard to months.

The Fixed Window Method

How do you fix the year 2000 problem? So far in this chapter you learned the depth of the problem and how a COBOL application captures date information from the operating system.

This information provides clues as to where to look in a program to find routines that perform date manipulation. However, what do you do to remedy the situation if you find the routine does not use the century digit?

The obvious solutions are to insert the century digit into the source of the date such as fields in a file, but sometimes you are unable to due to technical constraints or simply a lack of time to fix all the problems affected by the year 2000 problem.

A common solution to this dilemma is to rewrite the date routine that will adjust dates based on an assumption. Typically, the assumption is that a year of 50 to 99 is assumed to be 1950 through 1999. A year 00 through 49 is assumed to be 2000 through 2049.

This solution is called the Fixed Window Method of solving the year 2000 problem. An example of such a routine is shown on the opposite page.

The source of the date, such as a field in a file, is read normally and assigned to a record structure that contains a two-character date. The value and format of the date in the file doesn't change.

The Fixed Window routine evaluates the year characters of the date and compares the value against the previously mentioned assumptions.

Based upon the results of the evaluation, the Fixed Window routine stores the appropriate century characters into a variable that is then used throughout the program.

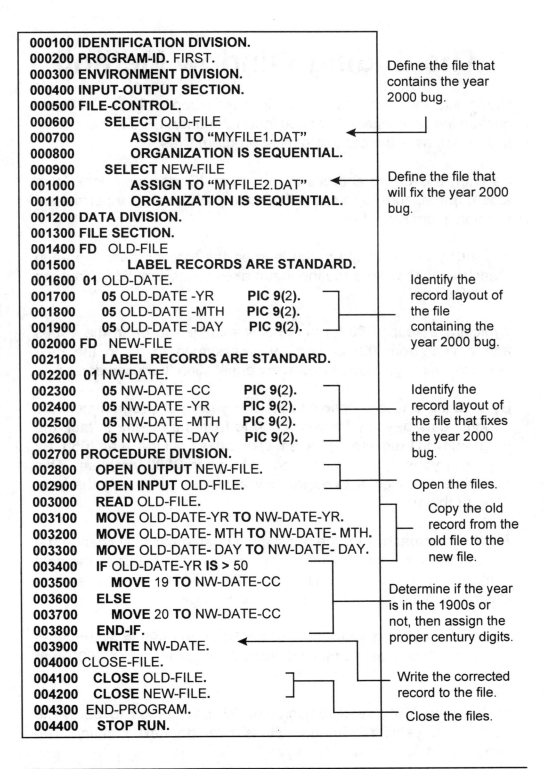

```
000100 IDENTIFICATION DIVISION.
000200 PROGRAM-ID. FIRST.
000300 ENVIRONMENT DIVISION.
000400 INPUT-OUTPUT SECTION.
000500 FILE-CONTROL.
000600     SELECT OLD-FILE
000700         ASSIGN TO "MYFILE1.DAT"
000800         ORGANIZATION IS SEQUENTIAL.
000900     SELECT NEW-FILE
001000         ASSIGN TO "MYFILE2.DAT"
001100         ORGANIZATION IS SEQUENTIAL.
001200 DATA DIVISION.
001300 FILE SECTION.
001400 FD   OLD-FILE
001500         LABEL RECORDS ARE STANDARD.
001600 01 OLD-DATE.
001700     05 OLD-DATE -YR     PIC 9(2).
001800     05 OLD-DATE -MTH    PIC 9(2).
001900     05 OLD-DATE -DAY    PIC 9(2).
002000 FD   NEW-FILE
002100         LABEL RECORDS ARE STANDARD.
002200 01 NW-DATE.
002300     05 NW-DATE -CC      PIC 9(2).
002400     05 NW-DATE -YR      PIC 9(2).
002500     05 NW-DATE -MTH     PIC 9(2).
002600     05 NW-DATE -DAY     PIC 9(2).
002700 PROCEDURE DIVISION.
002800     OPEN OUTPUT NEW-FILE.
002900     OPEN INPUT OLD-FILE.
003000     READ OLD-FILE.
003100     MOVE OLD-DATE-YR TO NW-DATE-YR.
003200     MOVE OLD-DATE- MTH TO NW-DATE- MTH.
003300     MOVE OLD-DATE- DAY TO NW-DATE- DAY.
003400     IF OLD-DATE-YR IS > 50
003500         MOVE 19 TO NW-DATE-CC
003600     ELSE
003700         MOVE 20 TO NW-DATE-CC
003800     END-IF.
003900     WRITE NW-DATE.
004000 CLOSE-FILE.
004100     CLOSE OLD-FILE.
004200     CLOSE NEW-FILE.
004300 END-PROGRAM.
004400     STOP RUN.
```

Define the file that contains the year 2000 bug.

Define the file that will fix the year 2000 bug.

Identify the record layout of the file containing the year 2000 bug.

Identify the record layout of the file that fixes the year 2000 bug.

Open the files.

Copy the old record from the old file to the new file.

Determine if the year is in the 1900s or not, then assign the proper century digits.

Write the corrected record to the file.

Close the files.

The Sliding Window Method

Removing the year 2000 bug in every application is a time-consuming task where the deadline of January 1, 2000 cannot be postponed as is the case with most program fixes.

As time runs out to address the problem, IS managers look for a stop gap measure to temporarily fix the problem until a permanent solution is firmly in place.

Previously in this chapter, you learned the tone of those stop-gap measures is to write a routine that makes an assumption about the year of a date.

Typically, a year of 50 through 99 is assumed to be in the 1900s and a year from 00 through 49 is assumed to be in the next century. This logic is built into every application that uses dates.

By creating an assumption about the year, the programmer has bought years beyond the year 2000 to fix the problem. In fact, the program won't run into a problem with dates until the year 2050. By then everyone hopes to remedy the year 2000 problem. This technique is called a fixed window approach to solving the year 2000 problem.

Another approach is for the application to automatically change the assumption each year by moving years from the 1900s to the next century. This technique is called the sliding window and is illustrated in the example on the opposite page.

For example, in the year 2000, years 50 through 99 is assumed to be in the 1900s and years 00 through 49 in the year 2000 and beyond.

In the year 2001, years 51 through 99 is assumed to be in the 1900s and years 00 through 50 is into the next century. The pattern continues to shift each year.

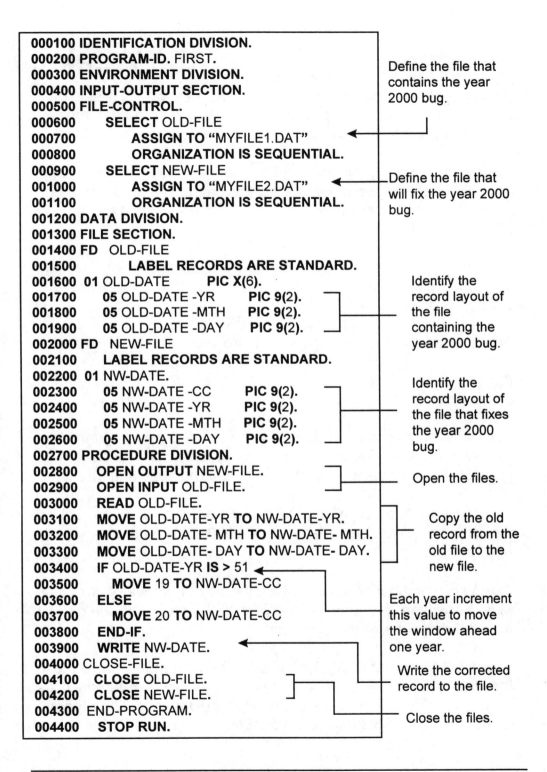

```
000100 IDENTIFICATION DIVISION.
000200 PROGRAM-ID. FIRST.
000300 ENVIRONMENT DIVISION.
000400 INPUT-OUTPUT SECTION.
000500 FILE-CONTROL.
000600     SELECT OLD-FILE
000700        ASSIGN TO "MYFILE1.DAT"
000800        ORGANIZATION IS SEQUENTIAL.
000900     SELECT NEW-FILE
001000        ASSIGN TO "MYFILE2.DAT"
001100        ORGANIZATION IS SEQUENTIAL.
001200 DATA DIVISION.
001300 FILE SECTION.
001400 FD   OLD-FILE
001500        LABEL RECORDS ARE STANDARD.
001600 01 OLD-DATE        PIC X(6).
001700     05 OLD-DATE -YR      PIC 9(2).
001800     05 OLD-DATE -MTH     PIC 9(2).
001900     05 OLD-DATE -DAY     PIC 9(2).
002000 FD   NEW-FILE
002100        LABEL RECORDS ARE STANDARD.
002200 01 NW-DATE.
002300     05 NW-DATE -CC       PIC 9(2).
002400     05 NW-DATE -YR       PIC 9(2).
002500     05 NW-DATE -MTH      PIC 9(2).
002600     05 NW-DATE -DAY      PIC 9(2).
002700 PROCEDURE DIVISION.
002800     OPEN OUTPUT NEW-FILE.
002900     OPEN INPUT OLD-FILE.
003000     READ OLD-FILE.
003100     MOVE OLD-DATE-YR TO NW-DATE-YR.
003200     MOVE OLD-DATE- MTH TO NW-DATE- MTH.
003300     MOVE OLD-DATE- DAY TO NW-DATE- DAY.
003400     IF OLD-DATE-YR IS > 51
003500        MOVE 19 TO NW-DATE-CC
003600     ELSE
003700        MOVE 20 TO NW-DATE-CC
003800     END-IF.
003900     WRITE NW-DATE.
004000 CLOSE-FILE.
004100     CLOSE OLD-FILE.
004200     CLOSE NEW-FILE.
004300 END-PROGRAM.
004400     STOP RUN.
```

Define the file that contains the year 2000 bug.

Define the file that will fix the year 2000 bug.

Identify the record layout of the file containing the year 2000 bug.

Identify the record layout of the file that fixes the year 2000 bug.

Open the files.

Copy the old record from the old file to the new file.

Each year increment this value to move the window ahead one year.

Write the corrected record to the file.

Close the files.

Fixing the Day of the Week

Some COBOL applications reference the day of the week of a date. A problem arises if the application isn't year 2000 compliant and assumes the date is in the 1900s.

January 1, 1900 is a Monday while January 1, 2000 is a Saturday. This difference is commonly called the day of the week problem. An application that assumes the year is 1900 will calculate the day of the week incorrectly.

This problem must be addressed by all applications that use the day of the week. Not all applications do this, so many applications will not be affected by the problem.

Applications that could be affected are those such as a payroll program that is likely to assume January 2 is a work day. In 1900, the second day of the year was a work day, but in the year 2000 it is a Sunday.

Another kind of program affected by this problem are programs that run other programs on a particular day of the week. These too will probably run on Sunday and shut down on Thursday and Friday.

You must write a routine that works around this problem, unless the program has been made year 2000 compliant by properly adjusting the date.

Whenever the application accesses the day of the week, a routine must be written to determine the year. If the year is in the 1900s, then the day of the week is correct.

However, if the year is 2000 or greater, then the routine must move the day of the week back two days. If the day is referenced as Friday, then the day must be changed to Wednesday. The program on the next page illustrates such a technique.

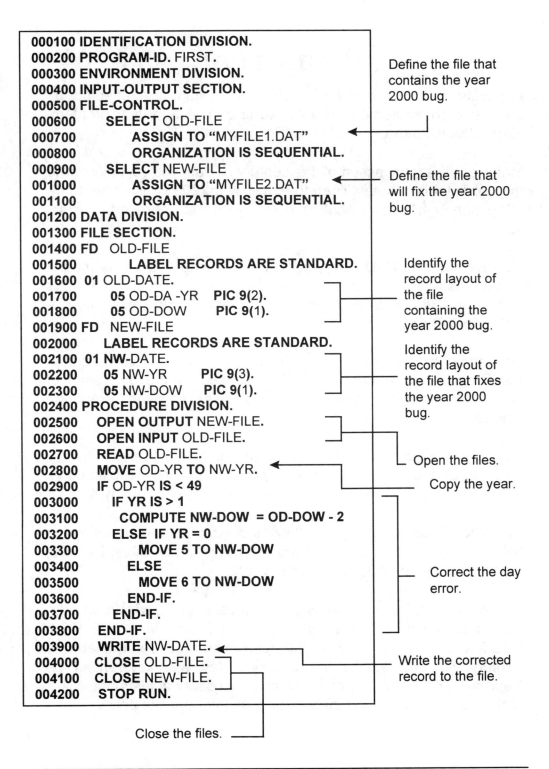

```
000100 IDENTIFICATION DIVISION.
000200 PROGRAM-ID. FIRST.
000300 ENVIRONMENT DIVISION.
000400 INPUT-OUTPUT SECTION.
000500 FILE-CONTROL.
000600     SELECT OLD-FILE
000700         ASSIGN TO "MYFILE1.DAT"
000800         ORGANIZATION IS SEQUENTIAL.
000900     SELECT NEW-FILE
001000         ASSIGN TO "MYFILE2.DAT"
001100         ORGANIZATION IS SEQUENTIAL.
001200 DATA DIVISION.
001300 FILE SECTION.
001400 FD   OLD-FILE
001500         LABEL RECORDS ARE STANDARD.
001600 01 OLD-DATE.
001700     05 OD-DA -YR   PIC 9(2).
001800     05 OD-DOW      PIC 9(1).
001900 FD   NEW-FILE
002000     LABEL RECORDS ARE STANDARD.
002100 01 NW-DATE.
002200     05 NW-YR      PIC 9(3).
002300     05 NW-DOW     PIC 9(1).
002400 PROCEDURE DIVISION.
002500     OPEN OUTPUT NEW-FILE.
002600     OPEN INPUT OLD-FILE.
002700     READ OLD-FILE.
002800     MOVE OD-YR TO NW-YR.
002900     IF OD-YR IS < 49
003000       IF YR IS > 1
003100         COMPUTE NW-DOW  = OD-DOW - 2
003200       ELSE  IF YR = 0
003300           MOVE 5 TO NW-DOW
003400         ELSE
003500           MOVE 6 TO NW-DOW
003600         END-IF.
003700       END-IF.
003800     END-IF.
003900     WRITE NW-DATE.
004000     CLOSE OLD-FILE.
004100     CLOSE NEW-FILE.
004200     STOP RUN.
```

Define the file that contains the year 2000 bug.

Define the file that will fix the year 2000 bug.

Identify the record layout of the file containing the year 2000 bug.

Identify the record layout of the file that fixes the year 2000 bug.

Open the files.

Copy the year.

Correct the day error.

Write the corrected record to the file.

Close the files.

Leap Year

Applications that are not year 2000 compliant are affected by another problem sometimes referred to as the leap year problem. Here's the dilemma.

Many applications assume the century 19 as you've discovered throughout this chapter. Therefore, the year 2000 is assumed to be 1900 although the application uses the 00 to represent the full year.

However, unlike 1900, the year 2000 is a leap year. This means one day is added to February. The last day in February in 1900 is February 28th. The last day in February in the year 2000 is February 29th.

Leap year was created in the 16th century to account for the drift in the Gregorian calendar. The drift is caused by the difference of about 11 minutes between the solar year and the Gregorian calendar.

Leap year occurs every four years and in years that are evenly divisible by four. However, years ending in 00 are the exception. They are not a leap year unless they are evenly divisible by 400.

This sounds as confusing to follow as directions for completing tax forms. The bottom line is 1900 isn't evenly divisible by 400, however the year 2000 is divisible by 400.

Unless the dates are adjusted to reflect the year 2000, the application must contain a routine that corrects for leap year. Each time March 1st is referenced, the application must determine if the century is 2000 and if the previous day was referenced as February 28th or 29th, then make any necessary adjustments. This technique is illustrated in the example on the opposite page.

```
000100 IDENTIFICATION DIVISION.
000200 PROGRAM-ID. FIRST.
000300 ENVIRONMENT DIVISION.
000400 INPUT-OUTPUT SECTION.
000500 FILE-CONTROL.
000600     SELECT OLD-FILE
000700         ASSIGN TO "MYFILE1.DAT"
000800         ORGANIZATION IS SEQUENTIAL.
000900     SELECT NEW-FILE
001000         ASSIGN TO "MYFILE2.DAT"
001100         ORGANIZATION IS SEQUENTIAL.
001200 DATA DIVISION.
001300 FILE SECTION.
001400 FD   OLD-FILE
001500         LABEL RECORDS ARE STANDARD.
001600 01 OLD-DATE.
001700     05 OD-YR     PIC 9(2).
001800     05 OD-MO     PIC 9(2).
001900     05 OD-DA     PIC 9(3).
002000 FD   NEW-FILE
002100         LABEL RECORDS ARE STANDARD.
002200 01 NW-DATE.
002300     05 NW-YR     PIC 9(2).
002400     05 NW-MO     PIC 9(2).
002500     05 NW-DA     PIC 9(2).
002600 PROCEDURE DIVISION.
002700     OPEN OUTPUT NEW-FILE.
002800     OPEN INPUT OLD-FILE.
002900     READ OLD-FILE.
003000     MOVE OD-YR TO NW-YR.
003100     IF OD-YR IS = 00
003200         IF OD-YR IS = 03 AND OD-DA = 01
003300             MOVE 02 TO NW-MO
003400             MOVE 29 TO NW-DA
003500         END-IF
003600     END-IF.
003700     WRITE NW-DATE.
003800     CLOSE OLD-FILE.
003900     CLOSE NEW-FILE.
004000     STOP RUN.
```

Define the file that contains the year 2000 bug.

Define the file that will fix the year 2000 bug.

Identify the record layout of the file containing the year 2000 bug.

Identify the record layout of the file that fixes the year 2000 bug.

Open the files.

Copy the year.

Correct the leap year error.

Write the corrected record to the file.

Close the files.

Finding Dates

Everyone knows how to solve the year 2000 problem by expanding the date variable or field, then inserting the century digits. However, one of the more challenging tasks is to locate where dates are used both in programs and in files.

Life would be easy if every programmer named date variables and date elements of data structures using the word date in the name. However, nothing is that easy.

Some programmers use such abstract names as D1, MONTH-END, or even identify it by a single letter. There is no easy way to locate every date by looking at a program.

The concerns of programmers working on solving the year 2000 program is that every date must be identified and analyzed to determine if the date could cause havoc with the program come the turn of the century.

Missing one date could possibly cause a program to abend that means the program abnormally ended typically caused by a run-time error. A run-time error occurs when an anticipated data value such as a date is inappropriate to an operation performed by the application such as subtracting years of two dates.

Your job is to look for clues throughout the code that will imply a date is being reference in the program. The initial step is to use the find feature of your editor and attempt to locate words that may have been used for dates. Some of those words are shown on the next page.

Next, either use the find feature or review the **Data Division** for variables that are defined as PIC 9(6) or PIC X(6). Typically, dates are defined with such a size. The final step is to give a quick review of processing routines for signs of date calculations.

Some YR 2000 Suspects

```
001100       MOVE 990504 TO CUR-DATE.
```

Any place where adapt is moved into a variable should be investigated.

The 99 year bug. The value 99 is assigned to the year field to indicate no year.

```
003000    IF HR-YR NOT = 99
003100       DISPLAY "First Name: ".
003200       DISPLAY FNAME.
003300       DISPLAY "Last Name:".
003400       DISPLAY LNAME.
003500    END-IF.
```

```
001200       ACCEPT CUR-DATE FROM DATE.
```

Using the DATE request to retrieve the operating system date.

Using the DAY request to retrieve the current day from the operating system.

```
001100       ACCEPT CUR-DAY FROM DAY.
```

A data structure or record layout containing an embedded date.

```
001300 01 CONTACT-RECORD.
001400       05 PRODUCT       PIC X(10).
001500       05 PROD-NUM.
001600          10 PD-SN      PIC X(5).
001700          10 PD-YR      PIC X(2).
001800          10 PD-MO      PIC X(2).
```

Hiding the Century Digits in the Existing Date

You don't need to increase the size of existing date fields beyond the standard six characters. Instead, you can encode the century digits within the month digits. This is called hiding the century digits.

Here's how it works. The first digit of a month is either a zero or a one. For example January is represented as 01 and December as 12.

Typical a date is defined as having a two-digit month, day, and year. However, the first digit of month is not limited to zero and one. Neither are the day or year; however, they are not used to hide the century digits.

The century digits can be encoded in the month digits by adding 20 to the value of the month if the year is 2000 or greater. For example, March in the year 2000 would be represented as 23 while March 1999 is represented as 03.

All date accessing routines must be rewritten to decipher the encode century digits. An example of such a program that encodes the date is shown on the next page.

To decipher the date, a program must determine if the value of the month is greater than 12 by using an **IF** statement. If so, then the program assumes the month is encoded with the century and proceeds to subtract 20 from the month to determine the correct value.

However, if the month is less than 13, then the program assumes the date is in the 1900s and does not decipher the month value.

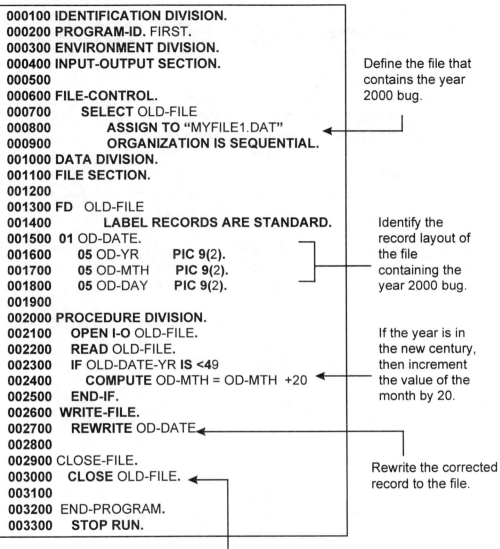

```
000100 IDENTIFICATION DIVISION.
000200 PROGRAM-ID. FIRST.
000300 ENVIRONMENT DIVISION.
000400 INPUT-OUTPUT SECTION.
000500
000600 FILE-CONTROL.
000700     SELECT OLD-FILE
000800        ASSIGN TO "MYFILE1.DAT"
000900        ORGANIZATION IS SEQUENTIAL.
001000 DATA DIVISION.
001100 FILE SECTION.
001200
001300 FD   OLD-FILE
001400        LABEL RECORDS ARE STANDARD.
001500 01 OD-DATE.
001600     05 OD-YR     PIC 9(2).
001700     05 OD-MTH    PIC 9(2).
001800     05 OD-DAY    PIC 9(2).
001900
002000 PROCEDURE DIVISION.
002100     OPEN I-O OLD-FILE.
002200     READ OLD-FILE.
002300     IF OLD-DATE-YR IS <49
002400        COMPUTE OD-MTH = OD-MTH +20
002500     END-IF.
002600 WRITE-FILE.
002700     REWRITE OD-DATE
002800
002900 CLOSE-FILE.
003000     CLOSE OLD-FILE.
003100
003200 END-PROGRAM.
003300     STOP RUN.
```

Define the file that contains the year 2000 bug.

Identify the record layout of the file containing the year 2000 bug.

If the year is in the new century, then increment the value of the month by 20.

Rewrite the corrected record to the file.

Close the files.

Facts You Should Know...

This example encodes the year in the month digits. However, modifications must also be made to routines that read the date from this file to decode the century and properly recognize the month by subtracting 20 from the month digits.

The Single Character Solution

There will be times when it is impossible to increase the number of characters used to represent a date that doesn't contain the century characters. For example, a date field in a file cannot be increased beyond 6 characters that consists of mmddyy.

A solution to this dilemma is to reduce the month and year to one digit each, then use the remaining four digits of the date to store the century and year digits.

Obviously, both the day and month exceed nine and typically require two characters to represent it. However, you can used a letter to replace numbers that are greater than nine.

For example, months can be represented as one through nine for January through September. Letters A, B, and C can be use to represent October, November, and December.

Likewise, days can be represented as one through nine for the first nine days of the month. Letters A through V can be used to represent the rest of the month.

While this method retains the size of the date field, it isn't without drawbacks. First, all the programs that access dates must be rewritten to accept the new date format. An example of such a program is illustrated on the opposite page.

The other drawback is with date data. Some programmers rewrite all the dates using the new format that can become time-consuming if dates are used in many files.

An alternative to changing all the dates is to use the new date format for dates that begin with January 1, 2000. Only those dates will represent days and months as numbers and letters. Dates in the 1900s remain unchanged. However, applications must be rewritten to recognize the two date formats.

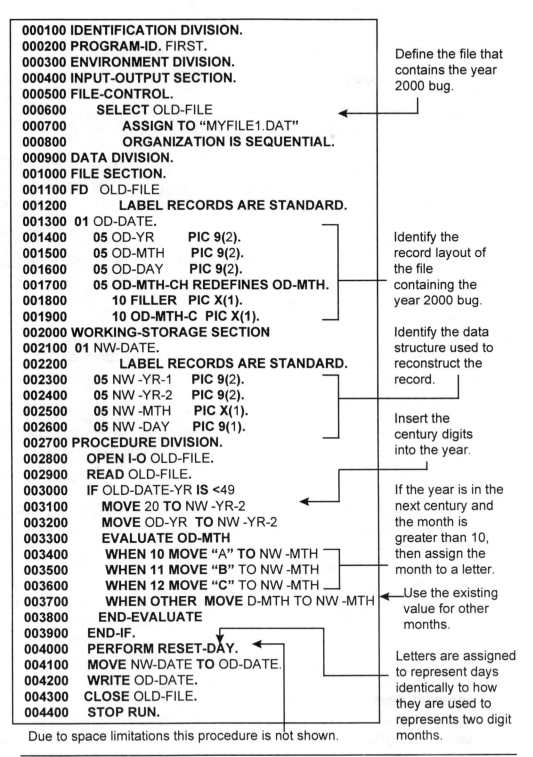

```
000100 IDENTIFICATION DIVISION.
000200 PROGRAM-ID. FIRST.
000300 ENVIRONMENT DIVISION.
000400 INPUT-OUTPUT SECTION.
000500 FILE-CONTROL.
000600     SELECT OLD-FILE
000700        ASSIGN TO "MYFILE1.DAT"
000800        ORGANIZATION IS SEQUENTIAL.
000900 DATA DIVISION.
001000 FILE SECTION.
001100 FD   OLD-FILE
001200        LABEL RECORDS ARE STANDARD.
001300 01 OD-DATE.
001400     05 OD-YR      PIC 9(2).
001500     05 OD-MTH     PIC 9(2).
001600     05 OD-DAY     PIC 9(2).
001700     05 OD-MTH-CH REDEFINES OD-MTH.
001800        10 FILLER  PIC X(1).
001900        10 OD-MTH-C  PIC X(1).
002000 WORKING-STORAGE SECTION
002100 01 NW-DATE.
002200        LABEL RECORDS ARE STANDARD.
002300     05 NW -YR-1   PIC 9(2).
002400     05 NW -YR-2   PIC 9(2).
002500     05 NW -MTH    PIC X(1).
002600     05 NW -DAY    PIC 9(1).
002700 PROCEDURE DIVISION.
002800     OPEN I-O OLD-FILE.
002900     READ OLD-FILE.
003000     IF OLD-DATE-YR IS <49
003100        MOVE 20 TO NW -YR-2
003200        MOVE OD-YR  TO NW -YR-2
003300        EVALUATE OD-MTH
003400        WHEN 10 MOVE "A" TO NW -MTH
003500        WHEN 11 MOVE "B" TO NW -MTH
003600        WHEN 12 MOVE "C" TO NW -MTH
003700        WHEN OTHER  MOVE D-MTH TO NW -MTH
003800        END-EVALUATE
003900     END-IF.
004000     PERFORM RESET-DAY.
004100     MOVE NW-DATE TO OD-DATE.
004200     WRITE OD-DATE.
004300     CLOSE OLD-FILE.
004400     STOP RUN.
```

Define the file that contains the year 2000 bug.

Identify the record layout of the file containing the year 2000 bug.

Identify the data structure used to reconstruct the record.

Insert the century digits into the year.

If the year is in the next century and the month is greater than 10, then assign the month to a letter.

Use the existing value for other months.

Letters are assigned to represent days identically to how they are used to represents two digit months.

Due to space limitations this procedure is not shown.

The No Date Problem

Programmers use flags to indicate a particular condition exists in an application or in data. A flag is a special value assigned to a variable or to data in a file.

One such flag common in applications that use date is the 99 flag. Many programmers assigned the year 99 to a date to indicate no date value is assigned to the variable or date field.

When the application reads a year 99, it may ignore the rest of the date or even the rest of the record assuming the information is test data.

It is difficult to conceive why a programmer didn't have the foresight to realize that 99 is a valid year in a date. However, many of the applications that contain the 99 bug were written decades ago when the assumption was made the application would likely be rewritten before 1999.

The example on the next page illustrates how the 99 bug can appear in an application. This is just one of many ways in which programmers wrote a routine to check for an invalid date.

The 99 bug poses two problems. First, the application will ignore dates and possible records that contains 99 as the year. The other problem exists in the data where date values that are to be ignored by the application contain the valid year 99.

The solution to these problems is to identify the files used by a program that traps the year 99, then find and review all the fields containing a year 99 to determine if this is a valid year. If not, then rewrite the routine to trap a value in a different field that indicates an invalid date.

The final step is to remove the routine that traps the year 99 in the application.

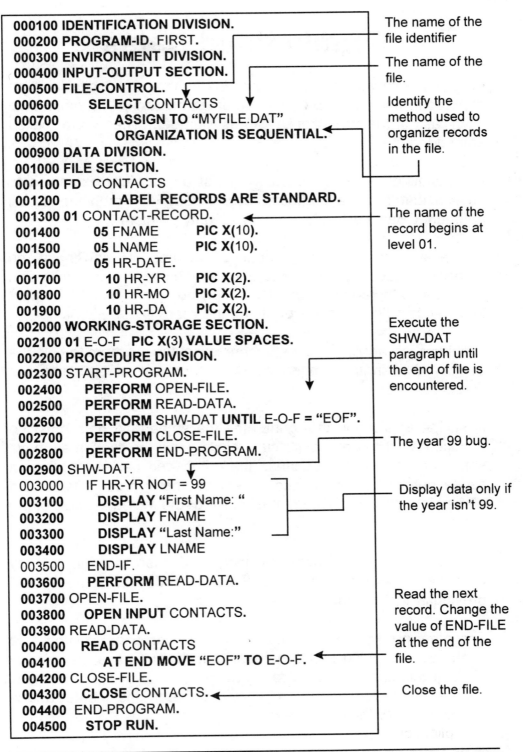

```
000100 IDENTIFICATION DIVISION.
000200 PROGRAM-ID. FIRST.
000300 ENVIRONMENT DIVISION.
000400 INPUT-OUTPUT SECTION.
000500 FILE-CONTROL.
000600     SELECT CONTACTS
000700        ASSIGN TO "MYFILE.DAT"
000800        ORGANIZATION IS SEQUENTIAL.
000900 DATA DIVISION.
001000 FILE SECTION.
001100 FD  CONTACTS
001200        LABEL RECORDS ARE STANDARD.
001300 01 CONTACT-RECORD.
001400     05 FNAME      PIC X(10).
001500     05 LNAME      PIC X(10).
001600     05 HR-DATE.
001700        10 HR-YR   PIC X(2).
001800        10 HR-MO   PIC X(2).
001900        10 HR-DA   PIC X(2).
002000 WORKING-STORAGE SECTION.
002100 01 E-O-F  PIC X(3) VALUE SPACES.
002200 PROCEDURE DIVISION.
002300 START-PROGRAM.
002400     PERFORM OPEN-FILE.
002500     PERFORM READ-DATA.
002600     PERFORM SHW-DAT UNTIL E-O-F = "EOF".
002700     PERFORM CLOSE-FILE.
002800     PERFORM END-PROGRAM.
002900 SHW-DAT.
003000     IF HR-YR NOT = 99
003100       DISPLAY "First Name: "
003200       DISPLAY FNAME
003300       DISPLAY "Last Name:"
003400       DISPLAY LNAME
003500     END-IF.
003600     PERFORM READ-DATA.
003700 OPEN-FILE.
003800     OPEN INPUT CONTACTS.
003900 READ-DATA.
004000   READ CONTACTS
004100        AT END MOVE "EOF" TO E-O-F.
004200 CLOSE-FILE.
004300   CLOSE CONTACTS.
004400 END-PROGRAM.
004500   STOP RUN.
```

The name of the file identifier

The name of the file.

Identify the method used to organize records in the file.

The name of the record begins at level 01.

Execute the SHW-DAT paragraph until the end of file is encountered.

The year 99 bug.

Display data only if the year isn't 99.

Read the next record. Change the value of END-FILE at the end of the file.

Close the file.

Embedded Dates

Programmers who set out to remove the Year 2000 bug from an application must alter it to identify dates hidden within other data such as is the case of a series number. These are called embedded dates.

Data containing embedded dates must be carefully examined to determine if the data is affected by the Year 2000 problem. Not all embedded dates will cause a data integrity problem.

For example, a series number of a product may have an embedded date represented with a four-digit year. The application that creates the series number will likely be able to handle the year 2000 since sufficient digits exists for the year.

Problems will arise, however, if there is insufficient room to hold the century digit in the embedded date. Two critical problems are presented.

First, the application that generates the embedded date must be modified to include the century digits. This in itself may have serious repercussions because the embedded date such as in a series number is reproduced in reports, metal product tags, and etched into products. Room must exist for the increased size of the number.

However, if the size cannot be increased, then months and day must be represented as single character codes as demonstrated previously in this chapter.

The other problem occurs when an application uses existing data such as an existing series number that doesn't have the century digit. In this case, the application must use one of the techniques such as the sliding window as shown earlier in this chapter and in the example on the opposite page.

```
000100 IDENTIFICATION DIVISION.
000200 PROGRAM-ID. FIRST.
000300 ENVIRONMENT DIVISION.
000400 INPUT-OUTPUT SECTION.
000500 FILE-CONTROL.
000600      SELECT CONTACTS
000700          ASSIGN TO "MYFILE.DAT"
000800          ORGANIZATION IS SEQUENTIAL.
000900 DATA DIVISION.
001000 FILE SECTION.
001100 FD   CONTACTS
001200          LABEL RECORDS ARE STANDARD.
001300 01 CONTACT-RECORD.
001400      05 PRODUCT      PIC X(10).
001500      05 PROD-NUM.
001600         10 PD-SN      PIC X(5).
001700         10 PD-YR      PIC X(2).
001800         10 PD-MO      PIC X(2).
001900 WORKING-STORAGE SECTION.
002000 01 E-O-F   PIC X(3) VALUE SPACES.
002100 PROCEDURE DIVISION.
002200 START-PROGRAM.
002300      PERFORM OPEN-FILE.
002400      PERFORM READ-DATA.
002500      PERFORM SHW-DAT UNTIL E-O-F = "EOF".
002600      PERFORM CLOSE-FILE.
002700      PERFORM END-PROGRAM.
002800 SHW-DAT.
002900      IF PD-YR = 99
003000         DISPLAY "Product recalled :"
003100         DISPLAY PRODUCT
003200      END-IF.
003300      PERFORM READ-DATA.
003400 OPEN-FILE.
003500    OPEN INPUT CONTACTS.
003600 READ-DATA.
003700    READ CONTACTS
003800         AT END MOVE "EOF" TO E-O-F.
003900 CLOSE-FILE.
004000    CLOSE CONTACTS.
004100 END-PROGRAM.
004200    STOP RUN.
```

The name of the file identifier

The name of the file.

Identify the method used to organize records in the file.

Embedded date in the product number.

Execute the SHW-DAT paragraph until the end of file is encountered.

The embedded date bug.

Display recall message only if the year is 99.

Read the next record. Change the value of END-FILE at the end of the file.

Close the file.

Programmer's Checklist

- General
- Keywords, Constants and Variables
- Expressions and Operators
- Program Control
- Input-Output
- Year 2000 Problem

General

☐ Do you have the four divisions in your program?

All COBOL programs must have **IDENTIFICATION DIVISION**, **ENVIRONMENT DIVISION**, **DATA DIVISION**, and the **PROCEDURE DIVISION** even if some of the divisions are not required by the program.

☐ Do you have a period after every sentence in your program?

Every sentence in a COBOL program must end with a period, otherwise a compiler error will occur.

☐ Do you have the **PROGRAM-ID** in your program?

Many COBOL compilers require the PROGRAM-ID followed by the name of the program to be included in the **IDENTIFICATION DIVISION**.

☐ Does the **PROGRAM-ID** have the same name as the source code file name?

You can avoid much confusion by making sure the name of the program specified in the **PROGRAM-ID** is the same name as given to the file containing the program.

☐ Do you have the **STOP RUN** sentence in your program?

All programs must tell the compiler when to end the program by using the **STOP RUN** sentence. You will receive an error message if the **STOP RUN** sentence is left out of your program.

☐ Do you have a hyphen in the **STOP-RUN** sentence in your program?

A common mistake among new COBOL programmers is to place a hyphen between **STOP** and **RUN**. No hyphen is necessary.

Keywords, Constants and Variables

☐ Is the name of any variable the same as a COBOL keyword?

Keywords cannot be used to identify variables in your program. Be sure to review the naming convention that you use for variables to be sure that no variable is named the same as a keyword.

☐ Did you use lowercase for any keywords?

A common typographical error in a COBOL program is to inadvertently write a keyword using lowercase. Remember many COBOL compilers require all keywords to be capitalized. These compilers will not recognize keywords written isn lowercase.

☐ Did you use a variable too small to hold a data variable?

There must be sufficient space reserved in a variable to hold the maximum number of characters that will be assigned to the variable. Data will be lost if the variable size is too small and no errors will be displayed either when the program is compiled nor when the program is running.

☐ Are all alphanumeric constants enclosed within double quotations?

A common error is to not use a closing quotation with an alphanumeric constant. Examine each occurrence where such a constant is used to make sure both quotations are present.

☐ Are all variables defined in the **WORKING-STORAGE SECTION** of the **DATA DIVISION**.

You must define the data type and size of a variable in the **WORKING-STORAGE SECTION** of the **DATA DIVISION** before the variable can be used in the **PROCEDURE DIVISION**. Otherwise, you'll receive a compiler error.

☐ Are all variables initialized?

Variables contain nothing until the program assigns a value to it. Another common mistake COBOL programmers make is to use a variable in the **PROCEDURE DIVISION** before it is assigned a value. Always initialize a variable when it is defined.

☐ Did you use spaces in the name of a variable?

Spaces are not permitted in a variable name. Use a hyphen in place of a space in the name.

☐ Did you use an underscore in the name of a variable?

Beginner programmers commonly make the mistake of using an underscore in the name of a variable when they intended to use a hyphen. Underscores are not permitted in the name of a variable and will cause a compiler error.

☐ Is the name of a variable more than 30 characters long?

No more than 30 characters can be used in the name of a variable. This is a common error whenever variables with slightly different data is used such as FIRST-QUARTER-REGIONAL1-SALES. This is likely to be first of a set of variables that contains data for the region. However, the variable name will exceed 30 characters when the 10th region is referenced or when the name of the data (i.e... SALES) exceeds five characters.

☐ Did you place a period outside the last double quotation in an alphanumeric constant?

A common typographical error is to reverse letters such as writing an alphanumeric constant such as "Please enter your name." Notice the period is after the last double quotation when it should come before the double quotation. This period tells the compiler the COBOL sentence has ended which is incorrect and causes a bug in the program.

☐ Does the variable have the same name as another variable?

No two variables defined at the same level can have the same name. However, variables defined at different levels can have the same name.

Expressions and Operators

☐ Did you begin all computations with the **COMPUTE** command?

Programmers who pick up COBOL as a second language frequently forget to preface all computational expression with the **COMPUTE** command that will cause a compiler error.

☐ Did you reverse characters in the operators >= and <=?

A common mistake is to reverse the characters in the greater-than-and-equal to operator (>=) and the less-than-and-equal to operator (<=). Remember the equal sign always appears on the right.

☐ Did you use the exclamation point or <> for reversing the logic of the operator?

When you want to reverse the logic of the operator such as the equal operator, some programming languages use the != or <> operators that says "not equal." COBOL uses the **NOT** keyword instead such as **NOT** = and won't recognize != or <> as operators.

☐ Is there an expression in the program that divides by zero?

A common run-time error occurs when a program performs a calculation that tries to divide by zero. Typically, a variable is used as the divisor, but prior to executing the calculation the variable is assigned the the value zero. This is a difficult bug to identify reading code because the value of the divisor variable isn't obvious.

☐ Will a compound expression execute in the order you except it to execute ?

One of the hardest bugs to locate in a program is caused by the misunderstanding of the order of operation of an expression. It is not uncommon for a programmer to assume particular order of operations that is contrary to the operator's precedence. When in double, always use parentheses to clarify an expression.

Program Control

☐ Did you use the **GO TO** command when you wanted the **PERFORM** command?

The **PERFORM** command is used to jump to a paragraph, then return control to the sentence following the **PERFORM** command when the next paragraph name is read by the compiler. However, the **GO TO** command does not return control to the sentence following the **PERFORM** command. Instead, the compiler continues by reading the next paragraph.

☐ Are you sure the expression in an **IF** statement will become true?

Sentences within a **IF** statement are executed only if the **IF** statement expression is true. A common error is to use an expression that is never true, then wonder way sentences with the **IF** statement are not executed.

☐ Did you end the **IF** statement block with an **END-IF**?

The last line in a multiple sentence IF statement block should be **END-IF**. This gives the program more structure and helps you find bugs.

☐ Did you use a hyphen in **END-IF**?

It is easy to become confused when and when not to use a hyphen between words. **END-IF** always require a hyphen, however it is common to assume **END-IF** has a similar structure as **STOP RUN** that does not use a hyphen.

☐ Did you use a period at the end of a sentence within the IF statement block?

All sentences end with a period. However, an exception to this rule is if the sentence is used within a block such as the IF statement block. Sentences within a block should not end with a period, otherwise the compiler will treat the period as the end of the block.

☐ Are you sure the condition in the **UNTIL** phrase will be met?

The **UNTIL** phrase is used to test whether or not a condition exists. When the specified condition is true, then the action ceases to continue as in the case of **PERFORM** ... **UNTIL**. Here, the specified paragraph is continually called by the **PERFORM** command until the condition specified in the **UNTIL** phrase is true. However, the assumption is made that at some point in the program the condition will be true. If not, then the program will be in an endless loop.

☐ Does the paragraph specified in the **THROUGH** phrase exist?

A group of paragraphs can be called using the **PERFORM** command be specifying the name of the first paragraph in the group to the right of the **PERFORM** command followed by the **THROUGH** phrase and the name of the last paragraph in the group. Make sure the paragraph name specified in the **THROUGH** phrase actually appears in the program, otherwise you'll notice unexpected results from your program.

☐ Does the program contain multiple calls to the **STOP RUN** command?

A program may unexpectedly stop running without performing the desired results. Once such cause of this condition is where the **STOP RUN** command is entered in more than one place in the program.

☐ Did you use the **EXIT PROGRAM** command to end programs that are called by other programs?

Another reason a program unexpectedly stops running, but fails to display an error, is when a program calls another program. The calling program is always terminated with the **STOP RUN** command. The called program is terminated with the **EXIT PROGRAM** command. Sometimes programmers end the called program with the **STOP RUN** command that terminates the called program and the calling program.

☐ Is the name of the called program within double quotations?

The name of the program being called from within another program must be enclosed within double quotations, otherwise the compiler might assume the program name is a variable that will cause a compiler error.

☐ Is the called program prepared to accept variables passed from the calling program?

The calling program can pass values to the called program by using the **USING** phrase followed by the variables, names with the **CALL** command. However, the same variables must be specified in the **USING** phrase to the right of the **PROCEDURE DIVISION** name in the called program. If not, then the called program will not be able to access the variable.

INPUT-OUTPUT

☐ Are you sure all files are opened in the proper mode?

It is not unusual for a program to try and write to a file that is opened only for **INPUT** or likewise a program trying to read from a file opened for **OUTPUT**.

☐ Is the file available to the program?

Another common mistake is to define a file within a program; however, the file isn't available in the operating environment. This will cause a problem whenever the program runs.

☐ Did you check the status of the file?

Each time the **OPEN** command is executed, the program should determine the return status of the command. You can't assume that the **OPEN** command successfully accessed the file. The return status of the **OPEN** command must be examined by the program, then the appropriate actions must be taken to address the status. This will prevent the program from abending (abnormal ending) when the program is running.

☐ Does the file definition match the layout of data in the file?

The program must create a file definition used when data is read from the file. Each field in the file definition must exactly match the layout of the file, otherwise the program could be working with inaccurate data.

☐ Did you redefine the alphabet before sorting a file?

Remember the default alphabet used by many compilesr does not properly sort values using the same upper- and lowercase letters. That is, a lowercase a appears in the sorted list following the letter capital Z. You would expect the letter a to appear in the list after the letter A. However, you must redefine the alphabet for this to occur as shown in Chapter 8.

☐ Are you using the proper file type when searching for information in a file?

There are three file types: sequential, relative, and indexed. Sequential files can only be accessed by reading one record after another. Records are accessed in a relative file by specifying a record number. Records are accessed in an indexed file by using a key field.

☐ Did you try to use a duplicate key in a primary index?

Only unique values can be used in the primary index of an indexed file. Duplicate values are not permitted. However, you can create an alternate to indicate which can accept duplicate key values by using the **WITH DUPLICATE** phrase.

☐ Did you specify the correct access mode when trying to locate a record by record number in a relative file ?

Records can be accessed in one of two ways from a relative file. This is by specifying the record number or by reading records sequentially from the file. However, the file access mode must be set to the proper mode. The access mode must be **SEQUENTIAL** if the file is the read sequentially. **DYNAMIC** or **RANDOM** is the access mode to read records by record number.

☐ Did you define a variable used to store the file status?

The file status tells you the condition of a file and is identified by a two-character file code. The variable that will house the file status is specified in the physical definition of the file using the **FILE STATUS IS** phrase. However, a common mistake is to identify the file status variable in the physical definition of the file, but fail to define the variable in the **WORKING-STORAGE SECTION** of the program.

☐ Did you open the file correctly before trying to rewrite a record to the file?

A routine that rewrites a record to a file must have both **INPUT** and **OUTPUT** access to the file because the record is typically read and modified before being rewritten to the file. You must open the file as **I-O** to properly rewrite the record to the file.

Year 2000 Problem

☐ Are you trying to rewrite a record to the same file, but the rewritten record is larger than the old record?

The record layout of a file may use a 6-digit date that means there isn't room for the century digits. A common mistake is to write a routine that reads a record containing a 6-digit date, increase the size of the record to accept the century digits, then rewrite the record to the same file. Instead, the resized record should be written to a new file to prevent possible data loss because of a misalignment of record size. The new file can always be renamed to the name of the old file after the old file is deleted.

☐ Did you assume the program is year 2000 compliant because the program was recently written?

All programs can contain the year 2000 problem regardless of when they were written and regardless of the language used to write the program. If the century digits are missing, the program is likely to be affected by the year 2000 problem.

Index